Searching for Normal

Searching for Normal

A new approach to understanding mental health, distress and neurodiversity

SAMI TIMIMI

FERN PRESS

3 5 7 9 10 8 6 4 2

Fern Press, an imprint of Vintage, is part of the Penguin Random House group of companies

Vintage, Penguin Random House UK, One Embassy Gardens,
8 Viaduct Gardens, London SW11 7BW

penguin.co.uk/vintage
global.penguinrandomhouse.com

First published by Fern Press in 2025

Copyright © Sami Timimi 2025

Sami Timimi has asserted his right to be identified as the author of this
Work in accordance with the Copyright, Designs and Patents Act 1988

This book is a work of non-fiction based on the life, experiences and recollections of the author. In some cases names of people, places, dates, sequences and the detail of events have been changed to protect the privacy of others.

No part of this book may be used or reproduced in any manner for the purpose of training artificial intelligence technologies or systems. In accordance with Article 4(3) of the DSM Directive 2019/790, Penguin Random House expressly reserves this work from the text and data mining exception.

Typeset in 12/14.75pt Bembo Book MT Pro by Jouve (UK), Milton Keynes
Printed and bound in Great Britain by Clays Ltd, Elcograf S.p.A.

The authorised representative in the EEA is Penguin Random House Ireland,
Morrison Chambers, 32 Nassau Street, Dublin D02 YH68

A CIP catalogue record for this book is available from the British Library

HB ISBN 9781911717126
TPB ISBN 9781911717133

Penguin Random House is committed to a sustainable future
for our business, our readers and our planet. This book is made
from Forest Stewardship Council® certified paper.

In memory of my father, Bakir Abood Timimi

Contents

	Preface: Encounters with the mental health epidemic	1
1.	Changing times	7
2.	What is mental health?	22
3.	Psychiatric diagnoses are facts of culture not nature	40
4.	Concept expansion	65
5.	The creation of ADHD	80
6.	Is ADHD an evidence-based construct?	102
7.	The creation of autism	124
8.	Is autism an evidence-based construct?	142
9.	Start them young	157
10.	Conveyor-belt therapy	174
11.	The mental health industrial complex (MHIC)	191
12.	Neurodiversity, gender and new human typologies	212
13.	Living in a compare-and-compete culture	234
14.	Colonial psychiatry	254
15.	Rehabilitating emotions	269
	Epilogue: The changing narrative	290
	Acknowledgements	295
	Notes	297
	Index	331

Preface
Encounters with the mental health epidemic

> 'The old world is dying, and the new world struggles
> to be born – now is the time of monsters'
>
> Antonio Gramsci

You can only ever be as happy as your least happy child

'Don't know,' utters fourteen-year-old Eleanor, after a pause, and in response to my asking what she hopes to get out of today's appointment.

Her nose piercing briefly glints in the mid-afternoon sun as she turns her head towards her mother. Arms folded, blue puffer jacket still on, Eleanor looks stern with lips pursed and eyebrows raised so that they disappear into the fringe of her dyed black hair. Her mother shrugs and gestures with her hands. 'We've talked about this. How can you be helped if you won't open up?'

'What's the point?' Eleanor replies. 'Nothing's going to work. No one can help me.'

I'm used to seeing angry and/or frustrated (and frustrating) teenagers. It's my first meeting with Eleanor, and her mother, Nicole. I usually start a first session by asking my patient what they hope to get out of the appointment. When they are unable or unwilling to answer, I invite the accompanying adult to respond.

Nicole explains that Eleanor has been self-harming for over a year, mostly scratching her forearms until they bleed, using items such as broken shards of plastic. She sometimes misses school because she feels too anxious. She complains of frequently feeling low and 'nothing helps her feel better' (Nicole's words). Then there are times when

Eleanor seems 'high, bubbly, excitable, chatty, and, then, a few days later, she will crash, sleep a lot and be irritable and moody', and Nicole feels like she's 'walking on eggshells'.

'And what do you hope to get out of today's appointment, Nicole?' I ask.

'Something to help her. Something to make Elly feel better.'

'Do you have any thoughts about what sort of help you imagine she needs?' I ask, as I look up from my notepad.

'We need to know what's wrong with her. Maybe she has depression or bipolar disorder. I've also wondered about autism. Maybe she needs some medication that will help her relax or feel better.'

'What type of help has she had already?'

'She went to a group for young people with anxiety. Then she saw a counsellor at school, and then I paid for her to see a private therapist. She still sees her once a week. I know she likes the therapist, but she's been seeing her for six months now. Then, a few weeks ago, Eleanor was crying and raging and telling me that there's no point in going on and that she's going to kill herself. I'm terrified because last year she took an overdose of paracetamol without telling anyone. A few hours afterwards she said she wasn't feeling well and told me what she'd done. We rushed her up to A&E*, but fortunately she hadn't caused any serious harm to herself. I've locked up all the medicine at home . . . but how can I stop her if she decides to do it again?'

Tears well up in Nicole's eyes. I get up out of my chair to reach for the box of tissues on the table, but Eleanor, reading my intention, takes a couple and offers them to her mum. I sit back down and pick up my notes. Nicole thanks her daughter and dabs carefully under her moistening eyes. As a parent myself, I feel for Nicole – that desire to do anything you can for your child.

Eleanor takes off her coat.

I ask them to help me create a family tree. This gives me the opportunity to talk about family relationships and history. Eleanor lives

---

* A&E refers to Accident and Emergency, the UK equivalent of the ER (Emergency Room).

with her mother, Nicole; her younger brother, Ethan; Nicole's partner, Justin; and their infant daughter, Jasmine. Eleanor loves Jasmine, with whom she often plays, but she has a difficult relationship with Justin. She didn't like it when he moved in and hates it when he tells her off or asks her to do anything.

Her biological father, Brian, left the family when Eleanor was eight years old. Eleanor becomes animated as we talk about him. She remembers coming home from school one day to discover that her dad had left, but she couldn't take in what was being said and instead kept looking at the shape of a stain on the sofa, thinking it looked like a teddy bear, or maybe Woody from *Toy Story*. She remembers it like it was yesterday. Nicole says that Eleanor used to be a daddy's girl when she was younger, but Brian had his own problems. He would go on drinking binges every now and then and would come home in a rage. Although there was no physical violence he would shout and break things.

After Brian left, he would collect Eleanor and Ethan and take them to McDonald's or the park, but these trips grew less frequent. When the first Covid lockdown came they lost touch with him. I ask Eleanor how she feels about that.

'I'm over it. He doesn't care about me; I don't care about him. If he got back in touch with us, I'd tell him to get lost. I don't want to see him.'

The Covid restrictions and lockdowns were particularly difficult for Eleanor. She started to lose a sense of structure and purpose to the point where sometimes she was neglecting to look after herself, often just staying in bed flicking through social media or YouTube videos on her phone. Nicole tried her best to keep routines and schoolwork going, but she was working exhausting shifts in an understaffed care home. Nicole was relieved when Justin moved in, just before the Christmas 2020 lockdown was imposed.

Eleanor fell behind with her schoolwork and, once school finally returned without any restrictions, she was plagued by a fear of failure and a sense of being judged. When I ask her how she feels about her school, she speaks about the lack of close friends. 'All the groups had formed. Everyone seemed to be getting on with their life and enjoying themselves and I just can't. I'm even a failure at therapy. There's nothing that's going to work to make me better.'

'Nicole, can you tell me what you admire or like about Eleanor?' I ask.

'Elly's amazing. I wish she could see it. She's kind, brilliant with Jasmine, always thinking about others. She's great at art. I wish she wouldn't keep screwing up the drawings she does. She's so hard on herself. When she's in a good mood she's funny, jokes around . . . It's horrible to see her hurting like this.'

More tears form, more tissues are passed by Eleanor to her mum, more dabbing under the eyes. We carry on talking. From a slow start with a reluctant teenager, there are now strong emotions, including fear and frustration, but also love and kindness flowing between mother and daughter.*

What should happen next?

The primary task of a psychiatric assessment in the mainstream model of practice is to enquire about, notice and analyse 'symptoms' to arrive at the correct 'diagnosis'. This will be used to guide the treatment plan towards interventions, considered to have a basis in evidence, that will improve the health of the person by reducing their symptoms. The treatment plan will typically include medication and/or specific therapies.

This does not mean ignoring other aspects, such as the family history, relationships, social situation and so on, but they become secondary concerns sitting in the shadow of the primary task of discovering the 'correct' diagnosis so that the 'correct' treatment can be given. It's the basis around which mental health services organise, categorise and deliver mental health care. This is what I am referring to in this book when I talk about 'mainstream' mental health practice.

---

* All case histories in this book are based around real clinical encounters with details changed to ensure confidentiality.

Is this the best way to understand what is happening?

Are what Eleanor experiences best thought of as 'symptoms'? What would a diagnosis tell us about her and how would it affect her beliefs about herself or others' beliefs about her? What is the scientific basis supporting (or otherwise) 'evidence-based' treatments?

Beyond the specific dilemmas posed by presentations like Eleanor's, there are also questions of public health, culture and other population-level trends of which Eleanor's story is a tiny part. Why are there so many more people receiving mental disorder diagnoses? Why are diagnoses like attention deficit hyperactivity disorder (ADHD) and autism becoming so prevalent? Is increasing recognition leading to better outcomes and better mental health in our societies?

Thinking more broadly, is there any connection to the perception that we are living in a time of crisis? Do these developments have a commercial function, helping companies to sell more drugs/treatments/self-help content? Could there even be some connection to government or political control lurking in the background?

This book delves into these questions without fear of where it might lead. Eleanor, and millions like her, may be at risk if we just take at face value that what is ailing her are symptoms (such as self-harm, depressive feelings and cognitions, irritability, mood swings and anxiety) that mean she has a mental disorder (such as childhood depression or a bipolar disorder) which requires specific treatments. With other cases I describe in this book, we will begin to learn what an alternative approach for Eleanor and countless others might look like.

I qualified as a doctor in 1988 and have been a consultant in child and adolescent psychiatry since 1997. I've worked in inpatient and outpatient settings, with urgent, crisis, eating problems and paediatric liaison services. I've been teaching, writing and lecturing for most of that time. I've published in many leading journals as well as chapters in numerous academic books. I've authored six books and collaborated with academics and service users from a variety of backgrounds in research, editing or co-authoring books, devising projects, writing documents and building new services. In this book I aim to bring those years of clinical and academic experience to a general audience to share what I have learned.

What the public is being told about the nature of mental health is misleading and may be harming our collective sense of well-being.

Mental health ideology may be the biggest and most powerful cause of mental health problems today.

I will explain why I believe this to be the case and what we could, at an individual and collective level, do about it.

1. Changing times

> 'Time changes everything except something within us which is always surprised by change.'
>
> Thomas Hardy

The changing face of autism

June 1998. It's a hot and sunny afternoon in east London. The tinted-glass windows of my consulting room don't stop the spaces on this side of the building from overheating, forcing me to open a window and let in a dusty breeze that's caked in the hum of the city. Traffic noise, regularly punctuated by the sirens of ambulances or police cars, is the soundtrack for my working day, something my mind seems to have learned to ignore. Like many UK National Health Service clinics, the walls are painted in standard magnolia with five lilac cushioned seats arranged in a semicircle on a bluish-grey carpet. I have been a consultant child and adolescent psychiatrist working here for nearly a year.

It's my first meeting with fifteen-year-old Ibrahim and his parents. Ibrahim is sitting opposite me, his mother and father either side of him. He's wearing a striped green-and-white T-shirt and grey shorts. His parents, immigrants from Bangladesh, are dressed smartly, in clothes that I imagine are uncomfortably hot. They are courteous, attentive and keen to ask lots of questions. Ibrahim has been referred by his school – a school for children with special needs and learning difficulties – as he has recently presented with an upsurge of behavioural issues. This once quiet and placid boy has started shouting and throwing things, sometimes in anger and sometimes through tears. It's not clear why he's doing this or how to help him.

Ibrahim received a diagnosis of autism when he was six years old. He also has significant learning difficulties. He has never developed the ability to communicate through language beyond a few basics, so it's hard to fathom what was behind this recent change in behaviour. Ibrahim is a well-built boy with a broad roundish face that regularly breaks out into a toothy smile that's hard to distinguish from a grimace. Early on in our session I realise that understanding through direct communication will not be possible. After attempting a few direct questions his answer to each is a polite 'yeeezz' with a nod of the head and a smile (or is that a grimace?). Every now and then Ibrahim leaves his chair, walks around the room making grunting noises while his parents are talking to him (maybe in Bengali), probably asking him to come back and sit down, which he eventually does while repeating 'yeeezz', nodding his head more vigorously and doing his smile/grimace. I imagine this session must be pretty boring for him.

I discuss with his parents the nature of the problems, recent changes, and his medical, social and educational history. They explain to me how they had to move house not too long ago after recurring trouble with their neighbours.

This is one of the more deprived areas of London, where social issues such as overcrowded housing, job insecurity and poor local infrastructure are prevalent. But it is also an area of vibrant diversity, full of the colours, sights and sounds of the varied cuisines, languages and religions. I have come to appreciate the greater sense of emotional openness here. I sometimes find it more difficult to work with polite, well-off families who are afraid to show how they feel, where emotions sit behind a commendable desire not to upset anyone, but which can make it hard to understand hidden undercurrents and discuss difficult issues.

I had been alerted to Ibrahim's case by teachers at his special school. I have an arrangement where, once a month or so, I attend their staff meeting. Here there is an opportunity to discuss pupils, ask questions and think together about broader issues of policy and environment. We talk about helping young people who have educational challenges and the many emotional dilemmas that come with that.

Recently the local educational authority had set up a support service for those who also had a diagnosis of autism. I remember the head teacher at one of these meetings saying that she now felt sorry for those who did not have a diagnosis of autism, because they wouldn't get the extra resources that children with the diagnosis would get, even though she didn't feel there was anything specific about the service that couldn't also be useful for those at her school who didn't have an autism diagnosis.

I met with Ibrahim and his family a few more times and he was discharged from our service a few months later much improved. What had helped and resulted in the improvement? Well, that's the thing about mental health care. You can't really tell. Perhaps it was the passage of time; perhaps it was that the parents felt listened to; perhaps he was settling into his new home; perhaps it was a better understanding of the effects of puberty (which I spent some time talking to his parents about); perhaps it was the school knowing he was being seen that helped them feel less burdened about trying to solve this problem. Perhaps it was discovering that he was good at riding a bike and seemed to really enjoy it. He started going out for regular bike rides with his sister and was eventually trusted to ride on his own around the local park and then started riding his bike to and from school.

Why has Ibrahim stayed in my mind for twenty-five years?

My first exposure to child psychiatry was as a trainee psychiatrist when, in February 1992, I was posted to a child and adolescent psychiatry placement. After passing my professional exams in late 1992 to become a member of the Royal College of Psychiatrists, I went on to complete higher training in child and adolescent psychiatry, by rotating through several inpatient and outpatient posts dotted around central London. After completing that training, I got my first consultant child and adolescent psychiatrist post in east London in October 1997. In all the years prior to meeting Ibrahim I had only encountered two other children who also had a diagnosis of autism.

Both, like Ibrahim, had significant learning difficulties and it was not possible to hold a coherent conversation with them. One of them would flap his arms and repeat everything I said to them — a phenomenon known as echolalia. The other one stormed around the room when I met him on a home visit, while making whooping sounds and other odd noises as his mother tried to concentrate on having a conversation with me.

In the year 2000, I moved to a new consultant post based in the cathedral city of Lincoln in the east of England. Shortly after moving there, I met with a clinical psychologist who wanted to discuss a case with me.* He told me that he had been on training and was learning to spot the signs of autism that he felt he had previously missed. He excitedly recounted the case of a fourteen-year-old young person he had recently seen, where this individual found it hard to talk about anything significant, until the topic of football, and particularly Liverpool Football Club, came up. This kid could talk endlessly about his team, as could his father who was also a LFC fan. The dad explained to the psychologist how the son followed all the matches, had posters on his bedroom wall and styled his hair in the same way as one of his favourite players.

To my surprise the psychologist had concluded that this was the symptom of 'restricted imagination' and the resulting repetitive behaviour characteristic of autism, which he suspected this kid, and probably his father too, may have. What about a father-and-son relationship bound by a common interest? Well, their common interest was apparently because they both shared the same disorder. What was this child referred about? Behaviour problems, mainly.

This way of thinking about autism was about to spread – big time.

The idea that autism exists in a spectrum, spreading from those with severe learning difficulties to geniuses in every cultural and

---

* A psychiatrist is a qualified medical doctor who then specialises in psychiatry. They can prescribe medication and should have good physical health knowledge. A clinical psychologist has a degree in psychology and then undertakes training in clinical applications of psychology. A psychotherapist is someone who has training in one or more model of therapy. Psychiatrists and psychologists may also be psychotherapists, but psychotherapists do not have to be either psychologists or psychiatrists. There are many other professions who may also work in mental health settings including psychiatric nurses, social workers, occupational therapists, peer support workers and educators.

scientific field, is now so embedded in clinical practice that many who now enter young people's mental health services as patients and who don't improve with the recommended treatment are at risk of being considered autistic. Autism is often proposed as the reason why they haven't got better whether the initial problem was anxiety, low self-esteem, behaviour problems, eating issues or, even, psychosis.

Autism is no longer what it was just over a couple of decades ago. Ibrahim is no longer the standard case of autism.

The changing face of ADHD

It's a typical English grey drizzly day in November 1995. I'm having my regular weekly session with my supervising consultant. I'm in my second year of higher training to become eligible to apply for consultant posts. My supervisor, a gentle bearded man with a soft but recognisably Persian accent, is discussing attention deficit hyperactivity disorder with me. There is growing interest in this latest American import. Stories about ADHD have been appearing in the UK press telling us how far behind we are in the way we practise. The articles inform us of families experiencing all manner of difficulties including child protection suspicions, educational failure and family breakdown. Then, one day, the problem child is diagnosed with ADHD and is started on stimulant medication. This transforms the child and their family's lives (or so the newspaper story goes).

In UK child psychiatry at that time, if you used a diagnosis for behaviour problems at all, 'conduct disorder' was the most common. Conduct disorder implied that there were social causes, and various types of family therapy or groups for parents were the usual recommended response. ADHD implied something different, that there was something wrong in the child, specifically in the child's brain. Some UK child psychiatry academics were starting to discuss and write about ADHD, and they began making recommendations to change existing practice.

My supervising consultant was interested in this emerging field. He sat back in his chair and, while looking wistfully out at the darkening skies, announced that it was time for us to properly explore this phenomenon. He asked if I would help him with doing some research on the topic. He wanted to deepen our understanding about the prevalence of ADHD among the local population that had a high number of Afro-Caribbean background families. There was a disproportionate number of black children who were presenting with behaviour problems in school and sometimes being expelled as a result. Perhaps this was a group of children who had undiagnosed ADHD. Perhaps there were also cultural issues that the emerging ADHD literature hadn't yet looked at. I was keen to be involved. I suggested I do a literature review to get us started.

I collected a big bundle of research papers, reviews, theoretical articles and historical tracts. The more I read, the more confused I became. Scrutinising paper after paper left me with a disturbing feeling of not being able to capture what this new concept of ADHD was. Perhaps if I had been exposed to it before starting training in child psychiatry, meaning that it was just part of my accepted common sense, I would have felt differently. But now I found myself unable to settle. What is meant by ADHD? Where did this concept come from? Why are behaviours that are part of what I would consider everyday behaviours children show, at least to some degree, considered part of a medical condition? And not just any condition, but one that is neurologically driven.

Try as I might to find some sort of empirical anchor to pin down this slippery concept, I just couldn't. Surely ADHD isn't just the behaviours of attention deficit and hyperactivity? The circularity inherent in a supposed medical condition that is defined by a description somehow causing itself seemed obvious to me. A behaviour cannot cause itself. Having hyperactivity cannot be the cause of a hyperactivity disorder.

In September 2000, by now witnessing the rise of ADHD in clinical practice and broader society, I attended the annual conference of the Faculty of Child and Adolescent Psychiatry at the Royal College of Psychiatrists. The keynote speech, delivered by the then chair of our faculty, discussed the recently published 'Multimodal Treatment of children with ADHD' (MTA) study.[1] This American study was about to become one of, if not the, most famous studies on the treatment of ADHD. Our esteemed professor stated that the implications were that we would have to prescribe stimulants for anyone diagnosed with ADHD and probably (given resource limitations) prescribed stimulants (such as methylphenidate, more commonly known by the brand name Ritalin) alone would be sufficient for most.

The MTA study was a fourteen-month multi-location trial where 527 seven- to ten-year-old patients were randomised to four treatment groups: medication (methylphenidate) only, behaviour therapy only, combined medication and behaviour therapy, and routine community care.

The authors concluded that after fourteen months of treatment, there was more reduction of ADHD symptoms in the medication only and combined medication and behaviour therapy groups than the behavioural therapy only group, who in turn did better than the routine community care group. A more detailed reading revealed some problems with this conclusion. For example, two-thirds of the routine community care group were also prescribed stimulants yet had the poorest outcomes. The behavioural treatment arm consisted of an intensive six-week course that was completed at any time during the fourteen months, so that by the time of the fourteen-month evaluation, some of the families receiving the behavioural therapy intervention had completed it up to nine months before the final fourteen-month assessments. The medication group had regular appointments throughout the study period. This raised the distinct possibility of a placebo response being the main reason for better outcomes in the medication and combined medication and behaviour therapy treatment arms, as, unlike the other two groups, they had regular reviews for all fourteen months of the study.

The fourteen-month MTA study became the most quoted study for ADHD treatments, regularly referred to in the treatment guidelines of many countries. But the story does not end here.

I was at a large psychotherapy conference in Phoenix, Arizona, in 2002. In a hall with several thousand people, I ended up sitting next to a psychologist from California. We chatted in between talks and discovered that we had a mutual interest in the subject of ADHD. I was intrigued to discover that he was involved in the evaluations of the MTA trial at one of the treatment centres. He had my total attention as we discussed over lunch what was happening in the trial now. He told me that the team he worked with had just completed analysing the data for the three-year follow-up. I remember him saying, 'Once these findings are published no one will want to have their child take medication any more.'

I was surprised by the clarity and certainty of this conclusion. He explained that in his centre a lot of the children who stayed on medication had got worse and experienced a variety of adverse effects, while those who had stayed off medication were doing better. He told me their results were like the other centres and it wouldn't be too long before they were published.

Years passed and there was no sign of this three-year outcome study. Maybe I had just imagined the whole conversation. Maybe the study had been abandoned.

It was five years later, in 2007, when the three-year follow-up of the MTA study was finally published.[2] Unlike the original 1999 study, this paper, published eight years later (allowing plenty of time for stimulant prescribing advocated by the 1999 paper to become the norm), had little accompanying press or professional coverage. After fourteen months, the participants in the study had been free to choose their ongoing treatments. It had, in effect, become a naturalistic study, similar to what happens in everyday clinical settings. The three-year outcomes could not find support for continuing superiority of medication regardless of the initial severity of ADHD symptoms. On top of that, those who were on continuous medication during the three years were more likely to experience a deterioration in ADHD symptoms, had higher rates of delinquency, and were significantly shorter (by an average of 4cm) and lighter (by 3kg) than those who had not taken medication.

By three years, then, the miracle story of stimulant medication is decaying. Those who continued to take it for treatment of ADHD were not doing any better and experiencing more negative effects than those who didn't. This supported my earlier hunch that placebo had likely played a role in the fourteen-month findings. What the psychologist told me five years earlier was right. Who in their right mind would now want to continue giving any child stimulants for ADHD?

Also in 2007, the National Institute of Clinical Excellence (NICE – now renamed as the National Institute of Health and Care Excellence) began work on developing the first UK guideline for the assessment and treatment of ADHD, which has since become influential in its impact on guidelines in many countries. I was invited to present to the guideline development group at a 'conference of experts' that they specifically set up to consider the question of the validity of the diagnosis. I had prepared a presentation based on my research that showed ADHD did not reach the standards for a valid medical diagnosis, let alone one considered neurodevelopmental in nature.

At the end of my forty-five-minute presentation, the five members of the guideline development group thanked me and then stared ahead blankly for what seemed like a lifetime. I gathered my notes, took a sip of water and prepared to head back to my seat, when one of the group said, 'Can I ask you, Dr Timimi, do you or would you ever prescribe stimulants?' I answered (truthfully), 'Yes, I have done, but hardly ever do it now.' There were no more questions. Nothing about the presentation I had just done or the question which the conference was meant to address about the validity of ADHD. I left that meeting later with a migraine, wondering about what had just happened.

When the ADHD NICE Guideline was published in 2008,[3] there was no mention of any of the content of the critiques I presented, just that ADHD was a valid diagnosis and the recommendation to use stimulants like methylphenidate (an amphetamine analogue) as a first-line treatment for those with 'severe ADHD'. What was the justification for this? *'Even the most ardent supporters of non-pharmacological interventions in ADHD recognised the importance of pharmacological treatment in the most severe cases.'* This referred to my answer to the single question I received. Another reason they gave involved a reanalysis of some of the data from the fourteen-month MTA study, which concluded that a subgroup of children with more severe ADHD symptoms showed a larger decrease in symptoms with medication than with behaviour therapy. Yet the three-year MTA outcomes did not show any beneficial long-term effects of medication over behaviour therapy, even in those with more severe symptoms at the start. In fact, they were more likely to deteriorate. That follow-up study was available to the guideline development group, but they had chosen to ignore it.[4]

I now wonder whether I unwittingly played a part in the spread of the medicalisation of behaviour. It is, I guess, difficult for a guideline group made of advocates for the concept of ADHD (many of whose careers are enhanced by their work in this area) to conclude that it doesn't reach the standards of a valid medical condition, or that the favoured treatment may be problematic. ADHD was here to stay, as was treatment with medication.

In the post-lockdown world there has been an extraordinary expansion in the numbers getting an ADHD diagnosis with one celebrity after another being diagnosed as having a brain-based disorder that apparently results from a chemical imbalance. I understand why people might seek such a diagnosis. It is something we in the medical profession have, after all, been promoting.

Like autism, ADHD has gone from a peripheral phenomenon in practice and culture to being something that just about anyone could have. The necessary bit in between – some empirical findings to support the reality of these conditions – is, as I'll discuss in subsequent chapters, pretty much non-existent. Sitting in my supervising consultant's office all those many moons ago seems like another era.

Times they are a-changing

February 1992. I'm in the consulting-room side of a one-way mirror divide.* Seated next to me is an experienced family therapist who

---

* A one-way mirror, also called two-way mirror, is a reciprocal mirror that appears reflective from one side and transparent from the other. When the room on one side of the mirror is more brightly lit than the other side it allows viewing through the mirror from the darker room into the lighter one, but not from the lighter one into the darker one.

gestures with her hands and sits forward in her seat as she talks with empathy and animation to the family we are seeing. Opposite us in the room are four people, thirteen-year-old Sofia, her older sister Julieta and their mother and father. The parents speak with a strong Spanish accent. The girls' mother has an anxious look on her face. She has one hand on Sofia's knee. Sofia looks away perhaps in embarrassment or disgust (at herself or her mother?), Julieta is looking at Sofia with a sharpness that suggests annoyance, occasionally rolling her eyes when Sofia or their mother speaks. Their father, physically separate, his chair being out of touching distance with the rest of his family, only answers questions if specifically asked. He seems somewhat peripheral to the charged relational dynamic in the room. They are here because Sofia has recently taken an overdose of paracetamol.

I'm feeling overwhelmed. I have recently started my first placement in a child and adolescent psychiatry service. This is the first time I am in front of the one-way mirror. So far in my psychiatry training I have managed outpatient and inpatient caseloads and completed individual psychotherapy interventions as well as assessments and medication reviews. I'm used to engaging with people in one-to-one meetings. Interviewing a whole family where intense emotions are swirling is new to me. How do I keep everyone in mind? Who should I ask questions to? How do I carry out an assessment?

I'm deeply impressed (and relieved) by the skill of the family therapist. She asks questions in an indirect way that I hadn't encountered before. For example, rather than first asking Sofia, she asks her mother how she thinks Sofia feels. Somehow, she manages to engage the four family members and, gradually, they all get involved in the conversation.

After about an hour we take a break and go to the viewing room behind the one-way mirror. Our supervising consultant and a senior trainee have been watching the session. We discuss what's happened so far. We talk about their history, the relational dynamic, the strengths in the family system and what sort of intervention we might recommend.

I am learning that in child psychiatry the 'identified patient' (in this case Sofia) is not the only, or even the main, focus of therapeutic efforts. Sofia exists within a relational network, particularly her immediate family, and working with this network may be more impactful than trying to adjust/treat something thought to be in her mind/brain.

This child psychiatry department was on the top two floors of a children's hospital in central London (the building, like so many other valuable sites, has since been sold off and is now luxury apartments). My supervising consultant was a tall, enigmatic and smartly dressed clean-shaven middle-aged man with wit, energy and more than a hint of mischief in his demeanour. He had an interest in culture and its intersection with mental health. His sharp intellect mixed with his impressive capacity to dissect dynamics and arrive at novel formulations and interventions made for engaging supervision sessions. The department employed family therapists, psychologists, social workers and child psychotherapists, as well as psychiatrists. They used a variety of therapeutic models and techniques. We had access to two inpatient beds in addition to the outpatient work and provided advice to paediatric staff in other departments of the hospital.

I recall being stimulated by the many interesting and creative interventions that were offered. From trying to improve communication in a family, to helping develop support networks around the young person; from individualised interventions around managing conflicts, to providing hope and creating safety. Some interventions were successful and proved helpful, others less so, and some interventions I would now view as problematic. What I don't recall is any importance being given to the question of what diagnosis anybody should have. Categorisation was mostly based on the face-value descriptions of the main problem that resulted in a referral. There were 'behaviour problems', 'eating issues', 'self-harm', 'suicidal feelings', 'overdoses' and occasionally 'psychotic' presentations. We never categorised anyone as having ADHD, or autism, or childhood depression. This was how I was taught child psychiatry.

My nine-month placement in the child psychiatry placement convinced me that this was the medical specialty for me. In adult psychiatry I had concluded that you spend most of your time as a glorified pharmacist. All I could see from adult psychiatry practice was a conveyer belt of changing medications and adding medications until patients were on multiple pills gradually cycling through all the limited number of drugs a psychiatrist can prescribe. The patients you then see in clinic have become numbers in a system, living a chronic relapsing course, spending year after year in psychiatric services, with many never really getting their life fully back on track.

The gift of child psychiatry to the rest of psychiatry, and indeed to medicine and health care in general, I felt to be twofold. First is development. Development in the broadest sense helps us appreciate that life is in constant motion, that change is the one predictable aspect of living. When dealing with young people you become familiar with the fact that their bodies will change, so will their interests, their relationships, their emotional depth, what they view as significant and important, their ambitions, their sleep pattern, their social and political beliefs, the music they like, their sexuality, and so on. The only thing I can predict with certainty when I see a young person is that they will change. However, none of us know in what way they will change. There's something quite marvellous about that.

The second gift is understanding that life exists in contexts. Most of the important decisions that affect children's lives are not made by them but by various people in caring relationships to them. Our life contexts simultaneously provide possibilities and limitations. There are material contexts, social contexts, historical contexts, cultural contexts, relational contexts, and our understanding of what is happening in our lives will be influenced by all of these. Each context contributes to the nature of the meaning-making frameworks through which we scaffold our experience and interpret the significance of all that happens to us.

I consider myself to be a traditional child psychiatrist. Respecting the twin pillars of development and context has allowed me to view what we consider to be mental health problems through the lens of the ordinary and extraordinary, rather than normal and abnormal. This means thinking systemically and developmentally about the dilemmas that people face at certain points in their lives. All we can do is generate various subjective hypotheses (which we often call a formulation) about the situation of a person/family, and the nature of that hypothesis will carry implications for how we then intervene. We cannot know the truth about their experiences.

Little did I know, when I first stepped into the world of child psychiatry three decades ago, how far and deep the tentacles of diagnostic mental health ideology would reach. That the diagnostic ideology – so demoralising in adult psychiatry – would start to strangle my adopted profession, bringing along with it a culture of pathologising, labelling and medicating. There has never been a generation of young people so colonised at such a young age by mental health propaganda.

Neither did I realise that child psychiatry itself would become an exporter to the world of adult psychiatry, causing the ballooning of concepts originally developed for the young, such as ADHD and autism. We have now long surpassed in mythology the phrenologists of the Victorian era and the quackery of astrological chart readings. People really believe that the developments in psychiatric diagnosis and treatment are the result of science. I hope this book will help disabuse some of you of that notion.

These days practice in child and adolescent mental health has been expunged of the curiosity and openness of a developmental and contextual backdrop, in favour of 'treatment pathways'. As mentioned in the preface, in the treatment pathway model, you get a diagnosis, which then informs you about the correct treatment. This individualised model has facilitated the growth of certain therapies, particularly cognitive behavioural therapy (CBT), on the one hand and medication use on the other. The idea of seeing young people, like Sofia, in the context of their family and community, is now relegated to a side show, where the young person might be referred to a 'family therapy clinic'. This is a model that sees the patient as the location of the problem when things don't improve after receiving what is considered the correct treatment for their diagnosis. When this happens you become at risk of accumulating new diagnoses, being labelled as 'treatment-resistant', and having medications added to whatever has already been prescribed.

Now people cling to their diagnoses. They have become woven

into their identities, as if it's like being a punk, identifying as an Australian, or as a fan of Southampton Football Club. The medical establishment has long been selling the story that each problem has a cause (a diagnosis) and a technical solution, whether pharmaceutical or psychotherapeutic. In a strange contortion of logic, it's not unusual to hear 'I thought it was just me, but now I know it was my ADHD', with ADHD then simultaneously occupying a role as an identity and the function of 'something that's not me'.

It seems a lifetime since the days I first encountered and found sanity in child and adolescent mental health. I can hardly picture those times any more.

2. What is mental health?

'Life is not a problem to be solved but a reality to be experienced.'

Søren Kierkegaard

Fen Su is sitting in my consulting room next to a member of her boarding-school support staff who is accompanying her to this initial consultation. She is dressed in her school uniform – a maroon blazer with the school emblem stuck to an upper pocket and a grey pleated skirt. She has straight black hair and a neatly cut fringe. She mostly stares at the floor, sometimes looking up and straight at me with a quizzical (can't tell if it's also hostile) look on her face. She also displays some humour, with the occasional sarcastic comment in her less than perfect (but nonetheless impressively good) English.

Fen Su is fifteen years old and this is her second year at the local girls' boarding school. Her parents live in Singapore. She's a very capable student and does well in her exams. A couple of weeks ago there was an incident that led to her being taken to A&E after an 'outburst' that resulted in her cutting herself with a razor.

The report from the on-call psychiatrist who saw her in A&E stated that Fen Su was presenting with a history of low mood and some difficulty sleeping. Fen Su had claimed that the reason for the self-harm was because she was feeling upset and annoyed with herself for a piece of schoolwork that she felt she had done badly. The report said that in her frustration she had broken a pencil, pulled at a wardrobe door until it came off its hinges, and this was then followed by cutting herself with a razor.

When staff found her, having heard the commotion, she was sitting on her bed crying and shouting 'leave me alone', while a couple of students were sitting next to her, trying to talk to her. Her forearm had blood dripping from it. In A&E she was also referred for a 'safeguarding' assessment because she mentioned that in the past her parents had physically punished her. However, when the social worker interviewed Fen Su later, she denied that she had ever said this.

The referring psychiatrist's conclusion was that Fen Su was likely experiencing an episode of depression and that as a result she should receive a course of cognitive behavioural therapy and medication such as fluoxetine (an antidepressant) should also be considered.

On meeting Fen Su a couple of weeks after the incident, she turns out to be, as so often happens, quite different from the person I had conjured up in my imagination. I am regularly reminded that one of the most important aspects of seeing people for mental health assessments is to approach each situation, each person, each family with an open mind, where curiosity and humility are, to me, vital ingredients enabling access to competing versions of the potential stories that might be told.

I discover that Fen Su is a lively and opinionated young person. She's not afraid to share her views or contradict the support worker accompanying her. Fen Su is adamant that she's fine, doesn't need any help, and doesn't want therapy or medication. She feels embarrassed about what has happened. She confirms that she did get very upset about the disappointing (to her) mark in a test and had been struggling with a new piece of work. She explains how her parents had sacrificed their own comfort to pay for her to go to this boarding school and that she doesn't want to disappoint them. She insists that she doesn't feel under pressure from her parents, that she loves them, and that she set the high standards for herself.

Her parents had wanted her to come home after hearing what had happened, but Fen Su does not want to do that, and she did not want them to come over to the UK either. She says that in a fit of anger at herself she self-harmed using a razor, because she had seen another girl in her dormitory do that and had heard that it helps with getting rid of horrible feelings. She's open about feeling low since the start of this school year because she was finding the schoolwork harder. She does have a couple of other girls in her year whom she is friendly with, but admits that she spends most of her time focusing on her studies. She wants to be able to go to one of the top universities and is hoping to study medicine in the future.

She doesn't think that she would self-harm again and denies having any suicidal plans. When asked about her parents sometimes hitting her, she replies that she used to get some physical punishment when she was younger, but this is not something that happens now and hasn't for many years. She adds that 'you don't understand how Asian parents show love to their children'.

In her opinion what would be most helpful for her now would be for the school to stop making such a fuss, stop taking her to appointments that she doesn't need, and instead give her more support with her studies. The school support worker, however, explains that the school is worried about Fen Su and about how she's feeling. They think that she needs a proper mental health assessment, and the report from the on-call psychiatrist had recommended treatment that they are happy to support Fen Su accessing. They feel that helping her with her mental health is the priority and believe that for her to be able to get on with her studies she first needs to improve her mental health.

What is the truth here? Indeed, is it possible to establish the definitive truth? Or is it even helpful to approach this situation with the idea that there is a truth to be uncovered? Perhaps a more useful question might be which version is going to be the most helpful. How should we go about the task of constructing this story? What meaning-making framework would enable progress, or at least minimise potential harms? Should we focus on what we might construe as symptoms of an illness or disease state and then provide treatments that aim to decrease, eliminate or otherwise better manage those symptoms? Should we frame this in more ordinary terms as a situation with a young person who is away from the familiarity of family and culture, who is experiencing a psychological crisis because of a disruption in her perceived sense of purpose? Do we need to go down a mental health framing as the school desire or abandon that framing as Fen Su wants us to do? Should the admission that her parents have sometimes, when she was younger, physically punished her require a safeguarding consultation, be perceived as 'trauma', or should we view this in more cultural terms?

Before returning to Fen Su's case at the end of this chapter, I want to explain why such questions are difficult to answer. Too often in our engagement with notions of mental health or illness, we act as if we can. But when it comes to what we consider to be mental illness or disorder, we literally don't know what we're talking about. Unfortunately, professionals, academics, journalists, teachers, politicians, etc., often act as if we do.

What is mental health or ill health?

Far from not talking about mental health, these days we are fed a saturated diet of mental health awareness, warning us of mental health pandemics, lack of services, and the importance of early treatment. But this explosion of interest assumes we know what we mean by mental health.

You'd be forgiven for thinking that there are specific targeted treatments out there and that people get better with interventions delivered by professionals with special expertise. You'd likely think that the main societal issues with mental health are stigma and lack of services, that there is woeful underfunding and long waiting lists, that the scandal is the lack of quick access and adequate availability of health care and support for those who have been struck down by a mental disorder, and that more needs to be done to educate the population about 'mental health'.

But these are not the real problems. Let's start by unpicking some basic assumptions, through asking the questions *what is mental health?* and, by implication, *what is a mental disorder or illness?*

These are the two related questions I have been posing for many years in workshops I run. I have asked lay audiences, psychiatrists, psychologists, teachers and psychotherapists, from trainees with little experience to others with many years working in health services. The answers I receive are revealing.

I am still waiting for somebody to give me an answer that

demonstrates they can pin down, with some sort of empirical anchor, a definition that reaches out beyond a subjective opinion and into the territory of measurable facts. The sort of answers I receive include references to getting or losing a sense of balance in your life, or the absence of a mental condition, or the ability to function, or a behaviour/experience that is considered outside of accepted cultural norms, or how you feel, or the absence of mental pain and suffering, to name a few. Some have put their definition in more medicalised terms, like having anxiety or depression; others have used more ordinary language, referring to being stressed, feeling overwhelmed or unable to cope. Try answering those two questions yourself.

Perhaps the closest I have come to what might be considered an attempt at a more empirical definition is referring to experiences such as 'mood' as existing on a spectrum across the population, with those who are on the statistical extremes of this spectrum being considered as mentally disordered/ill. However, this doesn't resolve the problem of subjectivity. What is meant by 'extremes'? What sort of distribution are we talking about? How are you intending to measure 'mood'? Why would 'mood' even be considered something to be framed as independent of context? When can mood be a symptom as opposed to an experience? You soon realise that attempts at grounding 'mental disorder/health' into existing in an objective factual world quickly disintegrates and dissolves back into the sea of subjectivity.

The World Health Organization defines mental health as 'a state of well-being in which the individual realizes his or her abilities, can cope with the normal stresses of life, work productively and fruitfully, and is able to make a contribution to his or her community'.[1]

This definition doesn't take us any closer to knowing what we mean by mental health. What does 'realize abilities' mean? Is it in the sense of being aware of them, or in the sense of putting them into effect? What are 'the normal stresses of life' and what do they mean by 'cope' with them? What does working 'productively and fruitfully' entail? How does a person know that they are contributing to a community? Which community? How do you define 'contribution' anyway? There must be many people who, for lack of education, money or opportunity, are in practice unable to do so. Are these unfortunates by definition mentally ill? I could go on.

The truth is that we are unable to escape something that all the definitions of mental health or illness I have encountered have in common. They are all subjective. They are constructed by a belief, an opinion, an idea. They are not phenomena that lend themselves to sitting in the world of objective facts in the same way that a broken bone does.

This is not to conclude that definitions of health in general don't also have a large element of subjectivity, but, as I will go on to discuss, it is possible to locate physical ill health and disease largely, but not exclusively, within the realm of the objective factual world. A broken bone or heart failure exists in a concrete form that is measurable and identifiable empirically and so beyond just the imagination of the person involved in identifying these pathologies.

So, what do people mean when they talk about mental disorder, mental health or mental illness? What sort of 'thing' is a mental disorder? Where are its boundaries? When does a behaviour become abnormal or disordered or pathological and who decides based on what? While the issue of how to define what is ordinary and what is not is something that most of medicine grapples with, when it comes to mental disorder, we have a whole new level of potential confusion, uncertainty and meanings to get through before we can assert something to be out of the ordinary, abnormal or disordered. In mental health the entire phenomena require interpretation, not just the boundaries.

A brief comparison between physical illness and mental illness

Take, for example, the relatively straightforward situation where there is minimal confusion about the nature of the problem we are dealing with. You were running, slipped on some ice and fell forward onto your outstretched arms with force. You feel a sudden extreme pain in your right forearm. Over the next hour you notice some swelling and bruising develop in that forearm. The pain is worse if you try and turn your arm from palm up to palm down or vice versa. It's also worse if you extend your arm, so you find yourself supporting the right arm with your left one. You decide you need to go to your local A&E.

At the hospital an X-ray reveals that there is a hairline fracture in the radius and ulna. In this scenario the medical model is working at its best.* You now have the explanation for why you have those symptoms of pain, swelling and inability to turn your arm. The fracture is what is known as a 'natural kind', so in terms of classification the diagnosis explains an abnormality in the person's physical body that can be empirically verified.

A 'natural kind' refers to something that exists in reality beyond our subjective hypothesis. It is a verifiable fact of nature. We can now develop knowledge that relates to this natural phenomenon. Just as the chair I am sitting on can be weighed, measured and analysed in all sorts of empirical ways, so we can build technical knowledge about fractures of the ulna and radius by comparing many people who have the same condition. We can investigate different treatment approaches and combinations, grade different types of severity and look at the various factors (in the fracture, the body of the person, the type of accident, and so on) which might affect responses to different treatments.

However, hairline fractures are easily missed, so there is a technical challenge here, too. There is also an important psychosocial dimension. For example, what does this mean for your income if you're a self-employed carpenter? Can you afford to lose that income, while your arm is in a plaster cast? Will you risk long-term complications by trying to return to work too early? These technical, psychological and social questions are always present in health care.

Notwithstanding these limitations, medicine is particularly good at such emergency scenarios where there is an identified abnormality and where the treatment period is relatively short. Here we can

---

* The medical model refers to the basic assumption that there are diseases that have some bodily causes enabling diagnosis to establish the cause and shape the resulting treatment.

gather data on the disease, treatment, recovery, complications, and so on, using empirical evidence. We know what sort of 'thing' a fracture of a bone is.

Not all presentations to doctors follow this easy-to-understand idea of what sort of thing we are dealing with. Let's take diabetes as an example. The connection between symptoms and the underlying cause may not be as immediately apparent. In diabetes a diagnosis refers to an abnormality of sugar metabolism and this can be measured mainly through blood tests but also in other ways, such as through testing urine for something called ketones. Some abnormality of blood sugar metabolism may exist for a period of time without any obvious symptoms. The sufferer may just have some non-specific symptoms such as generalised tiredness, particularly in type 2 diabetes, which has an onset later in life when the body becomes resistant to insulin or when the pancreas is unable to produce enough insulin. Type 2 diabetes could present just as a susceptibility to infections and so go unnoticed for months or even years.

Nonetheless, there is still a physical parameter that can be measured and there is a physiological process present in the body and that exists in the world external to the imagination of the doctor assessing the patient. Diabetes is defined as an abnormality that results in blood sugar being too high. It is then verifiable using data that is independent of subjective opinion. You have established a proximal cause – blood sugar that is too high – for the symptoms. There may be more distal causes (related to diet and lifestyle for example) but blood sugar is a measurable parameter, which when it's too high can cause a range of other problems. So, in this example, while the connections between symptoms and disease are not as clear and may be missed in the early stages or by a poorly trained doctor, the diagnosis is again explanatory. It is pointing to an abnormality that can cause symptoms in the patient and will cause more if not treated.

There are many disagreements in type 2 diabetes diagnosis and treatment; for example, when to consider the blood sugar has crossed a threshold justifying a diagnosis, whether to just use dietary approaches and for how long, when to use medication, how to deal with complications, the psychological impact of having a chronic disease, issues related to diet and lifestyle, the social dimension of long-term care, and so on. But still, we know what sort of 'thing' diabetes is.

So far so good. Now we start to get into medical conditions which can have recognisable symptoms and sometimes physical signs and some objective tests, but in which there are mysteries as to the initial cause. Many types of headaches, such as migraines, are good examples of this category. Diagnoses such as migraine are mainly based on a description of symptoms. We are now moving towards a descriptive rather than explanatory system. However, given that there are characteristic physical symptoms that justify being given the label of 'abnormal' (such as in migraine you may get blurring of vision, pain behind the eyes on one side of the face, and an enhanced sensitivity to light), it is likely that there is physical pathology involved. The presentation tends to be characteristic, has physical symptoms, and so it's reasonable to assume that it involves specific bodily processes.

So, we may argue that we know the sort of 'thing' migraine is, though we are now getting into some more fuzzy territory. We are beginning to move towards a more descriptive territory, where the proximal cause is less clear. With pain and the nervous system so involved, psychosocial aspects are becoming more prominent. But the idea of being a physiological condition (meaning medically it will be called a disease) still stands.

Once we come to talk about mental disorders, we start to get into a whole array of problems in order to support the idea that we have a 'thing' that can be considered in the same set of explanatory arenas as other 'natural kinds' found in medicine. The territory for what we have been calling 'symptoms' of a mental disorder are now experiences and behaviours that have meanings and that may be interpreted differently by different cultures, different times and in different settings.

This means we are shifting to an area of practice where there are not only disagreements and debates about where the boundaries are, but we must also take into account the significance and relevance of the diverse meanings that can be attached to symptoms, such that they are interpreted as symptoms in one setting, but not in others.

We have no signs, no tests, no physical correlates, and so are entirely reliant on observations and reports of the person and/or their significant other(s). It's all subjective and opinion based. We have now strayed into a different conceptual field.

The fact that health in general also has important dimensions involving subjective appraisals means we cannot escape the experiential realm when it comes to making judgements about the nature of all health and ill health. This is why I believe that a reformed psychiatry and reformed mental health services have an important – I would say vital – contribution to make to health care in general. Health care is a social activity which involves people in various caring relationships to others. Thus, while I am arguing that making some separation between mental and physical health is necessary (for example in what we label as symptoms or diseases), it is also potentially problematic to insist on complete separation and miss the important overlaps.

All health care involves engagement with the experience of suffering. The psychosocial contexts of people's lives, including the political ones that structure their experiences and beliefs, influence not only the types of diseases and distress they are afflicted with, but also a whole spectrum of health outcomes. Politics and subjectivity cannot be avoided. However, as I have been illustrating, in much of the rest of medical practice there is a significant technical component based on an empirical understanding that is beyond the subjectivity of the person doing the understanding. This technical knowledge then has a defining role in choosing specific treatments.

That we have not made (and probably will not make) progress in that technical understanding of what is happening in the bodies and brains of those we consider to have a mental disorder, marks an important difference that characterises mental health care. Far from something that we in my profession should feel embarrassed about, it's something that we should actively engage with if we're going to move health care in general, and mental health care in particular, to a kinder, more humane and collaborative footing.

Mental health, illness and disorder cannot be thought of as out there in the natural world, existing somewhere within the body of the person, in a way that is identifiable as a concrete 'thing'. It's not definable in a causal way in the same way as a fracture in the arm, diabetes, or even migraine. And yet this is the way we talk about mental health and illness, as if we know what sort of 'thing' this is and assume that it exists within a person regardless of their context. If you hear one in four of the population are possessed by or will be possessed by a mental disorder, be wary. It's an appalling mistake to make with appalling consequences for patients and professionals alike. One in four who have what sort of 'thing'? Where is this 'thing' located and how do I find it? How can I truly develop an accurate way of 'measuring' it if I can't locate it as an empirically knowable 'thing'?

What is 'mental'?

What do we mean by something being 'mental'? How is it different to other terms we might use like 'soul' or 'psyche'? Where is the 'mind', which apparently suffers disease, located? How does it relate to the concept of a 'self'? What do we mean by 'cognitive' and other commonly used terms in scientific writings? If they are all just as slippery as mental health or illness, what does it mean when we use those terms as if they are not constructs and abstract concepts, but scientifically known or knowable facts of nature?

Arabic is my second language and I have written a couple of papers for the *Arab Journal of Psychiatry* in the past. Their requirement is that you can write in English or Arabic but must have an abstract (a summary of the journal article) in both languages. I had to call on my father to help with this task as I immediately stumbled on a problem with the Arabic version of the abstract. There is no direct Arabic word for 'mental'.

My father and I concluded that there are three, maybe four, words that could be used. They refer to the brain, the intellect and a concept of self. The word I settled on, and is most commonly used in Arab psychiatry, is *nafseeyah*, which approximately refers to a soul-self (in translation from Arabic back to English it's also not easy to find an exact word). This word has roots in *tenafas*, which means 'to breathe'.

In language we can see how concepts such as self and mentalising draw on differing conceptual frameworks. The common word for behaving in a 'crazy' way in Arabic is *majnoon*, whose roots lie in the word *jinn*, which refers to supernatural spirits (which can be benevolent or malevolent) and therefore implies a possession state; whereas the English *madness* derives from *mad*, which we also use to refer to anger and/or foolishness.

References to breath and breathing figure prominently in many Eastern religious and spiritual practices. Theological conceptions of the importance of breath have led many of the world's traditions to feature respiratory exercises in their religious disciplines. The theme of breath, along with related notions of vitality and energy, has been associated with the 'soul' and with questions regarding the boundaries between mortal and immortal aspects of human life.

There are some biblical references to the connection between breath and the soul. In Genesis, God 'formed man of dust from the ground, and breathed into his nostrils the breath of life; and man became a living being'.[2] The Hebrew term *ruah* means breath, wind or spirit. The term also refers to the thing that animates emotions such as agitation, anger, vigour, courage, impatience, impulsiveness, jealousy and envy. As with the closely related *nafseeyah*, the Hebrew term *neshama* refers to a soul, spirit or breath.

The Arabic terms related to breath parallel the Hebrew ones. In pre-Quranic poetry, for example, *nafs* is the self and *ruh* is breath and wind. In the Quran, *nafs* takes on the additional meaning of 'soul'. Classical Islamic philosophy gives a central role to breath in the perfection of humanity within the cosmos and is identified with the force of life itself and a link between the bodily and spiritual aspects of an individual's being. Breath is thus closely aligned to soul, spirituality and a sense of self.

In the West we are perhaps most familiar with the role of breath in the Westernised versions of Hindu philosophy found in practices such as yoga. The Sanskrit term *prāṇa* can refer to breath, respiration, life, vitality, energy and strength. It's used to indicate the vital breaths in the body but also to the individual soul, its natural correlate the atmospheric wind and the broader cosmic order. These ideas influenced Indian medical theory and provided the basis for identifying a range of different types of breathing, with differing consequences, giving rise to a variety of health-related techniques.

My little sidetracking into breath, breathing, the soul, the mind and mental is to give you a tiny bit of the iceberg, showing where mining the assumptions constructing something as apparently simple as 'mental' can lead. There are millennia of thought and practice. These are rich, diverse and deep, with traditions that have delved into foundational questions concerning the essence of human experience. In such a historical context, the idea that we know what 'mental' is looks alarmingly superficial.

Where is the self?

Discussion about the nature of the self raises similar questions to that which I have introduced in relation to the concept of mental. Where is the location of the self? Is there such a thing as a 'true self'? If so, how do we find it and what does that mean for those experiences and behaviours that we do not consider part of that true self? When we talk about 'finding yourself', is there a self to find? Can a self exist in isolation from other selves or without a world to relate to?

Philosophers, theologians, sociologists, anthropologists and many others have been grappling with these questions for centuries. These technologies of self have emphasised all sorts of phenomena that are thought to shape how we experience and understand our being in the world. From the invisible hands of supernatural forces of ancestors and gods to the structures of social power that tell the public what the normal/common sense should be, to the potential for agency and resistance individuals have to dominating beliefs. We cannot escape subjectivity in our attempts to understand subjectivity.

Thus, the ways we imagine what the self is cannot be fixed but is fluid and changeable, with different cultures and different times having different ideals through which to interpret and understand our experiences. Perhaps the one thing we could reliably say is that the self is dynamic and therefore always in motion. Perhaps the idea of a fixed stable self is the one aspect of defining the self that we should reject. Indeed, perhaps the very preoccupation with a notion of the self is itself a product of a particular cultural fixation.

In very broad terms, sociologists and anthropologists have described a general tendency of cultures across the world to stress individualism (for example, in the Anglosphere West) or collectivism (for example, in most Asian and African cultures). They are created as concepts by contrasting their inclinations. Collectivism stresses the importance of the community, while individualism is focused on the concerns of each person. Where unity, selflessness and altruism are valued traits in collectivist cultures, autonomy and identity are promoted in individualistic ones. This can be further boiled down to emphasising responsibility and duty (collectivism) or rights and freedoms (individualism).

I'm acutely aware of how different my children's experience of growing up has been to my own. They grew up behind the closed doors of the play-by-appointment of a nuclear family, whereas my formative years were in the more collectivist environment in the dry heat of Basra in Iraq, surrounded by extended family with a free flow of people between families, and where one of my matriarch aunts treated me as just another of her children.

Although you can make a sort of translation of self-esteem into Arabic, it doesn't really exist as a concept. Personhood in the Iraqi culture of my childhood is relational. The idea of self-care, self-love is not only culturally absent, but positively strange to someone whose concept of self is defined by relationships. How can you feel 'better in yourself' without others to feel better with?

With the dominance of a scientific cosmology in collaboration with an individual consumerist orientation, in modern (or even postmodern) Western individualism we tend to think about the self in more rational terms, often using the language of science. We believe psychology to be a branch of science (because it uses the language of research and numbers) that helps us understand the human condition. Problems of the self (what we often see as the remit of 'mental health' services) are then dealt with by experts who use this language of science and logic. Furthermore, identity and a belief in a unique and separate 'you', which must be known and discovered in order to function within society and find a place in it, takes on an importance that is marginal for more collectivist selves.

Many consequences flow from this way of understanding the self and its problems. For example, it results in an obsession with classifying individuals and their experiences as a starting point for making sense of their problems. The process we use starts with analysing the individual for signs of 'psychopathology', 'dysregulation', etc., and then uses these to slot them into a 'typology' (which, as I discuss in the next chapter, we mistakenly call a diagnosis). The typologies we developed in this mental health ideology have since migrated into the lucrative and on-trend fascination with identity.

These political and cultural inclinations create an internal world, increasingly viewed as fixed and unalterable, where relationships, together with cultural and material contexts, are secondary in shaping our experience of the world we move through. This view then constructs emotions as an obstacle to be tamed to achieve a rational way of living. Thus, much of psychiatric and psychological technology is suspicious of what emotions do to us and uses interventions whose *raison d'être* is ultimately the control of emotions.

Another consequence of this way of constructing 'what it means to be human' is that we have outlined, classified and advertised all sorts of ways that human experience can go wrong. This creates a sense of vulnerability for most of us as we are sensitised to the ever-expanding possibility that something has gone wrong in us, or that we have some essential hard-wired difference that makes us unable to function in certain environments (rather than the environments themselves being hostile to the way many humans function).

We do not have access to infinite ways of making sense of our experiences and will inevitably draw on the making sense efforts of those we grow up with and other influences we are exposed to (such as the media including social media). In any society at any one time there will be a variety of ways available to make sense of any dilemma, but some will be more dominant than others. Those with more power to sell their version of reality will have more influence on what that dominating story will be.

So, what does all this deconstruction that I have embarked upon in this chapter mean? It means that when it comes to mental health or mental illness/disorder we literally don't know what we're talking about.

What happened to Fen Su?

Let's return to my first meeting with Fen Su. She is living away from her parents at a boarding school and recently attended A&E after self-harm. The psychiatrist who assessed her at A&E thinks she has depression, but Fen Su doesn't want any 'treatment'. Now that I have disrupted the idea that there is a truth to uncover, I will discuss how this helps me move beyond the standard psychiatric assessment I outlined in the preface (of noting symptoms and using that to make a diagnosis and treatment plan).

The potential harms of taking Fen Su down the diagnosis/treatment path are enormous. Not only does it indicate to her and those around her that her emotional reactions were abnormal and a sign of a disease/disorder (depression), thus creating a goal of getting rid of or suppressing/controlling these upsetting emotions, but it may expose her to medications (such as the fluoxetine that was recommended) with little evidence of producing lasting benefit, but much evidence for potential harms (see Chapter 11).

But this is not the approach I chose. I treated Fen Su's version as having some face value, while also silently wondering about the role shame might have to play (shame is more common in a collectivist culture, as opposed to guilt, which is a more individualist concern).

My favoured construct, which I drew upon to help move the dominant narrative from a mental disorder needing treatment, was that Fen Su was reacting in an understandable manner to a dilemma she was facing. I asked more questions about her evident talent, her strengths, how she'd responded to what had happened and, to further bring out her loyalty to her parents and family, by asking more about them and what she admired in them.

Through an exchange following my curiosity about what coming to the UK was like for her, a story of courage, insight and initiative emerged that was buried inside the expected narrative of grief, homesickness and culture shock. After she first arrived at her boarding school, she had a couple of weeks of barely leaving her dormitory and trying to suppress her grief and loneliness through studying. Then Fen Su made a decision. She decided that she had to force herself to go out, to try talking to others, and to be more part of the school community. She went out for walks and made friends with another of the new girls – Fiona.

Unfortunately, Fiona fell ill during the summer holidays at the end of their first year at the school and could not return for the start of the new school year. Then Fen Su got a message from Fiona explaining that she would not be returning to the school at all. Fen Su, once again feeling lonely, turned to what she knew best – studying. A few weeks later Fen Su had the self-harm incident that resulted in the trip to A&E. Fen Su then told me that she had again decided to take matters into her own hands and extend her life beyond that of study. Once again, she had compelled herself to talk to her peers. She wasn't sure it would come to anything yet, but she had been talking to the two girls who had come to her aid after she'd cut herself. Fen Su felt ashamed about what she'd done, but also grateful for their concern.

These subplots in people's life stories will be overlooked if we focus not only on what is going wrong, but also on how to categorise the problem in order to tackle it. Here Fen Su was demonstrating something that we all have and cannot, and indeed should not, be taught – resilience. Resilience is something we discover when we must get through a difficult situation. Now there was a new story to add to Fen Su's library. Alongside her understandable human reaction (not the result of a 'disorder') was a capacity for foresight, action and courage. Far from indicating that there was something going fundamentally wrong, she was showing what a resilient young woman she was.

As the expert, this feedback (in verbal and letter form) helped (I hope) the school, Fen Su and her parents out of the paradigm of a mental disorder requiring treatment and into the realm of an understandable response to a human dilemma by a person with considerable strengths, knowledge and skills.

I gave no specific advice — I rarely do these days. We had a few more sessions to review, which afforded me further opportunities to note her progress and problem-solving abilities. She was discharged a few months after that initial meeting.

3. Psychiatric diagnoses are facts of culture not nature

'Science is an ongoing search for truth and such truth has little to do with consensus. Every major scientific advance involves challenges to a consensus.'

Aaron Kheriaty

Sixteen-year-old Adam is sitting in front of me, head in his hands with his elbows on his knees. I think he's crying; I'm not sure. His mum tries to put her arm round him; he flinches and moves away from her. He's definitely crying.

Adam was seen by our child and adolescent mental health crisis team after a friend of Adam's had alerted his mother that he had sent a goodbye message on their WhatsApp group. This friend also told her that Adam had recently said to one of the group that he had been hearing voices. They didn't know what he meant by that, but he had sworn this friend to secrecy.

Adam asked to talk to me without his mother present. Initially he's reluctant to explain what's going on. He starts a sentence then shakes his head and tears well up. I try to make it easier for him by asking 'yes' or 'no' type questions, in other words questions that only require a nod or shake of the head to answer. I then follow this up with some speculations about what he might be experiencing that Adam can agree with or tell me I've got wrong.

I wonder out loud if Adam is scared about what's happening to him and maybe he's afraid that he's going mad. Adam responds positively to these suppositions, and we gradually get a conversation going. Adam explains that he first heard a single voice about six months earlier after he was attacked by a group of peers outside a shop. There had been some kind of ongoing, mainly verbal, bullying from them at school, but this was the first time it turned physical. They surrounded him and a few kicks and punches were thrown before two people came and the attackers left. He remembers feeling scared. The two adults who broke up the attack asked him if he was OK. He said he was 'fine'. He didn't want to press charges because he thought his situation would get even worse if he went to the police.

On his way home that day, feeling embarrassed, angry and shaken, he heard very clearly a voice. This voice he described as being like an angry and demanding military sergeant. 'You pathetic fucking weakling,' the snarling voice said. He looked around thinking there was somebody behind him and was shocked when he realised nobody was there. He couldn't understand what had just happened.

After that he started hearing the voice occasionally saying the odd derogatory thing to him. He couldn't tell anyone what was going on, and worried he was going mad. He thought he would be 'locked up' if he told anyone. He even wondered if someone had somehow put a radio chip in his brain.

He told his parents about the bullying at school (but not about being beaten up) and that he couldn't go to that school any more. His mother helped him to change schools and initially things improved. He was able to concentrate, his work improved, and he even made a couple of new friends.

About a month after transferring school, he had a nightmare. In the nightmare he was waiting at a bus stop for the school bus, when a group wearing balaclavas and wielding batons came running after him. He jumped over a wall and ran into a house that reminded him of his grandfather's house. A door shut behind him and he realised he was trapped in a prison-like room and was now tied to a chair. The door to the prison room opened and the balaclava-clad group came in holding cases that he knew contained torture implements. At this point he woke up sweating, with his heart racing. It was 3 a.m. but he couldn't get back to sleep. At an English lesson the next day, he suddenly heard the sergeant voice say something like 'absolutely pathetic' and then a female voice he'd never heard before said (as if she was talking to the sergeant), 'I know he is, but you shouldn't be so hard on him.' He was startled and looked around trying to reorient himself to the lesson. He felt a rising sense of panic. Not only was the sergeant voice back, but a new one had joined him. In the following weeks these two voices became more frequent. They mostly appeared at night when he was on his own in his bedroom, but also at school, particularly in lessons he found boring or otherwise difficult to concentrate in.

By the time of our appointment a third voice had emerged. All three voices would tell him that he was a good-for-nothing pathetic person, though the female voice would sometimes plead with the other two to go easy on him.

The newest of the three voices reminded him of his grandfather. This grandfather had since passed away. He was a very unpleasant person. There were times when he was younger and his (now separated) parents were having one of their many arguments, that he and his brother would be sent to their grandfather's. This grandfather had a short temper, would often be drunk and would sometimes physically chastise them. He remembers being very scared of his grandfather. He even wondered if this third voice was his grandfather now haunting him as a spirit.

At his old school he had taken part in some antisocial behaviour and had been involved in taking various illicit substances, mainly cannabis. Since the deterioration of his mental state, he had started getting hold of cannabis again and was smoking this regularly to try and calm down.

On the day that he sent the message that found its way to his mum, he'd had a particularly bad day at his new school. The voices were overwhelming, he was not getting much sleep and felt that the only way to resolve the situation was to kill himself. There must've been a part of him that wasn't totally convinced by the need to kill himself as he did reach out and send this message. He agreed with me that this was a call for help. He was scared that if he told anybody about the voices, he might end up being sent to hospital and locked up there.

What sense can we make of Adam's story and situation? How do we choose a framework to give meaning to his experiences in a way that might be of help to him?

With a presentation like this it is entirely possible this might end up with an admission to a psychiatric hospital for safety reasons, for a more in-depth assessment, and to commence treatment. What might be the types of diagnoses considered? There are several options: psychotic depression, post-traumatic stress disorder, a psychotic episode, schizophrenia, schizoaffective disorder, there may even be a case to make a diagnosis of drug-induced psychosis. This is not an exhaustive list of possibilities. Could any of these diagnoses approximate to some sort of truth that points to what might be causing Adam's experiences?

Before returning to Adam's story at the end of this chapter I want to interrogate the type of assumptions we make when we assign someone a psychiatric diagnosis. The diagnosis plays an important role in structuring the type of intervention services then make, meaning this issue of diagnosis will be crucial to understanding what might (and might not) now happen to Adam.

There is no such thing as a psychiatric diagnosis

In the last chapter I explained why we literally don't know what we're talking about when it comes to mental health. This is because we can't escape subjectivity. We create rather than discover meanings, through how we choose to make sense of experiences and behaviours. Unlike much of the rest of medicine, we have no access to objective empirical tests that can help us capture what might be going on in our mentally distressed patients' brains and bodies, beyond excluding possible physical ailments that may be contributing to their distress. In this chapter I want to take the reader further into the territory of mental disorder diagnoses to see what such an insight might reveal about common practice that is structured around a belief that we deal with specific diagnoses in a similar way to diagnoses found in the rest of medicine.

We are always classifying phenomena. Language itself is a system for categorising, with words used to represent all sorts of things and occurrences. Classification systems are based around the process of creating classes according to some sort of common relations or affinities. The type of classification system we use depends on what we intend to classify and what the purpose of that classification is.

Diagnosis is a system of classification based on cause. More specifically based on initial (proximal) cause. We can take a car to a garage to run diagnostic tests. Computer technicians will run diagnostics looking for software faults or computer viruses causing a program to malfunction. In medicine, diagnosis is the process of determining which disease explains, i.e. has caused, a person's symptoms and/or signs.

Diagnosis therefore points to causal processes. Making an accurate diagnosis is a technical skill that enables effective matching of treatment to address specific pathological processes. That's why someone might say, 'My doctor said that the cause of my chest pain was acid reflux, not a heart attack.' We usually go to the doctor to get the 'why' question answered and in the hope that this will then guide the treatment.

But psychiatric diagnoses cannot point towards any causal agent (apart from a few such as those related to forms of dementia). Consider the following example: if I were to ask 'what is depression?' it would not be possible for me to answer by reference to a particular known abnormality. I cannot say that depression is a disease that occurs due to having abnormally low levels of serotonin in the brain. I cannot say that because no one has found this (despite extensive research) and so there are no tests done to confirm or refute this (see Chapter 11). Instead, to answer the question I will have to provide a description such as 'depression is the presence of persistent low mood and negative thinking'.

Contrast this with asking 'what is diabetes?' If I were to answer in the same manner by just describing symptoms, such as needing to urinate excessively, thirst and fatigue, I would be in deep trouble as a medical practitioner, as there are plenty of other conditions that may initially present with these symptoms and diabetes itself may not present like this.

Instead I must refer to its pathology involving abnormalities of sugar metabolism, as in 'diabetes is a disease that occurs when blood glucose is too high'. To move from a hypothesised to a confirmed diagnosis, I would get independent (to my subjective opinion) empirical data to support or otherwise my hypothesis about what may be causing the patient's described experiences (such as testing the urine for ketones and/or blood for levels of fasting glucose). A diagnosis of diabetes doesn't answer more complex questions such as why your blood glucose has become elevated, but it provides what can be referred to as an 'empirical anchor' – something objective, external to imagination, and measurable. A high blood glucose means diabetes whether you have a British or Sri Lankan cultural background.

There are many psychosocial challenges that affect treatment and the consequences of living with a chronic illness, but the empirical anchor means we know how to define a case. Once we have an objective, factual basis for defining a case, we can build technical knowledge based on knowing that the group we are researching with the type 2 diabetes label share something essential and characteristic. In scientific terms we can extrapolate our research findings about treatment and prognosis (the long-term outlook) to all those with the diagnosis (this is known as essentialising) and to people from a variety of different backgrounds (this is known as universalising).

The problem of using a classification like 'depression' to explain an experience (i.e. as a diagnosis) can be illustrated by asking another set of questions. If I was asked why someone is feeling low and I answered because they have depression, then a legitimate next question to ask is 'how do you know that this feeling low is caused by depression?' The only answer I can give is that I know it's depression because they are feeling low. In other words, if we try to use a classification that can only describe in order to explain, we end up with what philosophically is known as a 'tautology'. A tautology is a circular thinking trap, a statement that repeats an idea effectively saying the same thing twice.

A description cannot explain itself. Low mood and depression are synonymous; you cannot use one to explain the other. It's troubling when doctors use a descriptive category like depression to explain and cannot see this problem of tautological circularity. Using depression to explain low mood is like saying the pain in my head is caused by a headache. In psychiatry therefore, what we are calling diagnosis will only describe but is unable to explain. This means that psychiatric presentations are not amenable to being put into a diagnostic system of classification.

If the rest of medicine were practised like psychiatry, then when you go to your general practitioner because you have a recurrent cough, the GP would just ask you questions about your cough and then get you to fill in a questionnaire. They would then pronounce that you have a 'recurrent cough disorder – RCD'. The 'diagnosis' would be a description, with the word 'disorder' added onto the end. Notice that in the rest of medicine we don't have the word 'disorder' as part of the name – we don't say asthma disorder or diabetes disorder. Psychiatric diagnoses, by contrast, nearly all end with 'disorder'. This, I think, is an attempt, to create an imagined boundary with normal.

But you wouldn't expect your doctor to behave like that. At the very least you would expect them to listen to your chest with a stethoscope, to seek out signs, and perhaps arrange further tests (like a chest X-ray) if they remain uncertain as to the cause of the cough. In the rest of medicine diagnosis really matters. It will guide the doctor towards a treatment that addresses the initial cause of the cough.

The failure of decades of basic science research to reveal any specific biological or psychological marker that identifies a psychiatric diagnosis is well recognised. Unlike the rest of medicine, which has developed diagnostic systems that build on a causal and physiological framework, psychiatric diagnostic manuals have failed to connect diagnostic categories with any causes. Thus, there are no physical tests that can help establish an actual diagnosis.

Technically speaking **there is no such thing as a psychiatric diagnosis**.

Psychiatric diagnoses are best thought of as facts of culture rather than facts of nature.

Is that patient in front of me who reports intense sadness, difficulty getting to sleep and a poor appetite suffering from the disease of 'depressive disorder' or experiencing understandable heartache and grief after the break-up of a long-term relationship a few months back? If you argue both can be true, then sure, it can be said to the patient depression or grief may be what they have. However, one (depression) cannot be a diagnosis as it explains nothing, just describes some aspects of the patient's experiences; the other (grief) could be a diagnosis as it has explanatory pretences. Grief (unlike depression) is, in this scenario, being used as an explanation.

But I have no access to the patient's inner mental workings – none of us do. With grief and/or depression, I still do not know what sort of a process is going on. Is there a physiological process in her brain? Is it the psychological process of grief? Is it the loss of a social network that she had with that partner? Is it her concern about how this is impacting her son? Is it the fear of returning to work after a long absence? Is it her embarrassment about what happened? Is it raising questions about whether she is lovable, interesting enough or able to sustain an intimate relationship? Is it all of these things or some of them in combination? The truth is that I don't know. Neither does she. I cannot escape my subjectivity in the same way she cannot escape hers. I can only guess at the 'diagnosis' (proximal explanation), something that attaching the words 'major depressive disorder' (MDD) cannot provide.

When it comes to our emotional experiences, we just have an experience. We then use words connected with cultural meaning-making systems to attach to that experience. The meaning-making scaffolding can itself transform our experience of the experience. 'You are broken-hearted' creates a different scaffold to 'you're suffering from a depressive disorder' or to 'you are surviving and recovering from a painful experience', or even to 'I really admire you for the great courage you've shown in keeping going for the sake of your son despite how difficult this is for you'.

Defenders of psychiatric diagnosis respond to such criticism by explaining that psychiatric diagnosis relies on recognition of a pattern of symptoms that go together to form a syndrome. They may also point out the limitations of diagnosis in other branches of health care to suggest the rest of medicine is just as imperfect as psychiatry. Finally, they may argue that historically pattern recognition of symptoms provides a basis for research into treatment and eventually into understanding the physical causes of that syndrome, pointing out that much medical practice involved pattern recognition prior to understanding the causes.[1]

I don't believe such a position stands up to scrutiny. Firstly, prior to discovering causes and understanding what is referred to as the pathology of a disease (the science of the causes and effects of diseases), medical practice involved not only ineffective but positively harmful interventions. For example, before germ theory, operations were not carried out in sterile environments. Instead, post-operative infections were put down to 'miasma' (unpleasant or unhealthy smell or vapour), so the post-operative wards would have windows wide open, meaning that if you didn't die from septicaemia you could die from hypothermia. Leeches were used for bloodletting, and the famous 'snake oils' for all manner of ailments. The history of medicine is littered with such examples. Technical progress only became possible once the pathology was better understood.

Secondly, the pattern recognition argument is weak given the way we categorise psychiatric diagnoses based essentially on symptom counts. Take MDD, one of the most diagnosed psychiatric conditions. In a study with over five hundred real-world patients, the authors identified 1,030 *unique* symptom profiles. The most common symptom profile exhibited a frequency of only 1.8 per cent.[2] Such extensive variation within just one diagnostic category means that without any objective empirical anchor it is impossible to conclude that those given the label MDD are suffering from the same condition.

Psychiatric scientism

How could we have ended up calling something a 'diagnosis' that is not a diagnosis? Surely there must be some scientific basis to it? Sadly, there isn't. Rather than science, what we have is scientism (science as a system of faith).

Science is generally regarded as the intellectual and practical activity encompassing the systematic study of the physical and natural world through observation and experiment. Science uses a methodological approach involving hypothesis generation (suggesting a theory) and then testing that hypothesis through experimentation. The best scientists can live with and accept uncertainty as a prerequisite to being objective in the pursuit of knowledge. In the natural sciences, which most of medicine relies on to develop a system of categorisation based on cause (diagnosis), knowledge develops and builds through carrying out a particular type of investigation, which is aimed at proving something called a 'null hypothesis' can't be true. The null hypothesis is a general statement or default position that there is no relationship between certain measured phenomena. Rejecting or disproving the null hypothesis – and thus concluding that there are grounds for believing that there is a relationship, and the actual hypothesis may be true – is a central task in modern medical science.

Before any finding can be accepted, you also need other independent research teams to replicate your results using the same or similar methods. This is because one team may have biases, inadequate sample sizes, technical issues with the accuracy of their equipment, made errors in the analysis, and sometimes they may have even manipulated results. The 'replicability crisis' is a major problem in psychiatric, psychological and neuroscience research. One team announces it has found something (say, an area of the brain is smaller in ADHD patients compared to a healthy age-matched group), but two other teams carrying out a similar study come up with different findings.

Disproving the null hypothesis – meaning therefore that there is evidence that your theory may be true – must happen before you can then move to the next stage of allowing other research teams to do the same or similar experiments to see if they get the same findings as you. If at any stage in this process your theory is not getting support, you must go back to the null hypothesis and assume your theory is not true. It is not scientific to ask someone to prove that the null hypothesis is true.

This means we cannot take at face value that what we are calling diagnoses in psychiatry represent naturally occurring categories similar to other diagnostic categories found in the rest of medicine. We must start with the null hypothesis and assume that each category we are calling a diagnosis (implying an identifiable proximal cause) is not diagnostic until we prove that the null hypothesis can't be true. We cannot proceed with research that assumes that MDD, ADHD or autism are concepts that have any explanatory power for the behaviours they describe, until we are satisfied that the null hypothesis (that they do not explain the experiences or behaviours they describe) cannot be true.

Applying this scientific methodology is the basis of evidence-based medicine (EBM). In its broadest form, EBM is an approach to improving health care that uses the application of the scientific method for decision-making. For much of its history, medicine relied more on the subjectivity of 'clinical judgement' and medical students learned this or that professor's favourite theories and practices. Medical practice used to develop more through anecdote and assumed authority of the doctor or professor.

The shift to EBM as we now recognise it didn't really occur in a systematic way until the 1980s. I remember one lecturer when I was at medical school then telling us that 50 per cent of what we learn will turn out to be incorrect, we just don't know which 50 per cent it is!

The EBM movement wanted to systemise and collate all the available research on causes and treatments, so that broad conclusions on important clinical questions could be made and continually updated. This led to the formation of international institutions such as the Cochrane Collaboration and new analytic approaches (such as meta-analysis and systematic reviews), enabling researchers to pool the results of many studies. By doing this, benefits, but also harms, that result from treatment could be assessed.

EBM was an important step forward in developing a more scientifically rigorous approach to health care. However, scientific endeavour is ultimately a human activity and thus what counts as 'science' and how we interpret it is also shaped by broader cultural and political processes.

In his 2013 book *Deadly Medicines and Organised Crime*, Professor

Peter Gøtzsche suggests that the definition of organised crime closely matches the activities of some of the largest pharmaceutical companies.[3] They design clinical trials to emphasise benefits; they control the data, do the analyses in-house, and employ professional writers to write the papers. They select outcomes that demonstrate the greatest differences to suit their marketing needs, rather than the most important outcomes for patients. They pay academics to become 'opinion leaders' who are then listed as authors when they had little input and cannot vouch for the data. Trials with negative results are buried and not published. Several books and articles in recent years have levelled similar criticisms at the way the pharmaceutical industry and regulatory authorities operate.[4] Thus, the profit motive acts to bias the evidence base towards the products they make. EBM itself fell victim to these broader market-powered political forces and so any statements on causes or treatments that claim to be evidence-based need to be carefully scrutinised.

Mainstream psychiatry has been infected by at least two types of scientism. Firstly, it parodies science, using scientific language and the language of EBM, and carrying out research that looks scientific (such as brain scanning). Psychiatry wants to be seen as residing in the same scientific cosmology as the rest of medicine. Secondly, as I discuss later in this chapter and throughout the rest of the book, it ignores much of the genuine science there is and instead goes on supporting and perpetuating concepts and treatments that have little scientific support. It means that psychiatry likes to talk in the language of science and treats this as more important than the actual science.

Psychiatry, and mental health ideology more broadly, keeps faith in scientism despite these obvious flaws because we live in a culture where technology and technological achievement are highlighted and promoted. This helps it to connect to that broader cultural imperative of wanting to use science to explain everything. With this type of scientism so prevalent, eventually what the science says is almost irrelevant as long as you can look like you're doing something that you call science and you can bullshit in a way that convinces others (who are excluded from the language and actual findings) that the knowledge you possess is based on a truth (because you are a scientist and you do science).

I have had debates with fellow psychiatrists and other mental health professionals on the evidence base in mental health. Two defences against the scientism accusation have become familiar to me. The first is use of anecdote – such-and-such a patient got better with such-and-such a treatment; therefore, this treatment works. Anecdote is precisely what EBM was trying to get away from. The second is an appeal for me to take a balanced perspective. Each person's idea of what a balanced position is depends on where they are sitting. We get our ideas on what is balanced from what is culturally dominant, not from what the science is telling us. At one point Nelson Mandela was painted as a terrorist; later he became the embodiment of peaceful reconciliation and forgiveness. Which view was more balanced? Providing an interpretation consistent with the facts is more important than any one person's notion of what a balanced position should look like.

If there is disorder what is order?

How do we arrive at an understanding of 'normal'? Our psychiatric classification of behaviours and experiences considered disordered relies on an idea that the person's presentation sits outside an imagined normal. How is this defined, by whom, and in what context?

Psychiatric and broader mental health logic inevitably reflects the social dynamics of the society it originates from. As the field of psychiatry developed out of European and North American societies in the mid to late nineteenth century, it should not surprise us that the preoccupations of those societies found their way into psychiatric concepts. There was an accepted belief that members of the 'African' races had smaller brains, a natural instinct for physical labour and were psychologically primitive compared to members of the 'European' races. You see these assumptions throughout the early psychiatric and psychoanalytic writings.[5]

German psychiatrist Emil Kraepelin (1856–1926) is considered the father of biological psychiatry. His system for categorising psychiatric presentations still forms the backbone of the diagnostic systems we use today. He was a keen eugenicist and racist. Kraepelin complained about a steady increase in psychiatric disorders in civilised people and believed that this was the effect of large numbers of 'idiots, epileptics, psychopaths, criminals, prostitutes and tramps' who descend from alcoholic and syphilitic parents, and who transfer their inferiority to their offspring.[6]

Kraepelin's pupil and successor Ernst Rüdin (1874–1952), whose influence also continued into the post-Second World War era, advocated eugenic theories of degeneration, alleging that bad genes entering the gene pool was the main causal factor for the assumed increasing prevalence rates of mental disorders. Kraepelin and Rüdin were both advocates of 'racial hygiene' and came to see people with mental illness primarily as a burden on society.

Rüdin was involved in the introduction of the 1933 Nazi 'Law for the Prevention of Offspring with Hereditary Diseases', which allowed for the forced sterilisation of a range of people, including those with a diagnosis of schizophrenia or manic depression. This law paved the way for psychiatrists to eventually become involved in the most shameful episode in its history, involving systematically exterminating their patients. Nazi-era psychiatrists were instrumental and often enthusiastic advocates for a system of identifying, notifying, transporting and killing tens, possibly hundreds, of thousands of those considered 'mentally ill' and 'racially' or 'cognitively' compromised individuals in settings ranging from centralised psychiatric hospitals to prisons and death camps.[7]

Their role was critical to the success of Nazi policy, plans and principles. Many of those involved were senior professors in academia who sat on the planning committees for developing the euthanasia processes and who provided the theoretical backing for what transpired. They developed the first gas chambers used for mass murder, before the plan to annihilate the Jews, Gypsies, homosexuals, communists and other 'undesirables' was put in place. The killing of psychiatric patients was a key mediator in the development of the eugenic logic and the technology that facilitated the Holocaust.[8] In

Chapter 7 we will also look at the Nazi roots of the concept of autism. A concern with human typologies, hierarchies and the gene pool has been present throughout psychiatry's history.

Psychiatry is not just a medical discipline; it's also a social institution. There was always a strand concerned with social control. Psychiatry represents and reflects, through its diagnostic system, the power structure in the society in which it functions. In the nineteenth and early twentieth century, a woman having a child out of wedlock might have been admitted to an asylum with a diagnosis of moral insanity, where they might have found other female inpatients with a diagnosis of hysteria, reflecting the patriarchal nature of that society (see Chapter 5).

This legacy of institutionalised and institutional discrimination persisted after the Second World War. Civil rights movement leaders and protesters in the 1950s and 60s were often labelled as mentally disordered due to their supposed 'pathological' reaction of 'emotionality', hostility and aggression. We find higher rates of diagnosis of a psychotic disorder, use of mental health acts, forced treatments and deprivations of liberty, among black patients in countries like the US and UK, even though such high rates are not similarly seen in black-majority countries in the Caribbean or Africa.[9]

Homosexuality was classified as a disorder in the *American Diagnostic and Statistical Manual of Mental Disorders* (*DSM*) right up until 1973, when it was narrowly voted out of the *DSM*. Out of the 17,910 eligible to vote in that decision, the vote was 32 per cent in favour of removal, 21 per cent against and 47 per cent not voting.[10] Prevalence of psychiatric disorders shows an inverse relationship with class. In addition, the greater the level of inequality in any society, the higher the prevalence of mental disorders (see Chapter 13).

Problems that are socio-political can easily be converted into problems that are psychological. The devastating consequences of discriminations, together with the persistent and pervasive inequities in society, are turned into mental disorders that need mental health care rather than political action. The diminishing boundaries for normal also mean that, over recent decades, the mental health industrial complex (MHIC) has continued to benefit from billions in revenue through individualising and psychologising mental suffering.*

We cannot escape the socially constructed nature of the territory that mental health ideologies occupy. The theories and practices that developed in the dominating professions of psychiatry and psychology have not arisen out of value-free scientific endeavour.

We create rather than discover a disorder by the way we choose to talk about and classify what patients bring to us. These days I prefer to use the two terms 'ordinary' and/or 'understandable' as my starting point for helping make sense of patients' struggles and dilemmas, rather than starting with the concept of 'disorder'. Just about everything I have seen in my thirty-plus years of working as a psychiatrist can be captured by those two terms.

The failure to improve outcomes

Award-winning journalist Robert Whitaker's first time of covering a story to do with mental health was in 1998, when he co-wrote a series for the *Boston Globe* on the abuse of psychiatric patients in research settings. At that time, he had a conventional understanding of mental health, believing that the drugs used in psychiatry fixed chemical imbalances in the brain, and that the newer generation of these drugs was much better than the older ones.

While doing his research, he came across a series of papers that didn't fit with these assumptions. The World Health Organization studies on schizophrenia perturbed him. They had found that outcomes for patients given a diagnosis of schizophrenia (considered the most severe presentation psychiatrists deal with) were much better in three developing countries (India, Nigeria and Colombia) than in the US and five other developed nations. Patients in the developing countries had lower relapse rates, were significantly more likely to

---

*The mental health industrial complex (MHIC) refers to the network of individuals and institutions involved in the production and proliferation of mental health-related products and the ideologies that accompany these.

have made a full recovery and showed lower degrees of impairment when followed up over several years, despite most having limited or no access to 'antipsychotic' medication that nearly all patients in the developed countries were taking.[11]

How could this be the case? The cognitive dissonance produced by this unexpected finding started him on a journey that was to influence the next two decades of his career. I have had many conversations with Bob about his journey, his research, and have watched him present on numerous occasions.

Bob took a deep dive and ended up writing three seminal books on the subject: *Mad in America*,[12] *Anatomy of an Epidemic*[13] and, with Lisa Cosgrove, *Psychiatry Under the Influence*.[14] Bob has spent two decades warning us that the outcome data from mental health treatments, particularly psychiatric medications, is troubling. Far from the story of progress we have been sold, the actual science tells a story of stagnation and, if anything, worsening outcomes happening in parallel with increasing volumes of mental health provision and psychiatric drug prescribing.

The academic world has gradually caught up with Bob. Not only are more papers acknowledging the poor record of mental health services in improving mental health being published in mainstream peer-reviewed journals,[15] but there has been a recent cascade of books written by psychiatrists, sociologists, psychologists and historians coming to the same conclusion: the current diagnostic paradigm has failed to improve our scientific knowledge or clinical outcomes.[16]

In 2021, *New York Times* reporter Benedict Carey, after covering psychiatry for twenty years, concluded that psychiatry had done 'little to improve the lives of the millions of people living with persistent mental distress. Almost every measure of our collective mental health – rates of suicide, anxiety, depression, addiction deaths, psychiatric prescription use – went in the wrong direction, even as access to services expanded greatly.'[17]

In 2023, *Time* reported that 'about one in eight US adults now takes an antidepressant'; however, 'mental health is getting worse by multiple metrics. Suicide rates have risen by about 30 per cent since 2000 . . . As of late 2022, just 31 per cent of US adults considered their mental health "excellent", down from 43 per cent two decades earlier. Trends are going in the wrong direction, even as more people seek care. That's not true for cancer, it's not true for heart disease, it's not true for diabetes, or almost any other area of medicine.'[18]

A 2023 study based on Danish population records found that about 80 per cent of the population will receive psychiatric drug treatment, with the likelihood of being treated in a mental health hospital being 29 per cent. Furthermore, after receiving treatment, they were more likely to experience new socio-economic difficulties, become unemployed or receive a disability benefit, earn lower income, live alone or be unmarried.[19]

Peter Gøtzsche is one of the most prolific researchers in medicine, with a record of groundbreaking publications in mainstream medical journals covering evidence on topics from mammography to vaccines. He is scathing about psychiatric science. In one of his books Gøtzsche concludes that biological psychiatry has been a failure, and that the frustration with lack of progress often leads to more diagnoses, more drugs, higher doses and more harm to patients.[20]

The actual evidence on outcomes from conventional mental health treatments provides a worrying picture for mainstream mental health services' real-world effectiveness. Although over-diagnosis and unnecessary care is recognised as a growing problem across medicine, the short- and long-term outcomes for many conditions dealt with by the rest of medicine have improved, often reflecting genuine technical advances. This is not the case in mental health.

Despite three decades of intense neuroimaging research, we still lack a neurobiological account for any psychiatric condition. Advances in scientific knowledge have helped cardiologists, oncologists and other medical specialists improve success rates for a variety of clinically important outcomes, confirming that current treatments are more effective than the ones that were available twenty or thirty years ago. Similar data is hard to find for psychiatric disorders. As a result, functional neuroimaging or other physical tests play no role in clinical decision-making.[21]

Research from several countries has found that, despite continuous growth in the availability of mental health services, only about

15–25 per cent of those referred significantly improve or recover in the long term.[22] This dismal picture is found in both child and adult mental health services. Non-attendance rates and numbers dropping out of treatment are also substantial. In most Western countries there has been a steep rise in the number of youths and adults categorised as disabled mentally ill (in other words those who require disability benefits because of a mental health condition).[23]

The likelihood of positive outcomes for those with mental disorders is further hampered by the stigma associated with the idea that mental distress is the product of a medically malfunctioning brain. Nearly all studies that have looked at public attitudes towards mental illness have found that the medical model for mental illness ('mental illness is an illness like any other illness') is associated with increased negative attitudes, greater fear of patients and a greater likelihood of wanting to avoid interacting with them. In contrast, the idea that mental distress, in all the variety of ways it may be expressed, is the outcome of adverse experiences is associated with empathy and a desire to help.[24]

Most people who attend standard community mental health services, it seems, either experience no lasting improvement or deteriorate. To cover up this disastrous situation the psychiatric profession has created the idea that the conditions we deal with are 'chronic'. This provides a framework for accepting as unproblematic the expanding numbers of people categorised as mentally ill who don't seem to get better or keep relapsing despite our treatments.

Here are a few more examples that further illustrate this worrying picture of poor outcomes:

Standard mortality rates (SMRs – a way of comparing death rates in a population) find higher mortality rates for mental health patient groups compared to the general population. For example, a 2007 study, using data from twenty-five countries, found an SMR of over 2 for schizophrenia patients (meaning that they were more than twice as likely to die over a set period of time than the general population) and that the differential mortality gap had worsened in recent decades.[25]

A 2017 study examining the mortality gap for people with bipolar disorder and schizophrenia in the UK between 2000 and 2014 found that the mortality gap between them and the general population was widening.[26] A review of multiple evidence sources concluded that 'antipsychotic medications' contribute to this mortality gap.[27]

Long-term use of antidepressants has been found to be associated with increased morbidity and mortality.[28] In a study of the ten-year outcomes of 222 people who had suffered a first episode of depression, researchers reported that 76 per cent of those not treated with an antidepressant recovered and never relapsed, versus 50 per cent of those initially prescribed an antidepressant.[29] A large study, published in 2024, that analysed data from 125 randomised controlled trials, involving 8,542 participants across various healthcare settings, concluded that the overall response rate for all treatments of depression was just 22 per cent.[30] According to a 2006 study, the natural history of untreated depression is an 85 per cent recovery rate in twelve months,[31] suggesting that antidepressant treatment may in fact reduce rather than improve long-term recovery rates.

In a study conducted in fifteen cities around the world and designed to assess the merits of screening for depression, the patients who were diagnosed by their GPs and treated with an antidepressant were twice as likely to be depressed at the end of one year as those who weren't diagnosed and treated, even though there was no difference in initial levels of severity (according to the rating questionnaires used).[32] In a Canadian study that charted outcomes for over 9,500 depressed patients for five years, those taking antidepressants were depressed on average nineteen weeks per year, versus eleven weeks for those not taking antidepressants.[33]

In the early 1990s in the UK, the Royal College of Psychiatrists and Royal College of General Practitioners launched a 'Defeat Depression' campaign. Evaluations of this campaign found no evidence that it led to any significant improvements in clinical outcomes, but instead was associated with a rapid increase in antidepressant prescribing.[34] Similarly, research evaluating the 'Beyond Blue' campaign in Australia, which aimed to increase awareness about depression and other mental disorders, demonstrated an increase in medical model beliefs about depression and an increase in rates of diagnosis of major depression between 1998 and 2008. It also noted a decrease in mental health-related quality of life over this decade, and that having 'mental health literacy' (i.e. a belief that depression was a medical diagnosis requiring medical treatment) that was classified as 'poor' or 'fair' was a significant protective factor for recovery from major depression! In other words, those who rejected the idea that their mental suffering was the result of a disease called 'depression' were more likely to recover.[35]

Mental disorders have also become the most common reason for receiving benefits in the UK, with the number of claimants rising by 103 per cent from 1995 to 2014, while claimants with other conditions fell by 35 per cent.[36] This pattern is seen across developed countries. Wherever you find a rising rate of antidepressant prescribing, you find a rising rate of people receiving disability benefits for mental health difficulties, with depression being the most common diagnosis.[37]

Perhaps one of the most instructive studies on this mismatch between what is advertised and the actual findings is one regularly used to justify the routine use of antidepressants. The Sequenced Treatment Alternatives to Relieve Depression trial (STAR*D) was published to much acclaim in 2006 and is still referred to today as an example of success in treating mental illness.[38]

The STAR*D is the largest antidepressant trial ever conducted. There were nearly 4,000 patients with what was classified as depression enrolled who could receive between one and four successive treatment steps. Those not achieving improvement with, or unable to tolerate, a treatment step, would have a change of treatment (for example, being put on a different antidepressant) to see if it would improve their symptoms. Once the person was categorised as receiving benefit, preferably symptom remission, from any particular step, they entered a twelve-month naturalistic follow-up phase to assess whether they stayed well or not. The STAR*D investigators triumphantly reported that the cumulative remission rate was 67 per cent.

That finding is still cited today by many as evidence of the effectiveness of antidepressants. But in reality, the STAR*D study revealed more about the failure of these drugs to make lasting improvements. An independent team of researchers subsequently obtained access to the STAR*D data and their analysis revealed a recovery rate of just 26 per cent.[39]

But even this doesn't reveal the full picture. Buried in their report the STAR*D investigators published a table on the one-year outcomes across the four steps; it was difficult to decipher, though, and they did not detail the one-year results in their written text. However, a group of independent psychologists subsequently determined that the one-year table showed that only 108 patients (3 per cent) of those enrolled had remitted and then stayed well until the end of the one-year follow-up.[40]

Psychiatrist John Rush concluded after his reanalysis, 'Only 26 per cent of the real-world patients responded to the antidepressant during the first year of treatment (meaning their symptoms decreased by at least 50 per cent on a rating scale), and only half of that group had a sustained response. Even more dispiriting, only 6 per cent of the patients saw their depression fully remit and stay away during the year-long study. These findings reveal remarkably low response and remission rates.'[41]

The dissection of the STAR*D trial has continued. A team of researchers used a Freedom of Information Act request to obtain the STAR*D protocol and other key documents. Their analysis of these documents, published in the *British Medical Journal* in 2023, concluded that the investigators had deviated from the original protocol which caused them to inflate the remission rate they published.[42] Following this latest critique, Dr John Miller, editor in chief of the respected and mainstream magazine *Psychiatric Times* published an opinion piece in which he concluded, 'For us in psychiatry, if the *BMJ* authors are correct, this is a huge setback, as all of the publications and policy decisions based on the STAR*D findings that became clinical dogma since 2006 will need to be reviewed, revisited, and possibly retracted.'[43]

While the history of psychiatry is one of consistent scientific failure, for such practice to become so dominant means it's also one of notable political success.

What happened to Adam?

At the start of this chapter, I told you about Adam, who had presented with hearing voices, feeling suicidal and possibly having some delusions. The conventional approach would likely be for him to be diagnosed as having a first psychotic episode, followed by prescribing what is labelled as 'antipsychotic' medication.* The diagnostic label may change at some point to schizophrenia, particularly if these voices are persistent despite ongoing treatment. In this framework, the voices he experiences would be viewed as 'auditory hallucination' and conceptualised as a symptom of a disease. Success of the treatment would be evaluated by whether symptoms were eliminated or noticeably reduced. The possibility that the voice hearing is meaningful is excluded through categorising this as a symptom rather than an experience.

Given the problems associated with diagnosis and some of the poor real-world outcomes I have outlined above, I feel it is my professional duty to do what I can to uphold the 'first do no harm' principle we in the medical profession are meant to follow. If there was a way to help Adam without needing to go down the diagnosis and medication route, I should make sure this is exhausted first.

That medication may be useful at this stage is an important consideration. If I am unable to hold some sort of at least partially coherent conversation with Adam, I may wonder how emotionally agitated he is and whether it may be necessary to prescribe something, particularly if he is experiencing sleep deprivation. However, my clinical experience with many people who hear voices is that using medication, even in these initial stages, is often unnecessary. Indeed, there is an international 'hearing voices' movement which recognises that many people can hear voices, and this is not always a sign of a

---

* Antipsychotic is more of a marketing term suggesting these medications have disease-specific effects. They should be referred to by the more generic term 'neuroleptic' because they have general effects on everyone of reducing levels of brain activity and arousal, often causing a numbing of feelings that many patients find unpleasant but can be helpful when you are in a state of high emotional arousal.

psychiatric problem. It may be part of a distress response that can be meaningful and reflects one of the many ways that humans respond to adversity.

I assumed that Adam was experiencing an understandable response to a difficult life circumstance – that it was a distress response. I framed his voices as an externalisation of unconscious feelings that were too unbearable to contain at the time. When we experience powerful emotions (such as fear) as a young child, we don't have the intellectual machinery with which to take a step back and see it in its broader context (this is hard to do even as an adult). Children are in that egocentric phase of growing up and, as a result, experience the world as an extension of themselves. This results in them feeling like they cause the (bad) things that happen to them. If you have experienced a situation of great fear as a youngster, you can then feel that the world is a scary place and that somehow you are the person who causes bad/scary things to happen.

Adam had some horrible experiences with his grandfather. Home life didn't sound too great, either. This may well have primed him to feel threatened and insecure. If you get another experience such as the bullying and attack he had to endure, then this can further confirm that deep sense you've had for a long time – that horrors are destined to happen to you. The world takes on an eerie and foreboding character.

The voices then become manifestations of unconscious feelings made conscious. Adam's attempt to suppress his fears has spilled out. In this way of imagining, the voices are embodiments of parts of the self that are now experienced as disembodied and disconnected from him. They start to push into consciousness his inner conflicts.

In subsequent sessions Adam and I spent time getting to know the different voices, giving them names and trying to understand what they were communicating. One voice represented his grandfather, who belittled him from a young age. He labelled this voice 'Joe'. The first voice he heard he labelled the 'sergeant major' – this voice is essentially encouraging him to stand up for himself. The second voice he heard he named 'Julie' (after an ex-girlfriend whose feelings towards him he found confusing). We concluded that she represented his feeling of not being protected, particularly by his mother, when his parents were going through their divorce and he was being sent to his abusive grandfather. Adam's mother did attend a number of the sessions, as did his father. They were both supportive of this work and felt that this way of structuring Adam's experiences made sense to them, too.

Framing Adam's experience in this way began to change his relationship to the voices and therefore the power they had over him. Recognising them as part of his own thoughts and feelings, giving them names and encouraging Adam to talk about them, and also to talk to them when he was on his own, as opposed to trying to suppress or ignore them, contributed to a reduction in their power. In some ways the voices had been a help to Adam and brought to notice conflicts and feelings that he could now get a better handle on and integrate into his sense of self.

I followed Adam up for another year and a half and, by the time he was discharged, he was doing well at a new college. He still experienced the three voices, but they were much quieter now, didn't happen as often and he had no fear of them. Indeed, the voices now became his barometer, informing him of when he was getting stressed about something. Adam did not make any further suicidal gestures and my expectation is that he will be OK.

4. Concept expansion

'Choice – sexual, consumer or emotional – is the chief trope under which the self and the will in liberal polities are organized.'

Eva Illouz

It's my first meeting with seventeen-year-old Andrew. His notes still have his birth name, Andrea, on them. Andrea has been seen in our service on and off for many years. Our Child and Adolescent Mental Health Service's (CAMHS) previous involvement has been mainly related to behavioural problems. She had been diagnosed in the past with ADHD and then autism.

I collect Andrew from the waiting room. He's tallish and slim with a fading pink dye to his short hair on one side, contrasting with the straw blond on the other. He wears jeans with designer holes and patches and a loosely fitting long-sleeved T-shirt. Andrew has come to the appointment on his own. He looks a little anxious as we walk up the stairs to my consulting room on the first floor. He takes a seat and leans forward. He wanted to come on his own as he does not want to burden his parents with his problems. He's now seeking help for himself, whereas for most of his past he felt that he was being brought to services by his parents because of their concerns.

Andrew explains that about a year ago he finally understood that one of the issues that he has been dealing with is that he is trans and that he identifies with being male rather than the female body he was born with. He came out to his parents as a trans male and they seem to have accepted this, although his dad keeps asking him whether he's really sure about it. He said that he'd attempted to be a woman and tried to convince himself that his discomfort going through puberty was just because he needed to get used to it. He now believes that the reason things never felt quite right was that deep down he was playing a role and felt compelled to adhere to it by what he labelled as 'society'. When he realised that he was really a man trapped in a woman's body he felt a sense of relief. Most of his friends have accepted him as a trans man.

He now believed that he had suppressed his feelings of not fitting in. He realised that he often looked at men and other boys as he was growing up with a sense of jealousy and a longing to be like them. He had tried really hard to love himself as a woman and accept the body he had, but despite all his efforts he had this inescapable feeling that there was something wrong, something deeply rooted, that was not just ADHD or autism. After coming out as a trans man his life started to make more sense, but the feeling of not fitting in, not being good enough and not being able to 'make it' had persisted. He still gets bad 'mood swings'. He and his parents felt that this was because there was something else wrong, like maybe a bipolar disorder. His moods have been a roller coaster, one day feeling on top of the world, the next day it all comes crashing down and he feels suicidal.

He knew there was a long waiting list for medical treatment for 'gender dysphoria', although he was unsure about how far he wanted to go with treatment, particularly any surgical procedures. The main reason he is attending now is that he couldn't shift a feeling of anxiety and depression and was wondering if he also had bipolar, or some other disorder, and needed medication for this. He often didn't attend sixth-form college and had lost motivation to keep up with his college work. He said that he also got 'paranoia' – a strange feeling that there was someone following him to school even though he knew there was nobody there. He increasingly stayed away from college and spent his time playing online video games.

When he was Andrea, the family had much adversity to contend with. Her father, who was a pilot in the Royal Air Force, was involved in a near-death situation when his plane developed a fault while flying over Syria. He managed to successfully land the plane as the cockpit was filling up with smoke. According to Andrew, his father used to be away for long periods of time on duty, but after that incident he became moody, prone to shouting and started drinking a lot. Andrea's parents separated for a period of time during which there were several house moves. Eventually they got back together, and Andrew's father was now accessing therapy for himself. Since then home life had been better and more stable.

Andrew's dilemmas are familiar to those of us who work in the mental health field. Patients often report that they sense that something's not right that you can't quite put your finger on. A yearning to find the reason for that feeling that you're different and/or don't 'fit in' to the world around you. The mental health industrial complex offers an array of possibilities that appear to offer you potential reasons for why you might feel like that. Trouble is, once you enter this hall of mirrors, whenever you think you have found your true reflection in a diagnosis, over time new distortions appear that lead you to looking for new potential reasons. I will return to Andrew's story at the end of this chapter.

The rising tide of mental problems

In the first chapter, I explained how practice had been transformed over the last thirty-plus years of my career, as marginal concepts expanded beyond what I could have imagined when I first trained as a child and adolescent psychiatrist. In chapters 2 and 3 I discussed how mental health is a slippery concept and how what we call psychiatric diagnoses are not really diagnoses in the medical sense. Because mental health ideology is carved out of subjectivity, it is vulnerable to what I call the elastic band effect – that diagnoses are elastic and can expand (or contract) in response to social forces.

According to US government data, 'nearly three in five high school girls reported feeling sad or hopeless in 2021, representing a 60 per cent increase over the past decade . . . The data shows a dramatic rise in experiences of violence, poor mental health and suicide risk in teens . . . About 57 per cent of the female students reported "persistent feelings of sadness or hopelessness", up from 36 per cent in 2011, according to the data.'[1] A 2023 survey in the US found that 40 per cent of parents report being either extremely or very worried that their child is struggling with anxiety or depression. Suicide is now the second-leading cause of death among people aged fifteen to twenty-four.[2] According to data from the National Survey on Drug Use and Health in the US, rates of major depressive disorder in US teens increased by over 145 per cent between 2010 and 2021 to 30 per cent of that age group and by 161 per cent in boys where 12 per cent can now be diagnosed with this.[3]

According to a report from the office of the US surgeon general, 'The COVID-19 pandemic brought the relationship between work and well-being into clearer focus for many US workers: 76% of US workers in a 2021 survey reported at least one symptom of a mental health condition (anxiety, depression), an increase of 17 percentage points in just two years.'[4]

The British Medical Association reported that 'In the UK the number of children and young people in contact with mental health services has increased by 309 per cent since April 2016 . . . In July 2022, the 10 per cent of areas with the highest levels of economic deprivation had over double the number of people in contact with mental health services compared to the 10 per cent of areas with the lowest levels of deprivation.'[5]

And the Royal College of Psychiatrists (in 2021) opined that 'England is in the grip of a mental health crisis, with under-18s suffering the most . . . Record numbers of children and adults sought NHS help last year for problems such as anxiety, depression and eating disorders, or because they ended up in a mental health crisis . . . NHS services were struggling to cope with the demand.'[6]

In Canada the prevalence of mood and anxiety disorders increased substantially between 2012 and 2022, particularly among women and those aged fifteen to twenty-four. For example, the one-year prevalence of generalised anxiety disorder among young women tripled from 3.8 per cent in 2012 to 11.9 per cent in 2022.[7]

International studies show a decline in mental health across all age and gender groups, with English-speaking countries (which tend to have the most comprehensive mental health services) having the lowest levels of mental well-being, and the eighteen to twenty-four age group having the worst mental health of all age groups.[8]

Wherever you look across the Western world you will find stories about mental health epidemics and data that shows more people being diagnosed, more services being created, and more psychiatric treatments being consumed.

Like the economy, what you publicly pronounce has an effect on how we collectively feel, how we interpret our experiences and, ultimately, how we behave. A kidney does not get anxious about the results of kidney function tests, because it is not the site that generates meaning. The person who has the kidney might. When it comes to the inescapable subjectivity inherent when we use the term 'mental health' and the collection of terms that come under its umbrella, the meaning-making scaffolding you choose can have a profound impact on how we interpret, experience and then act in response to our distress. Which interpretive framework would become hegemonic? There is money to be made through financialising emotions.

Even trauma can be marketised

Gabor Maté is a well-known Canadian-Hungarian physician who argues that the culture we live in is trauma-genic and responsible for most of the mental and physical health problems we experience. In a presentation discussing his 2022 book *The Myth of Normal*, he noted that mental disorders are rapidly increasing in Western societies and describes the case of an adolescent who is prescribed ten different psychiatric medications.[9] He points out, correctly, that this rapid increase cannot be the result of genetics as genes cannot change that quickly. Instead, he concludes that the alarming rise is due to a toxic and trauma-genic culture. He alludes to the promotion of greed in our society, but also targets child-rearing and its impact on brain development as an important pathway through which these traumas manifest in the bodies and minds of individuals. He argues that a disconnect between body and mind causes a 'loss of authenticity' – meaning individuals have this nagging feeling that they can't be themselves, don't know who they 'really' are and have lost that intuitive connection with their emotions.[10]

I agree with much of Dr Maté's analysis on the structural contributors to distress and the insecurities so many of us feel. I have a great deal of respect for his work and for his compassion and humility. But it seems to me he falls into the same cultural individualist trap when he sees trauma everywhere and constructs this as leading to a loss of something as hard to define as 'authenticity'. Trauma itself can become a new source of mental health expansionism. It is commodifiable and easier to marketise than a more nebulous and nuanced articulation of distress. It fits in perfectly with the cultural trend to notice our vulnerability more than our resilience.

In 2014, at a conference in London, I attended a lecture by Camila Batmanghelidjh – founding chief executive of a charity called Kids Company. Her fans included the prime minister of the time, David Cameron, along with a host of other famous people. Her lecture contained a parade of pictures of the brain and long explanations about how childhood trauma affected this or that area, suggesting that traumatised people are brain-damaged in some way, and the importance of therapy (such as that provided by therapists at Kids Company) for healing. For years Kids Company was kept going via its wealthy and influential donors together with sizeable government grants. At its height it employed more than six hundred people, had eleven centres, in London, Bristol and Liverpool, and was involved in multiple school outreach programmes.

Then, in August 2015, it suddenly collapsed. Police investigations into financial irregularities, poor management and suspect work practices had forced them out of business and revealed the charity to be bankrupt. What it seems had sustained them for the two decades they were operational was the popularity of the idea of treating trauma. For politicians keen to promote 'Third Way' or 'Big Society'* voluntary action beyond the state and the market, Kids Company appeared to fit the bill.†

---

* This idea emerged as the Conservative buzzword of the 2010 general election, when David Cameron, the soon to be prime minister, proposed to redistribute power to communities and to promote volunteering, in order to reduce the role of the state within them (for a brief critique, see https://blogs.lse.ac.uk/politicsandpolicy/big-society-social-capital).
† A 2022 report by the charity commission (https://www.gov.uk/government/news/official-report-criticises-former-trustees-of-kids-company) found that Kids Company

Even when protagonists point to social causes of distress, as long as there is an individualised technology (i.e. potential commodity) suggested as a cure, it can gain literal purchase within our societies. Anything that has the scent of mental health and the idea of helping vulnerable and suffering people is an attractive balm for the guilt of the wealthy. I am not suggesting here that such concepts and interventions are not helpful for many people; I am suggesting that they may act to distract from socio-economic injustice.

Even something as apparently politically neutral as treating 'trauma' may provide protection from class injustice by providing a vehicle for do-gooding philanthropy. After all, it's easier to rule over a population constructed as needing paternalistic care and sympathy than one made of people who are intelligent, capable and resilient.

Psychiatric brands

I have already explained why we don't know what we're talking about when it comes to mental health and why technically speaking there is no such thing as a psychiatric diagnosis. So, if they are not diagnoses and yet have such high and rising visibility in our culture, what are they?

They are what sociologists refer to as 'social constructs'.

Social constructionists view much of the knowledge we might take for granted as common sense, or simply accept as true, as being constructed. This happens through having the power to create the ideas that become dominant in any society. This means much of what passes for widely accepted concepts, beliefs, norms and values are formed through continuous interactions among society's members, instead of through objective observation of physical reality. There are many influences at play in how we then develop our cultural

---

had repeatedly failed to pay tax it owed and sometimes failed to pay its own workers. It owed £850,000 in taxes when it collapsed in 2015. A 2021 High Court ruling cleared Camila Batmanghelidjh and the seven others of personal wrongdoing.

beliefs and practices about what we consider to be 'normal' or expected.[11]

So what sort of a social construct are psychiatric diagnoses? Since mental health social constructs have emerged through marketisation, psychiatric diagnoses are not diagnoses – they are marketable brands. Each brand has a collection of products that sit within its field. Assessment protocols, questionnaires, medications, courses, books, experts, institutes, therapies, support groups, and so on.

Some brands are more popular than others. The main mental health customer base in childhood is boys, often brought to services by their mothers. Conduct disorder (CD) has diminished as a brand as it does not appeal to the main consumer base (parents) as much as other brands for kids' behaviour. CD suggests the environment, not the child, is the location of the problem. Behaviour problems in children are highly marketable and so ADHD and autism have become more consumer-friendly brands. In adults, mood, anxiety and self-doubt are highly exploitable. Depression, anxiety and bipolar disorder are strong brands for adults, but changing criteria for diagnosing ADHD and autism to capture more adult consumers has also resulted in brand expansion into adulthood for what previously were considered childhood-based diagnoses (see chapters 5 to 8).

In the capitalist societies that created it, the arena of mental health, and associated technologies of the self, cannot escape the logic of the market. As these brands spread and become more familiar, associated concepts, language and practices find their way into everyday life. Children no longer have tantrums, they have 'meltdowns' (from feeling overwhelmed). We don't feel miserable, we become depressed. Feeling stressed isn't enough, we're traumatised. We go for walks because it's 'good for our mental health'. If we're worried about how secure our job is and fear asking for a pay rise, don't worry, you can see someone from the staff well-being service (before we sack you).

The expansion has also soaked through mental health professional culture. We now routinely talk about 'overthinking', 'emotional dysregulation' and 'masking', concepts that I'd never come across in my earlier years of practice. Strange inventions like pathological demand avoidance, which are not even found in diagnostic manuals, have nevertheless found their way into clinical practice.*

Loopy concept creep

Many years ago, when my children were at our local primary school, great excitement occurred after reporters from a couple of the national papers turned up with cameras and started interviewing parents and children about a new policy that the head teacher had implemented to try and deal with bullying. She had banned any form of physical contact at playtime. Playtime monitors were tasked with policing the children, looking for any form of contact, from holding hands to playing 'tig'.† If caught, the offenders had to sit on a bench for the rest of that playtime. This policy was reversed soon after the press had a field day of mockery. It wasn't the last school to try something like this. In one of the most recent examples (April 2023), a school in Leeds banned all games that involve physical contact because of a 'high number of minor injuries'.[12]

The concern with harm and vulnerability, particularly of children, is visible not only in every institution you can think of, but also within many families. I am not minimising here the real and terrible effects of abuse, but I do wonder whether we now have a culture where parents are so afraid of intervening in any way that might be construed as non-consensual, that this then sets children and families up for more drastic and explosive encounters. This new form of 'cognitive parenting' sees a father trying to negotiate with their three-year-old who does not want to leave the park, treating her as if she has the adult capacity of reasoning. This can lead to upside-down hierarchies in some families where parents walk on eggshells around

---

*Pathological demand avoidance refers to resistance to doing something that is requested or expected of you that is meant to be persistent and includes marked resistance to 'the demands of everyday life', such as eating and sleeping, as well as expected demands, such as going to school or work.

†A children's game in which, in its simplest form, the player who is 'it' chases the other players, trying to touch one of them, thereby making that person 'it'.

a child who has more emotional and practical power than the child can, or should, handle.

Our expanding sense of vulnerability and the potential for harm carries over into expanding boundaries for what we consider to be a mental health problem. Philosopher Ian Hacking labelled the rather obvious dynamic connected with the social contagion of concepts as 'social looping'.[13] As a population's understanding of what is or isn't a mental disorder changes, people shape their behaviour, experiences and self-understanding in response. As a result, evolving concepts of mental disorder, carried by language, make up new kinds of people. A 'looping effect' means that what can be imagined to be a potential psychiatric disorder does not simply 'slide frictionlessly over an unchanging social reality . . . but rather they alter that reality'. In effect, 'changing ideas change people'.[14]

A looping effect also describes the process where growing interest in a subject (such as mental health in general or a particular brand like ADHD or autism) means that some academics might start writing papers on it. It then reaches the media who report on it, inspiring other academics and some professionals to become interested. Then members of the public start taking up the concept and looking for a professional who might examine them for that. Demand is created, attracting more professionals who will become 'experts', then more people are talking about it and so more research gets funded. Now institutes and courses and books and documentaries start emerging, leading to more talk, experts, reports, and so on.

We are a long way down the road of the looping process that has created psychiatric brands and eventually the MHIC. The emotional roller coaster involved in growing up is no longer in the realm of the ordinary. A 2019 survey of one thousand young people found that 68 per cent thought they have had or are currently experiencing a mental health problem and, of those, 62 per cent thought that destigmatisation campaigns have helped them identify it.[15] It also found that there had been a 45 per cent increase in mental health referrals of under eighteens in the previous two years.

This means that, in 2019, more than two-thirds of British youngsters believed they have or have had a mental disorder. This figure is not far off an academic paper that came out the same year and used a child self-report questionnaire methodology, which came up with a prevalence figure for mental health problems in eleven- to fifteen-year-olds of 42 per cent.[16] These are pre-Covid figures.

In an online survey conducted in spring 2020 of 583 adolescents in the US, 55 per cent reported symptoms of moderate to severe depression, 48 per cent reported anxiety, 69 per cent sleep problems, and 38 per cent suicidal ideation or behaviour.[17] As with the UK, these seem like extraordinarily high rates. What is happening here?

Sociologist Nick Haslam[18] coined the term 'concept creep' to refer to the gradual expansion of what he called 'harm-related' concepts. He argued that many psychological concepts had undergone a process of inflation whereby they identify an increasingly wide range of phenomena. That broadening, he said, occurs in two directions. Concepts creep horizontally by coming to refer to qualitatively new phenomena, and vertically by coming to refer to less extreme states.

The concept creep happening in mental health is part of this tendency for ideas about harm, suffering and maltreatment to expand their meanings over time. A few decades ago, bullying referred only to peer aggression carried out by children. It was intentional behaviour repeated multiple times and done in the context of a power imbalance. Over time, bullying expanded horizontally to include adults in workplaces who carry out exclusionary rather than intimidating behaviour (such as shunning) and intimidation carried out online rather than only in person (referred to as 'cyber-bullying'). Bullying also expanded vertically to include acts that were unintentional, unrepeated and directed at people of equal or even higher power than the perpetrator.

This outward and downward spread, Haslam argued, results from a rising cultural preoccupation with vulnerability and risk. This then problematises previously tolerated behaviour and reflects a growing sensitivity to suffering. What counts as suffering and sources of suffering expand and get incorporated into socially progressive politics and a liberal moral agenda. It can result in better recognition of harms that may have previously gone unnoticed. On the other hand, it can also lead to trivialisation of more severe harms, constraints on expression and a polarised view of a world that becomes populated by victims and villains (rather than, for example, antagonistic social classes).

Concept creep is rife in mental health ideology. People who hold more inclusive concepts of mental illness, categorising a wider variety of experiences and actions as disordered, are more likely to identify an experience or behaviour as a problem potentially requiring professional attention.[19] This type of psychiatrisation leads to category inflation and as a result increases the prevalence of psychiatric conditions and levels of service utilisation.

The ways of thinking about, defining and experiencing what is labelled as a 'mental disorder', 'trauma' and specific diagnostic entities have thus broadened in recent years, alongside what is considered as 'abuse', 'bullying', 'harassment', 'hate', 'prejudice', 'violence', 'discrimination', 'addiction', and so on.

There's an array of potential implications for lowering the threshold in what counts as a mental health problem. If the concept of trauma (for example) is broadened, then more people may see themselves as 'traumatised', and while it may help with creating a narrative that brings empathy, help and support, it may also lead to a sense of being damaged, particularly when constructed as trauma causing brain damage. If you're broadening what counts as disordered, then it could even reinforce a fear that you are potentially dangerous or unpredictable.

It may also have direct effects on how you experience the world and how you react to events. A 2022 study, where participants were asked to rate and discuss their reactions to a film, found that individuals with broader beliefs about trauma experienced more intense negative emotions and were more likely to report viewing the film as traumatic. Moreover, those who saw the film as traumatic reported more event-related distress (such as intrusive images and nightmares) in the days after they watched it.[20]

Talking in terms of well-being may not solve this problem of concept elasticity. Well-being may set unrealistic expectations if we get caught up with needing to have well-being to be 'well' and the absence of well-being then being interpreted as illness. We are then mired in the quicksand of fuzzy concepts, with visceral reactions to imagined loss of sanity or wellness and with no external anchor to hold on to as you sink further into the linguistic slush that sucks your soul/mind into its abstraction. In such a world suffering can no longer be ordinary, meaningful, or even sometimes instructive or revealing.

I think the accelerating spread of mental health ideology, as part of the growing sense that harms, dangers, traumas and personal injustices are everywhere, is a reflection of the pervasive injustice that our economic structures produce when they create glaring inequalities. In the logic of individual consumerism, that sense of injustice is pushed out of something that can lead to class consciousness and into individualised battles, insecurities and the sense that 'there's something not right' in the person. The political establishment can then take up sides in what is often referred to as the 'culture wars' and individuals can take up grievances as personal.

What happened to Andrew?

In recent years I and my colleagues have been seeing an increasing number of young people who are presenting with a belief that they are in the wrongly gendered body. In the first couple of decades of practice in psychiatry I only encountered two people who were questioning their bodily sex in this manner. Both were young males who wanted to become female. They both had an experience of feeling like that from a young age. Both also had some difficult and traumatic events in their histories. Both eventually came to accept themselves as gay men and lost the desire to transition.

Andrew has come to our service with an established set of cultural identities. He wants to identify as a 'he', and at least this is a label/construct that he has chosen. He already carries signifiers that were applied to his female body through the agency of her parents and the professionals who diagnosed her with ADHD and then autism. I don't see it as my place to start challenging these culturally available and common labels, but I do see it as my role to try and broaden the conversation away from an idea that the process of identifying such pseudo-diagnostic formulations will provide any explanations that enlighten the labelled.

Andrew is wondering if he has bipolar disorder. I ask what difference a diagnosis of bipolar disorder would make to him. He says that he would understand what was wrong with him. I ask what difference it would make to his life if he understood what was wrong with him. He says he would feel better. I ask, if he felt better, what would he be doing that's different to what he's doing now. You get the picture. This type of Socratic questioning provides a mechanism for trying to get beyond the abstract and closer to the concrete and material reality of Andrew's life. It also helps Andrew to visualise what change means to him. Trying to construct what change might look like in real life moves the conversation beyond a diagnostic framework, where diagnosis paints experiences and behaviours as potential symptoms and thus a successful intervention as one that gets rid of symptoms. If he was feeling better, Andrew explains, he would be able to get to college, see his friends and complete his transition. We talk about what was reasonable to expect and what might need to change for this to happen.

One of the things I am always on the lookout for in the people I see is evidence of what they are capable of. Aspects of their story that go beyond the problems they feel they carry. I discuss the concept of resilience with Andrew. I explain that resilience is a word that comes from engineering. It refers to the capacity of different metals or other materials to withstand pressure on them without breaking or bending. In mental life it refers to our capacity to keep going despite how bad we feel. Some of the most resilient people I've come across in my life have been those who have come to us as patients.

I was able to comment on the immense resilience Andrew displayed. Despite the many challenges that he has had to face he is clearly quite a capable young person. He had made it into college that day before coming to the appointment. We spoke about how he had decided to return, where he had found the courage to do that, how he had dealt with his anxiety on returning, and how he had got through the day. Andrew was pleased with himself for managing to do this. The fact that the decision to seek help from us had been his demonstrated a desire in him to take some control over the situation. Perhaps being more in touch with that hopeful part of him had enabled him to get to college before coming to the session.

He enjoys art and is a highly creative person. I can see he has a large book with him. I ask if he has any of his art on him and he opens the book to show me some beautiful and very individual stylised drawings. Some of the themes in those drawings seemed to reflect some of the challenges he feels he faces. We talk about the possible meanings in his drawings. For example, in many of them he has faces and even landscapes where one side of the picture contrasted sharply with the other. We speak about some of the conflicts these represent for him. I hear how proficient he is on his computer games. Although there is a downside in that he is playing them late into the night, he talks with pride about some of the high scores he is achieving in a certain online game, where he is beating most of the other players.

At our second appointment we speak a bit more about what he feels are signs of 'paranoia', the most glaring example of which is this sense that there is a presence he feels is stalking him, particularly on his way to college. I ask him to describe what he imagines this stalker looks like and what they are doing. The stalker is a female of a similar age who simply stares at him. I wonder whether this is the embodiment of his previous self, 'Andrea'. 'Perhaps she felt that you had tried to kill her, but she wasn't ready to die yet. Perhaps Andrea felt betrayed or misunderstood,' I suggest. Andrew seems shocked at this idea, and so we talk more about it.

We discuss medication and I explained the lack of evidence for medication in his age group and that we would normally offer therapy first. He seems to understand and accept this. Since the first appointment he has managed some further days in college and is trying to catch up with work he has fallen behind on. This gives me further opportunities to notice and comment on his growing agency and capacity to reconnect with his natural resilience. He didn't ask again about diagnosis, so I didn't bring it up. I think the conversation had naturally moved on.

Andrew requested to see a female therapist and so was passed on to a colleague. She discharged him about a year later much improved and still wishing to carry on with his gender transition.

5. The creation of ADHD

'The social media app TikTok figured out I had ADHD before I did.'

Matilda Boseley

It's my first meeting with Jordan and his mother Miriam. Jordan is an eight-year-old boy of British Afro-Caribbean background. He's growing up in an area where there are few other black children in his school and neighbourhood. Jordan was referred to us after his school expressed concerns about his behaviour. They complained that he has problems with concentrating, sitting still, has few friends, and often falls out with his class teacher. They think he may have ADHD or perhaps an attachment disorder. Miriam is not happy with this opinion and is not happy with the school for suggesting it. She feels Jordan is being labelled by them instead of helping him with extra support.

After coming into the consulting room and sitting quietly next to his mother for a few minutes, his legs swinging under his chair, I notice that he's looking at the toys and books that sit on a shelf in the corner of my room. I ask him if he wants to have a look at what's there. He nods and politely says, 'Yes, please.' Jordan then sifts through a box of toys that he carefully takes down from the shelf, some books and jigsaws. He takes out one of the jigsaws, sits down with it on the floor, empties the pieces out of its box and starts sifting through them. As I talk to Miriam, I notice how he quietly gets on with putting the pieces of the puzzle together. Once he finishes, he breaks up the puzzle, puts the pieces into its box and puts it back onto the shelf in the spot where he found it. Next, he takes out of the toy box some Duplo Lego and builds a house with a garden in front and a fence that surrounds it. He takes his time, searches through the

Lego pieces, and puts them together without getting frustrated when they don't fit, or he doesn't like the outcome. Throughout the session he is polite, answers some of my questions as he works, and was an absolute pleasure to have in the consulting room.

I have had many experiences like this where the person that I see in clinic bears little resemblance to the person who is described in the referral. Here is a young lad who seems perfectly capable of being cooperative, of concentrating, of remaining calm, and in the context of the consulting room at least, presents with no recognisable challenges.

When it comes to diagnosing ADHD, these observations have become redundant. The 'official' criteria state that the 'symptoms' of ADHD need to be present in at least two different settings (such as at home and at school).[1] Observations in consulting rooms, one of the few tools of my trade, are rendered irrelevant to making an ADHD diagnosis. Instead, parents and teachers are meant to fill in questionnaires about the child's behaviour and the diagnosis is based on scoring their answers.

I will return to Jordan's story at the end of this chapter.

So far, I have outlined how mental health and psychiatric diagnoses are best understood as the outcome of subjective processes, leading to the social construction of what we consider to be a disorder and by implication our concept of normal. In the last chapter I demonstrated how this renders mental illness/disorder vulnerable to expansion of its boundaries, particularly in the current risk-averse era.

TikTok diagnoses

In a 2021 article in the *Guardian*, Melbourne-based reporter Matilda Boseley described how TikTok helped her discover that she had ADHD: 'For 23 years my parents, my teachers, my doctor, my psychologist and my own brain all missed the warning signs, yet somehow it only took that app's algorithm a few days to accidentally diagnose me.' All her life she 'had a nagging feeling that everyone else in the world was coping better than I was'.[2]

Explaining how TikTok curates a stream of videos based on what you like, by building up a profile of you and your interests, Boseley started coming across 'ADHD content made by women and for women, for the very first time'. Now it occurred to her that 'maybe I wasn't somehow just "worse at being a person" than everyone else. Maybe I simply didn't have enough dopamine in my brain.' Boseley then got an ADHD diagnosis after paying for an online assessment and felt liberated by this.

Matilda's experience is increasingly common. It's understandable. Why wouldn't you seek an assessment for something that the medical community is telling you is a common and under-diagnosed condition? Article after article across countries and media is claiming that, because of TikTok, more young adults are learning about ADHD and seeking assessments for the disorder. According to a piece in *Cosmopolitan*, 'the hashtag #ADHD is the seventh most popular health hashtag on the platform, and there is a large ADHD community on the platform as well'.[3]

The trend in increasing numbers of women getting a diagnosis started long before the pandemic. Like many consumerist trends it started in the US. The percentage of reproductive-aged women there who obtained at least one ADHD medication prescription increased 344 per cent from 2003 (0.9 per cent of women) to 2015 (4.0 per cent of women).[4]

An NBC News article described how a growing number of adult women in the US have been diagnosed with and are seeking treatment for ADHD. This new gender-based bias is clear on TikTok, where videos list 'signs you might have ADHD' with women showing their messy rooms and sharing how they forget to do things. While the hashtag #ADHD has over 18 billion views, '#ADHDinwomen' has over 2.3 billion views, but the one for men, '#ADHDinmen', has just 8.3 million views.[5]

Other countries are now catching up. According to a report, in 2019 around 7,700 women in the UK took an online test to see if they had ADHD, but this figure soared to around 254,400 in 2021 – a spectacular 3,200 per cent increase. This trend of increasing numbers of women being diagnosed with an assumed brain-based condition is said to be because symptoms present 'very differently' in women, implying they had not been recognised as symptoms until recently. In addition, 'Men with ADHD often have women in their lives who look after them, but you don't get that if you are a woman ... ADHD is harder to spot in women due to them being more likely to internalise or camouflage symptoms.'[6]

Women and psychiatry

In May 1990, my first job after I had moved from Scotland down to London was at St Mary Abbots Hospital (a hospital made famous as the place where Jimi Hendrix was pronounced dead in 1970). My new post was as a junior doctor attached to the old age psychiatry team. There was one geriatric ward at the hospital – by then a mental health hospital that would soon be closed for good. My supervising consultant, a tall, elegant, compassionate man who always dressed immaculately in suit and tie and with a handkerchief protruding from the top pocket of his suit jacket, suggested I look at the notes of one of the oldest inpatients we had on that ward. I started leafing through the faded yellowing pages of the earliest entries dating back to the 1920s and 30s. I had never heard of the diagnosis 'moral insanity' before, but there it was in (faded) black and white.

Moral insanity was originally defined in 1899 as 'madness consisting in a morbid perversion of the natural feelings, affections, inclinations, temper, habits, moral dispositions and natural impulses, without any remarkable disorder or defect of the interest or knowing and reasoning faculties, and particularly without any insane illusion or hallucinations'.[7] As the twentieth century unfolded it began being applied to women who were considered emotionally volatile and sometimes to women who became pregnant out of wedlock. The Mental Deficiency Act 1913 allowed local authorities to certify and institutionalise unmarried pregnant women who were deemed 'defective', at this time of heightened panic over 'racial degeneration' and eugenic concern about the perpetuation of 'unfit' genes. A mental defect was believed by some to have caused these women's 'immorality'.[8]

Better known than moral insanity is the diagnosis of hysteria, made famous in the late nineteenth century by the father of psychoanalysis, Sigmund Freud. Hysteria was another diagnosis almost exclusively applied to women.

Hysteria was once a common diagnosis. It was described as exhibiting a wide array of symptoms, including anxiety, shortness of breath, fainting, nervousness, sexual desire, insomnia, fluid retention, heaviness in the abdomen, irritability, loss of appetite for food or sex and a tendency to cause 'trouble' for others. The physician Jean-Martin Charcot studied hysteria after creating a special ward for 'non-insane' females in mid-nineteenth-century Paris. His interest in hysteria and hypnotism developed at a time when the general public was fascinated by 'animal magnetism' and 'mesmerisation', and so his studies and public lectures (often including demonstrations of hypnotising a woman with 'hysteria') brought him fame and notoriety.[9]

News of Charcot's work led a young Sigmund Freud to want to study with him. During the winter of 1885 to 1886, Freud spent four months at the Salpêtrière hospital in Charcot's neurology service. He was impressed by Charcot's teachings (who at the time believed hysteria to be a neurological condition), and this proved instrumental in the shift in Freud's interest from general neurology to the study of hysteria, hypnosis and, eventually, the unconscious.[10] Freud's subsequent studies led him to conclude that hysteria is a disease of women where the symptoms were the result of the impossibility of fulfilment of the sexual drive, with the symptoms allowing for the 'discharge' of repressed libidinal urges. He also suggested that the hysterical woman is trying to use other subtle ways to achieve hidden objectives through the side benefit of manipulating the environment to serve her needs.[11]

Moral insanity and hysteria have both left the lexicon of psychiatric diagnosis, having largely been replaced by the pejorative and stigmatising diagnosis of 'personality disorder', and in particular 'borderline personality disorder', again a nearly all-female diagnosis. Although still prevalent, I think borderline personality disorder is now being replaced and expanded by ADHD, autism and bipolar disorder as more popular diagnoses.

Women and their emotionality has been a preoccupation of psychiatry and psychology for a long time, echoing Western cultural and political preoccupations. Freud developed the theory that women suffered from 'penis envy' early in their psychological development when they realised they were not going to grow one. He further suggested that much female behaviour could be viewed as the outcome of envy of males. Freud claimed that one way they could overcome this penis envy was to have a child of their own – even going as far as to suggest they wanted a male child, in their efforts to gain a penis. Women were thus viewed as forever feeling inferior to men.[12]

Thus, the patriarchy of Victorian-era Europe becomes naturalised as an inevitable outcome of the psychology of human development. By this logic, a person's psychology is not a reflection of social pressures and expectations, rather the opposite – the social arrangement we have reflects human psychology. It's understandable that women might feel envious of the power and prestige men have in most societies, from sexualised comments on the street, sexual and domestic violence, to the persistent wage gap women endure, despite doing better than men in educational achievement when they get equal access to it. There is a long history of problematising female emotionality, something many feminists (including critical psychoanalysts) have pointed out.[13]

The Power Threat Meaning Framework, published in 2018, has a very good summary of the research and theory on the social drivers of mental health presentations in women, helping explain why women become the main mental health consumer demographic. Here are some of the relevant points they make.[14]

Women are expected to take most of the responsibility for the domestic sphere, for cooking, cleaning, childcare, and for addressing and working on the quality of relationships. According to UK-based research, in 2019, despite a significant rise in the number of women earning the majority of the household's income (compared to 2014), even when male and female partners are both in paid work, women do much more childcare and domestic work than men, with male breadwinners twice as likely to do no household chores at all.[15] Especially after the birth of children, many women become economically dependent on their male partners. The expectation of domestic and caring responsibilities is accompanied by social constructions of idealised femininity as synonymous with suitability for these roles – expressing warm emotions, unselfish concern for others' feelings and needs and lacking competitive striving or aggressiveness.[16]

Some feminists argue that capitalist societies created an institutional basis for modern forms of women's subordination. Splitting off the labour involved in care and nurture from the larger universe of human activities, in which women's work previously held a recognised place, they relegated it to a newly institutionalised 'domestic sphere', where its social importance was obscured. In a world where money became the primary medium for demonstrating power, the fact that such domestic work is unpaid sealed the matter – those who do this work are structurally subordinate to those who earn cash wages and so many women's roles become saturated with and mystified by domestic ideals of femininity.[17]

Women's reproductive bodies – in menstruation, pregnancy, childbirth and menopause – have traditionally been strongly associated with psychological weakness, especially increased emotionality and irrationality. Girls' and women's frequent exposure to images portraying them as sexual objects, and frequent reminders that desirability is an important attribute, encourages them – especially heterosexual women – to adopt an observer's perspective of their bodies and selves; to see themselves as objects to be judged. This is reflected in a pervasive concern with appearance and in the belief that a woman's appearance is a measure of her worth and value.[18]

Girls and women worldwide, in public and private, experience high levels of harassment, abuse and violence from men, ranging from unwanted 'chatting up', name-calling, sexualised insults and threats, various kinds of control and coercion, to physical and sexual assaults, rape and murder. US studies on sexual harassment from the 1980s onwards continue to show that sexual harassment of women is widespread in public and workplaces and there has been no significant decrease.[19] The scope of harassment and abuse of girls and women has in fact been increased by technology and social media.

These are just some of the many background factors that may help explain why adult women have been, and continue to be, the predominant sex that ends up getting diagnosed with a mental disorder and subjected to the medical gaze (whether they have sought a diagnosis or others have referred them or suggested it).

Thus, women are found to be two to three times more likely than men to meet diagnostic criteria for anxiety and depressive 'disorders', the two most common psychiatric diagnoses. They are also more likely to be diagnosed with panic disorder, post-traumatic stress disorder and eating disorders.[20] In childhood it's mainly boys who attract diagnoses, usually related to behaviour problems (such as ADHD, autism and conduct disorder). As age increases, by the later years of adolescence, girls are more likely than boys to report being depressed and to start attracting the diagnostic labels of adulthood.[21]

Young women have also been identified as a group with increasingly poor mental health outcomes, with 16- to 24-year-old women in the UK being three times more likely than men to experience a common mental disorder.[22] According to a briefing paper from the Royal College of Psychiatrists, rates of self-harm among young women in the UK tripled between 2000 and 2014, with gender-based violence, harassment and experience of trauma often associated.[23]

Women, from mid to late adolescence onwards, are thus the primary consumer group for MHIC.

Selling ADHD

There has been a wave of celebrities 'coming out' as having ADHD. Prince Harry was diagnosed in a highly public way, during a live-streamed conversation with Dr Gabor Maté. Celebrities such as Rory Bremner, Ant McPartlin, Heston Blumenthal, Sue Perkins, Johnny Vegas, Adrian Chiles, Josie Long, Lily Allen, Mel B, Nicola Adams, Jermain Pennant, Paris Hilton, Tom Watson and Owen Jones (to name just a few) have all stated in recent years that they have been diagnosed with ADHD.

What such public figures, whose stories have appeared in the press, have in common is that they can be considered relatively successful.

Despite this, they apparently have a brain disease caused by a lack of dopamine. Of course, like all of us, they will have struggles, histories and stories to tell. I do not wish to minimise the challenges they have had to deal with in their lives. However, celebrities and journalists have cultural power. What they say will be listened to and become a source of admiration for their 'courage' in helping 'destigmatise' ADHD. Is there a risk that celebrity adoration could result in glamorising ADHD? Could that lead to unforeseen problems for non-celebrities who then become convinced that they may also have this condition?

Founded in January 2020, the San Francisco start-up Cerebral was touted as a mental health saviour for offering virtual diagnosis and prescription services to hundreds of thousands of Americans cut off from in-person doctor visits during the global pandemic. Two years later Cerebral was investigated for possible violations of a federal law that regulates the distribution of controlled substances, including stimulant medications used in ADHD (a legal case that is ongoing at the time of writing).[24]

This came after a Bloomberg report claimed that 95 per cent of Cerebral patients received a prescription and that care coordinators were assigned as many as a thousand patients at a time. ADHD diagnoses were their biggest trade.[25]

Customers, however, seemed happy enough. Cerebral earned high satisfaction scores according to a survey conducted by ADHD magazine *ADDitude*. Respondents rated the service from Cerebral 4.07 out of 5 for its evaluation and/or diagnostic services and 4.06 out of 5 for its prescription services.[26]

Cerebral responded by pausing the prescribing of controlled drugs for ADHD, and the CEO at the time, Kyle Robertson, denied that they set targets to clinicians to prescribe drugs and claimed that they follow clinical prescribing guidelines based on the latest research.[27] By June 2022 Cerebral began halting most prescriptions of controlled substances and had replaced Robertson. They announced a transformation plan that included reviewing its clinical and marketing practices; 15 per cent of the workforce was laid off, and many of the services that it offered were discontinued.[28]

The creation of ADHD

Psychiatry UK is a private company contracted by the National Health Service to provide adult ADHD assessments. It has seen referrals quadruple between 2020 and 2022 compared with the previous two years. As many NHS clinics have long waiting lists for ADHD assessments, people are turning to private clinics, where (in 2024) it costs between £600 and £1,800 for an initial consultation.[29]

A recent report found an estimated 170,000 identified patients were prescribed at least one drug for adult ADHD between July and September 2022 in the UK – a 20 per cent increase from the 141,000 identified patients during the same period in 2021. Dr Tony Lloyd, the chief executive of the ADHD foundation, said its own figures suggested a 400 per cent increase in the number of adults seeking a diagnosis since 2020, adding that prescription volumes did not take account of those who do not use medication.[30]

Diagnosing adult ADHD

How is adult ADHD diagnosed? Basically, it's a questionnaire. It's not that different to filling out one of those pop psychology quizzes you find in magazines but then injected with the sort of life meanings astrology charts might have for those who believe in them.

According to ADHD UK, adults with ADHD may have problems with organisation, time management, following instructions, focusing, completing tasks, coping with stress, feeling restless or impatient, impulsiveness, relationships and social interactions. They offer the online survey I've reproduced below (one of many free online 'tests' you can complete).[31] Here are the six questions which you must choose to rate as never, rarely, sometimes, often, or very often. You score 1 if you answer 'often', 2 if you answer 'very often' and 0 for the others). Have a go and see what you score:

1. How often do you have trouble wrapping up the final details of a project once the challenging parts have been done?
2. How often do you have difficulty getting things in order when you have to do a task that requires organisation?

3. How often do you have problems remembering appointments or obligations?
4. When you have a task that requires a lot of thought, how often do you avoid or delay getting started?
5. How often do you fidget or squirm with your hands or feet when you have to sit down for a long time?
6. How often do you feel overly active and compelled to do things, like you were driven by a motor?

If you score 4 or more, it's likely that you'll get a diagnosis of ADHD once you delve into your savings to get the 'formal' assessment. That's it, as far as the basis of diagnosis is concerned. The rest of the questionnaires and discussion of your personal history and so on is just the ornamental dressing to make it look like something medical, scientific and serious. The science (or lack of it) will be looked at further in the next chapter.

A brief history of ADHD

ADHD did not exist until it was imagined into being. There was no ADHD until someone called it ADHD (or its precursor names). This is not the same as saying there was no bacterial infection until Louis Pasteur described how small organisms called germs could invade the body and cause disease. Prior to this discovery doctors believed that foul odours could create disease, or priests may have pointed the finger at 'evil spirits'. In the case of bacteria, they always existed, and it was only after they were discovered that we could start moving to a scientifically valid explanation for certain diseases that were caused by bacteria. Infections became a diagnostic category and we have steadily built technical knowledge around different types of infection, different treatments, and so on. ADHD is closer to a belief in 'evil spirits' than bacterial infection.

Over-activity, poor concentration and impulsivity in children were first conceptualised as possible medical phenomena more than a century ago, when British paediatrician Frederick Still described a group of children who showed what he considered to be restlessness, fidgetiness and a poor capacity for sustained attention.[32] He went on to argue that these children had 'abnormal defects of moral control', although he generally assumed this was caused by pre-existing diseases affecting the brain, such as cerebral tumours, meningitis, epilepsy, head injury, typhoid fever or impairment of the intellect. Yet Still describes other behaviours that could be considered more appropriate to the category of conduct disorder (such as cruelty, jealousy, lawlessness, dishonesty) than ADHD.

The next important link in the developing ADHD narrative is a 1937 paper by American psychiatrist Charles Bradley describing a chance discovery at an institution for neurologically impaired children. Bradley tried a stimulant (Benzedrine) as a 'treatment' and it allegedly improved the behaviour, concentration and school performance of a group of them, at least in the short term.[33] These children often presented with restlessness, personality changes and learning difficulties, with many having previously suffered from encephalitis (inflammation of the brain, probably secondary to an infection).

Neither Still's nor Bradley's papers received much attention at the time of their publication and would have disappeared, like thousands of other ideas that come and go in medical and scientific literature, had the focus on understanding and intervening in children's behaviour not started to gain traction in cultural and political circles decades later.

In the post-Second World War years, psychiatry became involved in the treatment of many men and women traumatised by the experiences of war, and so began to expand its range of interests. The mental life of children – a group that had not drawn much interest from the psychiatric profession until then – started to attract increased scrutiny. Some doctors began to speculate that children who presented with what was described as 'hyperactive' behaviours might have organic lesions in the brain that was causing hyperactivity.

In 1947, Strauss and Lehtinen published a book about the education of children with brain injury and in it proposed a diagnosis of 'minimal brain damage' to explain the occurrence of hyperactivity in the absence of overt evidence of brain injury. Arguing that children who experienced identifiable brain injuries (from, for example, encephalitis, birth trauma and epilepsy) sometimes presented with hyperactivity, they suggested that those who presented with hyperactivity in the absence of readily identifiable brain injuries, may have some, as yet unidentified, brain damage.[34]

According to historian Matthew Smith, it was not until the mid to late 1950s in the USA when a group of physicians, along with some educators, politicians and parents, started to become more alarmed about children who had the behaviours that we now associate with ADHD. In 1957 a group of child psychiatrists at Emma Pendleton Bradley Home in Rhode Island coined the term 'hyperkinetic impulse disorder'. A group of childhood behaviours, mainly displayed by (as any parent or teacher would tell you) boys, were now brought under a medical gaze. There was to be no biological discovery either then or since to justify its entry into any system of knowledge as a 'neuro'-based thing.[35]

After 1957, the number of medical articles about children with what are reported as 'symptoms' of hyperactivity escalated, initially in the US, and later in other countries. In the previous half-century, medical literature, particularly that which was influenced by psychoanalytic ideas, was more concerned with withdrawn, shy, 'neurotic' children. The late fifties marked a turning point as interest transferred more to children who exhibited delinquent, violent and other antisocial behaviours.

What was behind this shift? According to Smith, it may have been related to fear, following the Soviet launching of the Sputnik satellites in the autumn of 1957, that the USA was falling behind the USSR in the race for scientific, technological and military superiority. There was concern that if changes were not made in the American school system to redress the situation, they might lose the Cold War. This caused a change in classroom structure, teaching methods and expectations with regard to pupil performance.

I am not entirely convinced by this suggestion and think that such events intersected with other changes taking place in the culture of the time, including (but not limited to): the growth of and fear of adolescent culture and rebellion, changes in family structure and community rootedness, growing size of an aspirational middle class, and greater concern about children both as perpetrators and victims of harm.[36] The important point here is recognising that ADHD emerges and gets popularised because of cultural, not scientific, reasons. Shifts in public and political concerns will shift interest, conversations, funding, service provision, and so on.

What was, up until then, a culturally non-existent condition was about to go through a growth spurt. The metamorphosis that ADHD undergoes over the next six decades is quite extraordinary. It enters the medical lexicon initially as a condition that is thought to be rare, predominantly found in young males, and something you are likely to grow out of. Sixty-plus years later it has spread out of its initial niche in the US, migrated geographically, demographically, experientially, behaviourally, and in its gender profile. By the third decade of our millennium the new customer base has become women with disposable incomes.

Diagnostic mutations

Evidence for underlying organic lesions in children who displayed hyperactivity could not be found, so definitions started to focus on behavioural descriptions rather than attributing a brain-related cause. In 1966 the North American-based *Diagnostic Statistical Manual, Second Edition* (*DSM-II*) coined the label 'hyperkinetic reaction of childhood'.[37]

Growing interest from psychologists meant that psychological mechanisms were being hypothesised as causing behaviours such as hyperactivity. The role of attention came to the fore as a new theory proposed that problems in sustaining attention were the drivers of hyperactivity. Thus, when *DSM-II* was replaced in the early eighties by the third edition (*DSM-III*),[38] it was called attention deficit disorder (ADD). This could be diagnosed with or without hyperactivity and was defined using three dimensions (three separate lists of symptoms): one for attention deficits, one for impulsivity, and one for hyperactivity.

ADD now sets the scene for a revolution to take place in Western child psychiatric practice, as the drug Ritalin joins the growing popularity of using psycho-pharmaceuticals to deal with life's challenges and becomes the first one aimed specifically at children. When *DSM-III* was revised (and became *DSM-III-R*) in the late 1980s,[39] the symptoms were all combined into one list (one dimension) and ADD was now changed to attention deficit hyperactivity disorder (ADHD), with attention, hyperactivity and impulsiveness now assumed to be part of one disorder with no distinctions, and thus the label ADHD was born.

When the fourth edition of *DSM* (*DSM-IV*) was published in 1994,[40] the criteria were again changed, this time in favour of a two-dimensional model with attention deficit being one subcategory and hyperactivity-impulsivity the other. With each revision, a larger number of children are found to be above the threshold for diagnosis. In 2013 the fifth edition of *DSM* was published (*DSM-5*) with some key criteria having been broadened to allow more adolescents and adults to qualify for a diagnosis.[41] For example, in earlier versions of *DSM* you had to have shown ADHD behaviours before the age of seven to qualify for a diagnosis; this was increased to twelve in *DSM-5*.

Childhood pathologised

The principal recommendation for treatment of ADHD became that of prescribing stimulant medication – namely, the use of the amphetamine class of drugs (such as Ritalin). I discuss stimulants mechanism of action and effectiveness as a treatment in the next chapter. However, the idea that there was a specific medical treatment helped popularise its adoption and created a foundation for imagining that ADHD is the result of some sort of chemical deficiency or imbalance.

By the 1960s and 70s the use of psycho-pharmaceuticals was expanding at the same time as scientific approaches to parenting were becoming fashionable. The ascendance of scientific ways of talking about children, child development and upbringing were now displacing more naturalistic approaches to child-rearing characteristic of earlier eras, pushing the task of child-rearing further towards ownership by professional groups.[42]

Prior to this, most Western countries viewed children as largely sturdy and resilient. An example of this can be found in the late 1950s/early 60s Fischers' New England town study. They found that families understood their children's problematic behaviours as 'stages' that most children could be expected to pass through. Viewing problems in this way meant that parents did not feel an obligation to seek professional help for them. In fact, to do so would run counter to another prevailing belief, which was that parents ought not to force children in case they damage their potential. Thus children's 'bad' behaviour was interpreted through a normative lens as expected and temporary.[43]

As childhood behaviour problems move away from the arena of parental and community common sense and towards ownership by a professional class, childhood psychiatric diagnoses and prescription of psychiatric medications to children, particularly stimulants, begin their ascent in the post-industrial West.

By the beginning of this century the concept of ADHD was migrating beyond that of a childhood developmental disorder to a lifelong and fixed brain-based condition as the idea of adult ADHD took off. The emphasis in adult ADHD moves from observations of external behaviour to perceived failings of internal regulation, highlighting problems with 'self-concept' and largely disregarding hyperactivity in its diagnostic criteria.

As Western culture has heightened its focus on the individual, it has emphasised the fragility of inner life, turned desires into commoditised needs, and taught people to measure their sense of self-worth through competitive achievements. Diagnoses that are framed in ways that blame the problem on biochemical dysfunction can appear to provide an avenue of relief from the struggles involved in keeping a positive sense of self. In a commodified culture, a sense of satisfaction, of being good enough and productive enough, is not only hard to achieve, but also hard to know what that means and what it should look or feel like. ADHD is one of the new commodities on offer promising to fill that sense of emptiness.

What we define as ADHD today has grown from nothing to a lifelong disorder that can be identified from the cradle to the grave with something believed to have 'neuro' roots.

ADHD is 'culture-bound'

Changes in cultural norms and concerns cause changes in what we consider to be a problem, in how we understand a problem once it is defined as such, and how we then seek to intervene to address that perceived problem.

The various ways ADHD itself can be constructed act as a window into the cultural dynamics of the society constructing it. We have already seen how shifting constructs first allowed for irritating childhood behaviour to be pathologised and, later, for women's sense of not being good enough to be exploited. Other definitional manipulations can also be seen.

In the UK, ADHD diagnosis and treatment is more likely to be given to children (mainly boys) from lower social classes and is associated with higher levels of behavioural problems, whereas in the US, middle-class children (again mainly boys), particularly in areas of lower academic achievement, are more likely to be diagnosed and treated, although this pattern may now be changing.[44] Interviews with young people diagnosed with ADHD in the UK and US have found that their beliefs about ADHD mirror these epidemiological findings, with UK children much more likely to view ADHD as a disorder of self-control causing them to lose their temper and get into fights, whereas US children are more likely to believe that ADHD is a disorder that causes them to fail at school.[45]

Cross-cultural ADHD studies find major and significant differences between assessors from different countries in what behaviours they rate as problematic. There are also significant differences between assessors when they assess children from different ethnic minority backgrounds. In a 1992 study, Chinese and Indonesian clinicians gave significantly higher scores for hyperactive and disruptive behaviours than did their Japanese and American colleagues.[46] While these may reflect cultural attitudes towards certain types of behaviour in children, it suggests as well that international comparisons based on observations or rating questionnaires are unlikely to be reliable.

A medical anthropology study published in 2003 looked at a group of middle-class children at a Mexican school. Using standard questionnaires, the researchers concluded that about 8 per cent of the children could be diagnosed as having ADHD, yet there was only one child in that school who had been given such a diagnosis. Through interviews with parents and teachers of those more active children who were not diagnosed, the researchers discovered that these carers regarded ADHD-type behaviours as within the boundaries of behaviours viewed as normal and expected for these children, particularly boys, at those ages.[47]

Race and ethnicity is another area where within-country differences in diagnostic patterns can be found. In a 2008 ethnographic study of families with children diagnosed with ADHD in a metropolitan area of north-eastern US, considerable differences between the beliefs and practices of 'Euro-American' families and 'African American' families were found. While Euro-American families voiced biomedical explanations and preferred to use a clinical lexicon of 'disorders' and 'conditions' or specific diagnostic categories to describe their children's behaviour problems, African American families resisted pathologising their children's experience. They used more diffuse vocabulary of 'issues', 'challenges' and 'difficulties' to describe problematic behaviours and feelings in their children. These African American families displayed active questioning of, and scepticism towards, mental health interventions whether these were medication-based or psychotherapeutic.[48]

It's worth remembering these older studies as they tell us something about the cultural ideology in the earlier phases of the growth and blossoming of the ADHD, and associated 'neurodiversity', industry. They remind us that the gap between observations of a child's behaviour and the meanings attached to them is vast and cavernous. In that space we construct our culturally biased interpretations with the consequences that then flow out of our choices.

Within-nation differences remain prevalent today. For example, the diagnosis is significantly lower among Hispanic- and Asian-background children, compared with Caucasian children in the US.[49] In Israel, the Jewish population can be classified into four relatively distinct levels of religiosity: secular, traditional, Orthodox (observant Jews) and ultra-Orthodox (devout observant Jews). Yaakov Ophir's research found that these groups show a linear trend in ADHD rates: whereas 6.7 per cent of the ultra-Orthodox sector received a diagnosis of ADHD, 16.4 per cent were diagnosed in the Orthodox sector, 25.7 per cent in the traditional sector and 26.0 per cent in the secular sector.[50]

How much ADHD do we now have?

One way to get a window onto the frequency of ADHD diagnosis is to look at global consumption of prescribed stimulants. While the US remains top of the table (along with Iceland) as the highest per capita consumers, global consumption of prescription stimulants has been steadily rising over the last decade. In one year between 2020 and 2021 the number of countries prescribing stimulants increased from sixty-two to sixty-seven, with consumption rising in several European countries (Belgium, Denmark, Estonia, Finland, Germany, Iceland, the Netherlands, Portugal, Spain, Sweden, Switzerland and the United Kingdom) as well as in Canada, China, New Zealand and the Republic of Korea.[51]

What proportion of the population is getting an ADHD diagnosis? According to the National Survey of Children's Health, conducted by the US Centers for Disease Control and Prevention, in 2016 in the US a total of 9.6 per cent of all children (six to eleven years) and 13.6 per cent of all adolescents (twelve to seventeen years) had received a medical diagnosis of ADHD.[52] Other national survey data found rates of ADHD exceeded 20 per cent among boys aged eleven to fourteen.[53] This far surpasses the 'official' rate for the prevalence of ADHD in young people of 3–5 per cent.

ADHD has become an MHIC monster: the more we throw its way to try and tame it, the taller, broader and more aggressive it becomes.

What happened to Jordan?

At the start of this chapter, I told you about Jordan, an eight-year-old boy of British Afro-Caribbean background, whose school thought that he may have ADHD. His mother, Miriam, was not happy with the school's opinion. In my consulting room Jordan presented with no challenges and concentrated on doing a jigsaw and building a Lego house.

Miriam separated from Jordan's father when he was a baby. The father no longer had contact with Jordan and Miriam didn't want him to. Before moving to the current area two years ago, Miriam and Jordan lived in London, close to her parents who provided a lot of ongoing support. Jordan was, and still is, close to his maternal grandfather but they don't see him as often now. Jordan didn't like his new school and felt the teachers and some of the kids 'picked on him'.

There are many different directions we could have taken our sessions. The house move, loss of a father early in Jordan's life, loss of extended family support, loss of a male role model, possible racism or, at least, an awareness of difference, the school's biases, and so on. I could talk more to Jordan to understand why he feels like he does, contact the school, meet with extended family, and so on.

In our second meeting Jordan repeated what he did in the first. He sifted through the toys, puzzles and books on the shelf. He got a joke book out and read it quietly to himself, smiling from time to time. Then he got out a jigsaw, sat on the floor and started carefully sorting through and putting the pieces together. Miriam and I talked during this time. After a while, Miriam went quiet and just looked at Jordan with what I interpreted as adoration. Jordan noticed his mum's silence, looked up at her and said, 'What?' Miriam smiled at him. 'Nothing, just watching you. It's nice to see you like this.' Jordan went back to his puzzle. I was curious. I wanted to find out more about that moment.

Miriam explained that she was enjoying how calm, polite and cooperative he was being. She was surprised at how he had behaved in our first meeting and now he was doing it again. At home Jordan could get oppositional and argumentative. She worried about him. She worried about what would happen to him in the future and how easy it was for young black boys to get labelled and dismissed. I wondered with Miriam why Jordan seemed, to her, so different when they came to these meetings. And so started the pattern of our sessions.

Miriam and I would talk, and Jordan would quietly and calmly occupy himself. He was clearly listening, judging by his occasional well-timed comment. Miriam and I spoke about the nature of emotions. Emotions are viral! We tend to 'catch' the emotions of those whom we are closest to (emotionally and geographically). An emotion can ripple out into those around you at alarming speed. Laughter breeds laughter like anger breeds anger, worry breeds worry and calm (sometimes) breeds calm. We discussed how she had been feeling about Jordan and about her life and their life together.

I spoke about how relationships settle into a kind of rhythm. I use the metaphor of a dance to think beyond behaviour and into the emotional flow that happens between two (or more) people. Relationships settle into a dance that involves our fears, joys and frustrations, which have their echoes in the responses we get back, which in turn creates responses in us. We talked about Miriam's fears, joys and frustrations and the nature of the emotional dance between her and Jordan. Did Miriam want to alter her side of the dance? Could she learn to step back from worry and frustration being such a big feature of their emotional dance? Could she notice and reinforce Jordan's abilities and skills, including his ability to be calm and concentrate as he was showing us in the sessions?

I compared how our emotional attention functions to a radar. Because she's worried, Miriam's internal radar scans the environment for signs in Jordan to be worried about. Over time this drives their emotional dance. Could she train her internal radar to notice, however small or infrequent, any events and actions by Jordan that demonstrated his abilities, maturity and aspects not to worry about but to celebrate? Could she learn to manage difficult situations without giving them much emotional energy at the same time? Miriam found that she could and the tension in their relationship eased. Jordan was always perfectly behaved, and I could sense Miriam's heart swelling with pride every time I commended Jordan for his behaviour and what a pleasure it was to have him in my consulting room. Miriam also moved Jordan to a new school.

When it was time for Jordan to be discharged, I asked Miriam what she thought had helped. She said it was feeling heard. It's rarely the clever stuff that makes a difference.

6. Is ADHD an evidence-based construct?

'I know that most men can seldom accept even the simplest and most obvious truth if it be such as would oblige them to admit the falsity of conclusions which they have delighted in explaining to colleagues.'

Leo Tolstoy

Yasmine, a fifteen-year-old girl in the care system for many years, has been referred to our service by her social worker. Her biological parents were substance abusers. She was taken into care as a two-year-old due to parental neglect and moved around foster-care placements until aged four, when she was finally adopted. Unfortunately, her adoption broke down after a couple of years and she was taken back into the care system. Inclined to frequent outbursts of anger and what was described as 'controlling' behaviours, she also ran away from time to time.

After going back into care, she did relatively well in a long-term foster placement and remained stable and able to cope in a mainstream school. Problems emerged again in adolescence. She became oppositional, prone to running away (resulting in police being called on several occasions) and aggressive towards a younger person newly arrived in the foster family. When the placement broke down, now fourteen years old, she was placed in a private children's home, which called itself a 'therapeutic' home.

Yasmine had grown up in the hubbub of London. This new home was in a rural area, where the company had taken advantage of low house prices and the high demand for places that care for difficult-to-place children. She was one of three residents in this home, which had round-the-clock staffing. She no longer had any contact with her biological, adoptive or long-term foster parents, but did still have some contact with her paternal grandparents.

Since being placed in the children's home several months ago, Yasmine had displayed intermittent difficult behaviour. She could be disruptive, rude to the staff, oppositional, unable to settle and complete tasks, and her access to the education on offer was sporadic.

What had been confusing for the staff at the home is that she can have good days where she is responsive, warm, appreciative and engaging. After a recent trip to the seaside, where she appeared to really enjoy herself – she even said, 'I love it here' – the next day she was 'uncontrollable'. She smashed a light bulb and used the broken glass to cut herself on the forearm and then swallowed some of the remaining shards, before running away. She was finally found by the police the next day, some thirty-two miles away. She had walked and walked and had blisters and cuts on her feet as a result.

Like most young people with an extensive care history, Yasmine had multiple psychological/psychiatric assessments over the years, often to try and save a placement. She had previously had therapy for 'attachment trauma'. While it was recognised that she had experienced trauma, her most recent assessment, from a private clinical psychologist, concluded that Yasmine probably has ADHD. Yasmine's social worker now referred her to our service to request an 'urgent mental health assessment' that included 'testing' her for possible ADHD.

What difference would a diagnosis make to Yasmine? Is there evidence that an ADHD diagnosis could lead to interventions that might improve her life? I return to Yasmine's story at the end of the chapter.

So, what is ADHD?

Having read this far, are you still struggling to know what ADHD is? Perhaps I haven't yet done it justice, so let me introduce you to some conceptual and scientific issues.

We are faced with some key concerns. What does it mean to have a diagnosis that is supposed to identify a specific and characteristic condition, and that can be pulled, stretched, expanded and then have the criteria changed?

How do we arrive at a scientific understanding of what makes up a 'case'?

In Chapter 3, I explained the principles of scientific methodology and how evidence-based medicine allows for the application of scientific principles to build technical knowledge based around a diagnosis. I explained that EBM relies on a process which starts with generating a hypothesis. This hypothesis needs to be testable empirically, through studies that can generate data that help us answer whether the hypothesis we are putting forward is supported and to what degree it's supported. If you cannot get empirical support for your hypothesis, you should maintain the 'null hypothesis'. The null hypothesis is always your starting point, meaning you always start by assuming that your hypothesis isn't true (null – there's nothing here) until you prove, with data, that this null hypothesis has been disproved and your hypothesis therefore has empirical support. Once you have data to support your hypothesis you need other research teams to replicate your results before it's possible to finally discard the null hypothesis.

It is up to those who are claiming ADHD is 'genetic' and 'neurodevelopmental' and the result of a 'chemical imbalance' to demonstrate this is the case before we can accept any of those propositions. As a scientist my only job is to scrutinise studies to see if such claims have been supported.

This is important to state as I regularly encounter supporters of abandoning this basic premise and stating that the 'absence of evidence is not the same as evidence of absence'. But in scientific terms, that's precisely what it is. So let me examine the evidence, with the null hypothesis in mind.

Has the null hypothesis been disproven for ADHD genetics?

The claim that ADHD is genetic has been extrapolated mainly from twin studies because identical twins are more often both diagnosed with ADHD than non-identical twins. In the twin method for estimating heritability, it's assumed that when a higher percentage of identical than non-identical twins are diagnosed with the same condition, this is due to genetics. This is because identical twin pairs will share 100 per cent of the genes whereas non-identical twins will share, on average, 50 per cent of their genes. Twin studies have led to the suggestion that ADHD is 75–80 per cent genetic. The researcher Jay Joseph has examined the question of heritability of psychiatric disorders (including ADHD) in detail in his books and articles and concluded that there is no scientific basis for genetic claims based on twin studies.[1]

Let me walk you through the problems with the twin study method and the subsequent research that tries to establish the genetic foundations of ADHD.

For identical twins to have a greater likelihood of a psychiatric disorder because of sharing the same genes, you must assume that the psychological and social environment is the same for identical and non-identical twins. This is known as the equal environment assumption or EEA for short. But EEA doesn't hold when comparing identical and non-identical twins. Identical twins are often treated more similarly (such as being dressed in the same clothes) and experience a unique psychological environment (for example swapping roles to confuse others). Identical twins will always be the same sex, unlike non-identical twins. Being one of an identical twin pairing is a different experience to being one of non-identical twins and so psychological and social factors, not just genes, could also be responsible for any greater behavioural or emotional similarity. This means the twin study method cannot disentangle genetic from environmental factors for psychiatric presentations, and so estimates of the genetic contribution to ADHD cannot be arrived at from this method.

There are other methods used to estimate genetic heritability such as family studies (looking at prevalence of ADHD symptoms in family trees) that also cannot disentangle environmental from genetic contributions. Another approach, which is more challenging logistically, is adoption studies. An ADHD adoption study would involve comparing rates of ADHD in adoptive parents' families with rates in the biological families of children who have been adopted and subsequently diagnosed with ADHD. There have been no adoption studies of this type in ADHD research. Methodological problems are numerous in adoption studies anyway, from the fact that most adoptees have already spent considerable time in biological families of origin or in foster-care placements prior to adoption, to the differences parents of adoptees as a group may have to the 'average' parent. Adoption studies, like family studies, are also not capable of distinguishing environmental from genetic contributions and so none of these methods used to estimate heritability can, on their own or together, disprove the null hypothesis that there is no characteristic genetic abnormality or difference associated with those who get an ADHD label.

The only way to reliably evidence a specific genetic contribution to ADHD is through molecular genetic studies, in other words to examine actual genetic material. Since faster and cheaper whole genome scans have become available, the molecular genetic evidence has been accumulating. This increasingly large volume of ADHD genetic research is not showing any unique findings, whether in relation to abnormal genes or consistent genetic differences.

In 2010, a study was published in the medical journal the *Lancet* claiming to have found molecular genetic evidence for ADHD.[2] This study has been, and continues to be, referenced as an important study that demonstrates the certainty with which we can call ADHD genetic. In the press release at the time the research team lead, Professor Anita Thapar, left little room for doubt, saying, 'Now we can say with confidence that ADHD is a genetic disease and that the brains of children with this condition develop differently to those of other children.'[3] This is what they found:

The study involved whole genome scans looking for something called copy number variants (CNVs). CNVs are abnormal bits of genetic code that are repeated where they shouldn't be or deleted where they should be. In the study, 366 children 'with ADHD' were compared to 1,047 'non-ADHD' children. The researchers found 15.6 per cent of the children with ADHD had CNVs compared with 7.5 per cent of the non-ADHD controls. This leaves an excess of 8 per cent in the ADHD group, hardly a significant figure (and nowhere near the 75–80 per cent heritability estimates from twin studies). If we are to accept standard 'mainstream' quoted prevalence for ADHD of 3–5 per cent of the population, it also means that if you come across a young person who has CNVs they are more likely not to have an ADHD diagnosis than to have it.

There is more, much more. When children with significant learning difficulties (LD) were excluded from the ADHD group, only 11.4 per cent of the remaining children had CNVs (now only 4 per cent above the 'non-ADHD' control group). However, 39 per cent (13 of the 33) of children with both ADHD and LD had CNVs. This evidence is more suggestive of a relationship between the presence of CNVs and LD (39 per cent) than CNVs and ADHD only (11.4 per cent).

The authors should have chosen a subgroup from their ADHD set that had the same intellectual level, in order to control for the effects of learning ability. This would then have made for a more legitimate comparison group to their controls. I can't help wondering whether they may have been left with no significant difference between the ADHD and non-ADHD groups once both groups were of similar learning ability (as measured by the IQ test used in the study).

Since then, there has been an explosion in well-funded genetic research into ADHD. Thousands of those diagnosed with ADHD have had their entire genome scanned to detect what is known as 'DNA variants' – bits of DNA that are different in persons with a condition compared to those without. These studies are called genome-wide association studies (GWAS). In GWAS, each person's DNA – which contains millions of genetic codes – is examined looking for a gene that occurs more frequently in people with a condition than those without. If a gene is found more commonly in people with the condition, it is said to be associated with that condition. It's important to note that these are not bits of genetic code considered to be abnormal (such as CNVs), just different.

GWAS are fundamentally different to methods that start with a hypothesis. A hypothesis-based approach puts forward a theory that a particular gene or set of genes are abnormal and then compares these in people with or without an ADHD diagnosis. GWAS are data-fishing exercises. They may lead to a hypothesis that can be further investigated if they reveal regions that may be of interest and seem relevant to the condition being studied, but on their own cannot tell you the relevance of a particular set of otherwise 'normal' genes occurring slightly more often in those with or without a diagnosis.

The initial GWAS of ADHD did not discover any DNA variants that achieved significance, even when most of these samples were combined into a study, including over 3,000 patients with an ADHD diagnosis and/or their parents. Later, using even larger samples going into tens of thousands of ADHD-diagnosed people, GWAS showed ADHD to be associated with many common variants, each having tiny effects, which are spread across the entire genome and cross over with other (so-called) psychiatric diagnoses (like autism, schizophrenia and bipolar disorder).[4]

What this means is that in order to pick up genes that occur very, very slightly more than chance in those with ADHD compared to healthy controls, you must have a very large sample size. Most of those with an ADHD diagnosis don't have any of the individual genetic differences picked up in the massive GWAS samples, nor do we have any reasonable biological theory to test from what is being picked up from these tiny, barely relevant, findings.

Having given up on ever finding any relevant hypothesis-driven molecular genetic findings, a new idea emerged. Instead of looking for relevant genes, let's create a probability-based 'algorithm'. Welcome to the world of polygenic risk score (PRS). PRS is based on comparing thousands or tens of thousands of whole genome scans of those with a particular condition compared to a 'healthy' control group. The starting point is the GWAS discussed above. PRS then applies the GWA profile of a particular condition to an individual patient.

Given that GWAS find hundreds of bits of genetic code scattered across the genome, the PRS is the process of looking at the individual's genome to see how many of these hundreds of potential variants can be found in this particular individual's genetic profile. The higher your PRS (the more of these tiny genetic differences you can find) the higher is the assumed risk.[5] But like any probability-based methods it tells you nothing about the cause.

Where has this got us? Well, here are the latest estimates for how much of the variance in cause the PRS method is achieving: for schizophrenia, it's about 6 per cent of the liability variance; for major depressive disorder, it's 2 per cent; for bipolar disorder, it's 5 per cent; and for ADHD, it's 6 per cent (again far off the 75–80 per cent heritability estimates). But wait, behaviours not considered psychiatric disorders have higher estimates using the PRS method: 10 per cent for externalising behaviours (behaviour problems in general), 11 per cent for years of schooling (a proxy for educational attainment) and 15 per cent for tested school performance at age sixteen, which is the most predictive polygenic score in the behavioural sciences (possibly indicating as before a higher potential genetic loading for learning difficulties).[6]

What does all that actually mean in real life? I think the only thing we can comprehensively conclude is that it means that genetics has made no progress in understanding ADHD.

But those who have spent their careers expounding that ADHD is genetic cannot accept this most obvious failure to find any reliable evidence (perhaps understandably, because they are humans first and scientists second). To deal with this conundrum they now refer to this problem as 'the missing heritability'. Because they assume ADHD must be genetic, they imagine the genes must be there somewhere; it's just that we haven't found them yet. The most likely reason for the 'missing heritability' is, of course, that it was never there in the first place. Scientifically speaking, we must assume that, as regards genetics, the cupboard is empty, and the null hypothesis stands: there is no characteristic identifiable genetic abnormality/profile associated with ADHD.

Has the null hypothesis been disproven in ADHD brain-imaging studies?

As with genetics, ADHD brain-imaging studies have not uncovered any specific or characteristic abnormality. The picture that emerges is of consistently inconsistent findings, which are statistical deviations (the brains would not be recognised by radiologists as being clinically abnormal), come from small sample size studies, don't always accurately match for age (and you'll see why this is important when I comment on birthdate research below) and typically don't control for IQ level (and any associated intellectual/learning difficulties), or for the possible effects of medication. One research team finds one bit of the brain smaller than 'healthy' controls and the next one doesn't, or even finds that bit is a little larger.

In 2017 *Lancet Psychiatry* published a study that the authors claimed provided definitive evidence that young people with ADHD have different and smaller brains compared to their healthy peers.[7] The lead researcher, Dr Hoogman, concluded that 'The data from our highly powered analysis confirm that patients with ADHD do have altered brains and therefore that ADHD is a disorder of the brain.'[8]

The authors call their study a 'mega-analysis', as they took data from twenty-three previous studies conducted in several different countries and 'number-crunched' all the different sites' findings as if they were all just one big study. This process is sometimes illuminating but can also make incidental findings look more significant than they are. In total they had data from the brain scans of 1,713 patients diagnosed with ADHD and 1,529 individuals who did not have this diagnosis. They claim that they found what amounts to tiny differences in some (not all) brain structures that become statistically significant when they add all the available recorded volumes from all the studies.

Other researchers saw problems with their claims.[9] The largest difference was found for a tiny brain structure called the nucleus accumbens (NA). The authors assert that children with ADHD have a smaller NA than non-ADHD children. However, if you look at the data by site you find ten of the twenty-three sites found an average smaller NA in the ADHD group, four sites found an average larger NA in the ADHD group, and six sites found no difference. This is the picture for the structure with the largest difference in the study. Staying with NA, you can also see that there are major technical issues with interpreting the scans that arise out of the different machinery and/or analytic algorithms the different sites used. For example, individuals in Bergen, Norway, have an average NA volume of 758 mm^3 v 805 mm^3 (ADHD v control), whereas in Würzberg, Germany, they have an average NA volume of 462 mm^3 v 449 mm^3 (ADHD v control). Perhaps Norwegian children have amazing NAs compared to German children, who by this standard must all have raging ADHD to contend with.

Here is yet another study that does not control for IQ differences (learning ability levels). Associations between brain volume and IQ levels have been shown across a range of studies with adults and children. A separate research group reanalysed the published data from this study and concluded that there was no significant difference between individuals with ADHD and those in the control group in any of the investigated areas of the brain once IQ differences is controlled for.[10]

One final issue in this mess of pretence that there is anything specifically 'neuro' about ADHD. What would it mean if you did find significant brain-size differences? Male brains are on average larger than females' from birth, stabilising at around 11 per cent larger in adults.[11] Yet wherever there is equal access to educational opportunity, females tend to score higher on average in tests than males. Does this mean a smaller brain is a cause of being smarter?

Here too then, as far as the science is concerned, the evidence cupboard is empty. No one has come near to finding a characteristic abnormality, and as a result there is no biological marker or brain scan used to diagnose ADHD. The null hypothesis stands – there is no characteristic brain abnormality associated with ADHD.

Has the null hypothesis been disproven for ADHD being caused by a chemical imbalance?

There is no shortage of 'experts' prepared to claim that ADHD is related to a chemical lack of the neurotransmitter 'dopamine'. As a significant effect of stimulant drugs (like Ritalin) used in ADHD treatment is to increase the release of dopamine, the theory that ADHD is the result of a lack of dopamine took hold. Yet, decades ago, studies found that if you take stimulants, regardless of diagnosis, it improves your ability, in the short term at least, to maintain concentration on a task. In other words, stimulants have a general effect on anyone who takes them rather than a specific effect on those who get the ADHD label.[12] Remember, stimulants like cocaine and amphetamines are widely used illicitly, so there is a vibrant black market as a result for ADHD drugs.

Despite no one ever demonstrating a lack of dopamine existed in ADHD-diagnosed individuals, the chemical imbalance theory was able to spread alongside marketing from drug manufacturers.

A study published in 2013, which was barely noticed in mainstream media, questioned 'previous suggestions that ADHD is the result of fundamental abnormalities in dopamine transmission'.[13] The researchers found that administering the stimulant methylphenidate to healthy adult volunteers, as well as to those who exhibit symptoms of ADHD, led to similar increases of dopamine in their brains. Both groups also had equivalent levels of improvements when tested on their ability to concentrate.

We should not be surprised by this. Amphetamines give you a kind of tunnel vision making you highly absorbed in what you are doing; thus, as well as taking them for their recreational effects, they are also used as exam revision aids as they increase concentration and keep you awake. Like all the other drugs we use in psychiatry they have general effects on everybody. They do not correct any disease-based chemical imbalances.

As no one has found the illusive lack of dopamine in ADHD, the null hypothesis stands – there is no characteristic chemical imbalance or lack associated with ADHD.

As confirmed by a 2024 review of all the biological research on ADHD, there is no biological difference that can be used to differentiate people with an ADHD diagnosis from those without it.[14] Scientifically speaking, this means that there are no characteristic genetic, brain or chemical differentiators between those with or without an ADHD diagnosis.

Young-for-class children are more likely to catch ADHD

Several studies conducted in different countries have found that the youngest children in a class year have a significantly increased risk (compared to the oldest children in a class year) of being diagnosed with ADHD and/or receiving medication for ADHD. These studies have found that whether you are in a country that has high rates of diagnosing or prescribing (like the US) or low rates (like Finland), this pattern is still evident.[15] Such a pattern of identifying ADHD suggests that relative immaturity to your peers is a risk factor for receiving this label.

Of course, children mature at different rates, raising an important question of whether a diagnosis of ADHD, even for older-in-the-class children, might also be reflective of their relatively slower developmental trajectory. Remember that, in children, this is a diagnosis mainly given to boys, and males, on average, develop more slowly than females.

For a while now I have thought that the growth of pseudo-diagnoses like ADHD reflects Western impatience with diversity among children, where, from an early age, children are given messages that they are valued for what they do (for their 'performance') rather than for just being. The finding that relative scholastic immaturity is associated with the likelihood of a subsequent ADHD diagnosis lends further support to my concern that the prevalence of diagnoses like ADHD acts like a barometer of how intolerant of children and childishness we are in modern Western culture.[16]

The problem of 'caseness'

The diagnosis of ADHD is supposed to depend on a set of criteria, where the young person should have six or more 'symptoms' of inattentiveness, and/or six or more 'symptoms' of hyperactivity and impulsiveness. According to the latest guidelines these should have been present for more than six months and evident from before the age of twelve. These symptoms should also be seen in at least two different settings (typically at home and at school) but it doesn't need to be seen everywhere.

What are these 'symptoms' that are found in the lists? Here are some of them:

- *Often* fails to give close attention to details or makes careless mistakes in schoolwork, work or other activities.
- *Often* does not seem to listen when spoken to directly.
- *Often* fidgets with hands or feet or squirms in seat.
- *Often* runs about or climbs excessively in situations in which it is inappropriate.
- *Often* has difficulty awaiting turn.
- *Often* interrupts or intrudes on others.

Notice they all start with the word 'often'. What does that mean? Let's take the third in that list: 'Often fidgets with hands or feet or squirms in seat'. What's a unit of 'fidget' or 'squirm'? How much movement and for how long does it need to last to qualify as a 'fidget' or 'squirm'? And how often is often? How many fidgets or squirms a minute or an hour or a day do you need to qualify as 'often'? Is there any difference in the number you need depending on age? As there are no age criteria in the symptom description, it seems not.

This means that the problem of what counts as a case (caseness) becomes impossible to solve. There is no external anchor. The definition of a case has little to do with the actual behaviours being displayed because we have no way of pinning them down, let alone having anything empirical to locate in the bodies and/or brains of those who get this label. What makes a case is based on how a particular person at a particular moment in time fills in a questionnaire (often about someone else, if it's a parent or teacher about a child) and then how the person who gives a diagnosis interprets these questionnaires and/or what they hear from talking to those seeking an assessment. Subjectivity and bias are present throughout and inescapable. We thus have no factual basis for defining a 'case'. This means those identified as a case may well have little in common beyond getting the label.

What would I predict if this is indeed the case? The research findings I've outlined above. Without a valid and reliable way to identify a case, meaningful technical knowledge cannot be developed.

An ill with a pill

The promise of a medication that treats a chemical problem assumed to cause ADHD is a powerful reinforcer of the idea that ADHD is a medical disease and one that resides in the brain. It's also a powerful incentive to get a diagnosis in the hope that there is a solution as simple as taking a pill. What we rarely hear about is what these pills are and what dangers come along with them.

In her 2003 book *More, Now, Again: A Memoir of Addiction*, author of *Prozac Nation* Elizabeth Wurtzel provides a brutally honest account of a descent into addiction after her psychiatrist prescribed the stimulant Ritalin (whose generic name is methylphenidate and is the most common medication used for ADHD).[17] Wurtzel was elated with the outcome. As far as she was concerned Ritalin 'worked'. She described Ritalin as her sugar – the sweetness in the days that had none. After a while she started taking more to keep that good feeling going. Then she found herself grinding up the Ritalin and snorting it. Finally, she moved on to cocaine (which has very similar mind-altering effects to methylphenidate), more Ritalin, and more cocaine. After many years Wurtzel eventually broke free from the cycle of addiction but looked back aghast at just how easy it was to convince doctors to continue providing prescriptions for her.

In an article in the *Daily Mail* in April 2023, 21-year-old Sara described her experience of taking methylphenidate (Ritalin) for her 'ADD'. 'I found it hard to focus or pay attention – it was a relief when I was diagnosed with ADD. At last people would no longer think I was being naughty or lazy. Everyone, including my parents, became more supportive.' Eventually the side effects became worse than the improved focus she had. 'I had heightened sound awareness: it felt like I could hear all the sounds around me piled into one. I couldn't sleep and turned to smoking marijuana to relax. I had no appetite. When a dose wore off, the effect was so severe that it felt like ADD times ten – I couldn't focus, felt sluggish, and found it hard to string words together. I started smoking more marijuana to cope with the come down and became addicted to it.'[18]

Joseph Pack was twenty-seven when he was diagnosed with ADHD in 2017. 'To begin with I thought: Wow, this is positive but between doses the withdrawal was awful, like a gin hangover.' Joseph founded an organisation with medication-free tips on managing ADHD. He has been contacted by people from all over the world who are experiencing the effects of prolonged use of stimulant medication who say they can no longer work without the drugs and feel hooked on methylphenidate for life. For others, ADHD drugs acted as a gateway to harder drugs. 'Last week I was contacted by a Canadian woman who gave her eight-year-old son Ritalin. By 15 he was crushing and snorting it and by 41 he was in rehab with a cocaine addiction.'[19]

The truth about ADHD treatment

In the 1970s, 80s and 90s, ADHD, as a concept, took off, aided in large part by the growth in the use of stimulants (amphetamine derivatives) for its treatment. Ritalin was the most recognisable brand name of these drugs and became a bestseller, making huge profits for Novartis Pharmaceuticals. Other companies soon realised the potential that comes from medicalising children's behaviours, particularly those that stress out parents and teachers. There is now a variety of short- and long-acting stimulant preparations available. While the prescribing of stimulants to kids started out and stayed for a couple of decades as an almost solely US phenomenon, it has since spread globally, and numbers being medicated continue to rise.

Of course, this trend has not been without controversy. After all, amphetamines are known to be highly addictive with many serious health risks. As central nervous system stimulants, they elevate life functions, such as blood pressure, body temperature and heart rate. Those using amphetamines will generally want less sleep, have less of an appetite, and be at higher risk of serious health consequences such as heart attacks or strokes.[20] How could we possibly justify giving to kids a substance we warn adults about taking because of the terrible long-term effects we know this can have on the body and brain?

This is where a chemical imbalance theory was needed. ADHD

medication enthusiasts spun a myth as a way of justifying what they were advocating. The argument was that those with ADHD react in a different way to stimulants than those without, because in ADHD there is a deficiency of dopamine, therefore stimulants are just replacing what wasn't there in the first place. This means stimulants are only dangerous if you don't have ADHD. As I've already discussed, there is no evidence that those who get the ADHD diagnosis have a dopamine deficiency.

Like most medications used in psychiatry, its use was based on anecdote and had started before studies to show that they were safe and effective had been done. The assumption was that because stimulants appeared to calm these children down, it must be working in a different way to those using it recreationally, who seemed more energised. The apparent calming effect is related to stimulants' generic effect of increasing the person's focus. When you see your child sitting down, apparently concentrating on schoolwork and following instructions in a way they weren't doing before, it can seem like this is a transformative treatment.

But this is a general short-term effect of a stimulant. It will do this for most children (and adults) who take it, regardless of the label they have. The studies that supported the use of stimulants as a treatment were nearly all conducted by pharmaceutical companies, were for a few weeks or months, and concentrated on rating ADHD 'symptoms' rather than other quality-of-life measures.[21] However, once children are prescribed a stimulant, the prescription isn't for a few weeks or months, but usually for many years and perhaps the rest of their lives. Thus, we need to understand what the potential long-term outcomes are.

Given that amphetamines are highly addictive, physical tolerance is likely to occur. Like many systems in the body, the nerve synapses (the connections between nerve cells) have homeostatic properties. This means they like to keep their chemical messenger amounts in a narrow range for optimal functioning. If there is more than the usual amount of dopamine (for example) being released because of taking an amphetamine regularly, the synapse will start switching off dopamine receptors to, in effect, reduce the overall amount of dopamine transmission back to within its usual range. This is why cocaine addicts find that, over time, to get the same 'high', they have to take larger amounts of cocaine.

Because of this homeostatic mechanism, after a while the problem behaviours start emerging in the child again, as that increased focus effect the stimulant was having begins to wear off. This is what we call becoming 'tolerant' to the dose of amphetamine. It means the synapses have switched off some of the dopamine receptors, so you no longer get the same effect. If you stop the amphetamine now, however, you will get withdrawal effects, as the nerve cells will get too little dopamine because of the reduced number of working receptors. The state of agitation that sudden or too fast withdrawal of the stimulant can induce will look like the 'ADHD' coming back with a vengeance, convincing all, often including the doctors, that the child really does need the amphetamine for more normal functioning.

Now, therefore, the dose will be increased and set in motion will be a process of physical (in the child) and psychological (in parent, teacher and doctor) dependence that leads to more increases in the dose over time. Temporary periods of improvement may eventually wear off, leading to another dose increase, alongside a solidifying of the idea that the child has a brain-based condition that requires amphetamines to keep it in control.

Interference with sleep often means that a sleeping aid will be added (like melatonin) and continuing behaviour difficulties often result in some children having the very heavy end of 'antipsychotic' medication added too. It's not unusual, therefore, after several years, to find ADHD-labelled young people who are taking several medications, often at high doses, and the problems keep coming back or never quite go away. This may then result in further assessments (such as for autism) because it is now assumed there must be some other disorder that needs identifying and treating and that's why they are not getting better and staying better. This is how long-term patients are created.

What does the research evidence say about long-term outcomes? Is there clear blue water between those who take stimulants for ADHD compared to those who don't?

In Chapter 1, I discussed the most referenced ADHD treatment study (the MTA study) and how the findings after three years of follow-up contradicted the well-publicised fourteen-month findings. At fourteen months the authors suggested that methylphenidate improved outcomes over and above other treatments, but by three years continued medication exposure was associated with worse outcomes and greater side effects. I also discussed how the first major international guideline on treating ADHD (the UK NICE guidelines), published in 2008, ignored the three-year outcome data, and based their advice that those with 'severe' ADHD should be prescribed stimulants as a first-line treatment on the fourteen-month outcome data. Follow-up of the MTA study participants went up to eight years after initial enrolment and confirmed most of the findings of the three-year outcomes – that the type or intensity of the fourteen-month treatments did not predict symptom severity or functioning eight years later.[22]

Science can't trump marketing in a free-market-driven economy. Prescriptions of stimulants hardly blinked after the publication of the three-year or eight-year follow-up studies. In guideline after guideline the fourteen-month MTA study outcomes kept being referred to and the three-year follow-up ignored. Other long-term follow-up studies did not show that long-term use of stimulants is associated with any improved outcomes compared to those diagnosed with ADHD who don't take them. On the contrary, often children on stimulants have worse outcomes than those not taking them, with physical (such as blood pressure), psychiatric (like mood disorders) and academic problems more common in those on long-term medication.[23]

A search of the Cochrane Reviews for ADHD* finds the one consistency in their conclusions is that the studies are at high risk of bias (primarily due to pharmaceutical industry funding), and despite stimulant treatment for ADHD being one of the most highly

---

* A Cochrane Review is a systematic review of research in health care and health policy and conducted using some standardised methods to take account of potential bias to try and make an objective conclusion based on available evidence.

researched psychiatric treatments, conclusive evidence that it leads to significant improvement, even in the short term, is missing.

Here are two examples. A 2022 review of 'Extended-release methylphenidate for attention deficit hyperactivity disorder (ADHD) in adults' concluded that 'We rated the certainty of the evidence as "very low" for all outcomes, due to high risk of bias, short trial durations, and limitations to the generalisability of the results. The benefits and harms of extended-release methylphenidate therefore remain uncertain.'[24]

A 2023 update of the 2015 Cochrane review, 'Methylphenidate for children and adolescents with attention deficit hyperactivity disorder (ADHD)', found that 'The majority of our conclusions from the 2015 version of this review still apply . . . the certainty of the evidence for all outcomes is very low and therefore the true magnitude of effects remain unclear.'[25] The 2015 review decided that they could not conclude that taking methylphenidate will improve the lives of children and adolescents with ADHD.

Further evidence on outcomes from diagnosis of ADHD and its treatment come from two studies of a different type. A publication in 2020 as part of the national longitudinal study of Irish children examined the sociodemographic, clinical and psychological variables that differentiate children with high hyperactivity/inattention symptoms, some of whom had received a diagnosis of ADHD, and some of whom had not. By age thirteen, those who had been given an ADHD diagnosis at nine years showed more emotional, peer-relationship problems, worse prosocial behaviour and poorer self-concept than those who did not receive a diagnosis despite similar levels of symptoms at nine.[26]

A similar study, this time as part of the Longitudinal Study of Australian Children, included a comparison of nearly four hundred children diagnosed with ADHD matched to a group who had similar levels of hyperactivity/inattention but did not get an ADHD diagnosis. By fifteen years old (an average follow-up of seven years), those with the diagnosis were doing worse on a number of variables including self-harm, feeling that they could succeed academically, sense of self-efficacy and demonstrating negative social behaviours.[27]

Both of the two above studies suggest that in the long term you may be better off not getting a diagnosis of ADHD even if your child shows all the behaviours that may lead to a diagnosis.

The dangers of prescribed stimulants go beyond those described above, as patients may continue to take them for decades with all the potential consequences this has for them. A population-based study from Sweden that looked at the medical records of nearly 280,000 individuals diagnosed with ADHD found that long-term exposure to ADHD medications was associated with an increased risk of cardiovascular disease, especially hypertension and arterial disease. With an average fourteen-year follow-up, each one-year of ADHD medication use was associated with a 4 per cent increased risk of such disease.[28]

Another study that followed up for several decades patients who were prescribed stimulants, found an over-eightfold increase in the likelihood that such patients develop neurological conditions such as Parkinson's disease.[29] Parkinson's is an illness that results from patients not having enough of the neurotransmitter dopamine in the nervous system. It's highly likely that this finding relates to long-term stimulant ingestion, given that stimulants mainly work by stimulating cells to release more than the usual amount of dopamine.

Hopefully this and the previous chapter have given a window into the truth about ADHD ideology. It has little to do with any genuine science. This is the case for the majority of what passes for mental health.

What happened to Yasmine?

At the start of this chapter I introduced you to fifteen-year-old Yasmine who has been referred to our service for an urgent mental health assessment and to consider whether she has ADHD. She has been in the care system since the age of two, having had multiple carer changes over her short life, and recently ran away from a children's home after what seemed like a positive period.

There is an understandable wish to deal with emotionally

challenging situations by framing it as being the product of a particular disturbance within the young person that can be given a name and then treated. Whether it's the idea that there is trauma that can be ameliorated through some type of trauma therapy or that she has ADHD that can be treated by the simple application of a medication, they serve the same function. In Yasmine's difficult situation, this supports the fantasy that the role of the staff at the home is to continue with a generic care function and make sure Yasmine gets the prescribed treatment that will fix her troubled mind.

A more systemic perspective involves thinking about not just the difficult history that Yasmine has been through, but also the current dynamics and what they may reveal. Our starting point, therefore, was to offer a consultation to the professional network rather than an assessment of Yasmine.

A colleague and I met with her social worker and a couple of senior staff from the home. We discussed how Yasmine's expectation will be that any placement she has will break down sooner or later. This means it's psychologically dangerous for her to have attachments to those she is living with, and it's particularly dangerous for her to start feeling happy or secure in any placement. Even though, deep down, she likely craves, more than anything else, to feel loved, to have a sense of belonging and feel that people caring for her see something likeable and valuable in her, admitting to those feelings exposes her to unbearable pain when the inevitable breakdown in placement happens.

This means that whenever she gets that feeling of being loved or happy, she becomes afraid. The process of distancing herself again from any sense of security acts as a protective mechanism. It's always easier to leave when you've convinced yourself that this is a place you don't like, that the people there are horrible, and that it's time to try a new placement. Feeling valued and loved is far more dangerous for her than carers hating her.

The problem with trying to deal with this dynamic through giving Yasmine a label and any particular therapy or medication is that it continues reinforcing a narrative that there is something deeply wrong in her, whether it's the result of her adverse life experiences or some sort of disease. It further solidifies the story of deficit and dysfunction. Moreover, in Yasmine's history, 'urgent assessments' have often been precursors to a placement breaking down. Going for treatment in which she is the only participant will also reveal to her that the staff at the home are not able to handle her. Just going through the process of offering an urgent assessment may further reinforce the belief that, like all other placements, this one will soon break down.

Our meeting with the social worker and staff from her home allowed us to discuss how her behaviour was understandable in the context of her history. It also allowed them to understand that far from Yasmine having a negative view of the home, the reason she presented with such a crisis may have been because of the opposite – that she was developing a positive view of the home and staff. Indeed, a couple of the staff regularly spoke in affectionate terms about Yasmine, whom they enjoyed engaging with because of her sharp wit and chatty nature.

We worked with the social worker and children's home over several subsequent meetings and Yasmine's behaviour did eventually settle. When she had good days, they knew to be aware that these are likely to be followed by a period of disruptive behaviour and that their task in those periods was not to panic but ride it out. No long soul-searching questioning or conversations with her when these happen, just manage situations, accept it, and allow everyone to move on. Yasmine was discharged from our service many months later without us ever having met her.

7. The creation of autism

'The time to worry is when the idea is so widely shared that we no longer even notice it, when it is so deeply rooted that it feels to us like plain common sense. At the point when objections are not answered anymore because they are no longer even raised, we are not in control: we do not have the idea; it has us.'

Alfie Kohn

In my second session with sixteen-year-old Oscar, he asks if he could see me on his own, rather than with his mother and younger sister as had happened at our first meeting. Oscar is a tallish lad with a few wisps of facial hair on a chiselled face topped with a thick mop of unbrushed black hair. He had been given a diagnosis of autism when he was six. He spends most of his time playing online games where he seems to have found a community of like-minded people who will play together for hours. He's been referred for suicidal impulses and anxiety.

Oscar wants to talk to me about his future. He explains that he knows he has autism and there's nothing he can do about it as it's a lifelong condition. Oscar feels trapped by this. His suicide attempt a few months ago was because he had lost all hope that there was a future for him. He was angry and resentful that he had autism and felt the burden of this condition weighing on his every ambition. He wasn't particularly academically gifted at school but really enjoyed working with computers and, in this subject area, he was very capable. He'd studied computer code in his own time and started writing simple programs. He was meant to be attending a local college after the summer holidays, mainly to study computing, but couldn't see the point.

Oscar was close to his mother, who had brought him and his sister up under difficult circumstances and with limited finances. She always put her children first. He didn't want to burden her with how hopeless he felt.

In our first session Oscar's mother, Sue, had spoken about Oscar as her rock – the one she felt was most in tune with how she was feeling. He always seemed to notice when she was feeling down and often asked her how she was and whether she was OK. Oscar was estranged from his father and hadn't seen him in many years. His father had moved away and now had a new family. Recently he had been wondering more about his father. He felt his father was nasty to his mother and admitted to being scared that maybe he was turning out to be a nasty person just like his father was. He felt he was making life for his mother harder, which really upset him.

I have seen a variety of reactions in young people like Oscar who were diagnosed with autism in early childhood, and who start to wonder about the meaning and significance of the label as they move through adolescence. Many ask existential questions about who they are, where they fit in and what having 'autism' means for their future. Others don't want to think about these questions, and others still embrace the diagnosis and identify as being 'autistic'. With the autism diagnosis becoming more common, it seems to me that a deep dive into the foundations and implications of this label is long overdue. I return to Oscar's story at the end of this chapter.

Autism and the Nazis

The word 'autism' was first used in psychiatry in 1911 by the psychiatrist Eugen Bleuler who used the term 'autistic' to denote the state of mind of psychotic individuals who showed extreme withdrawal from the fabric of social life. It's probably the most accurate use of the term as Bleuler used it to describe a state of mind rather than as a diagnosis.

In 1943, child psychiatrist Leo Kanner first proposed 'autism' as a diagnosis, to label a group of eleven children who were emotionally and intellectually impaired and showing 'extreme aloneness'.[1] It's possible that Kanner coined this new diagnosis to create a less stigmatising label than common ones used at the time (when eugenic theories about improving the gene pool were just as common in the US and Europe as they were in Nazi Germany) such as 'mentally retarded', 'idiotic', 'feeble-minded' or 'backward'.

For decades, autism remained a rare diagnosis given to young people who had considerable impairments in day-to-day functioning and moderate to severe learning difficulties. According to a 1966 study, the prevalence rate for autism was four in 10,000 (0.04 per cent).[2] Kanner's definition remained the dominant one until the 1990s.

In 1944, the year after Kanner first proposed 'autism' as a diagnosis, Viennese paediatrician Hans Asperger published a paper, largely ignored at the time, in which he described four children with no easily recognisable intellectual impairment, but with social communication problems.[3] At the time he wrote his seminal paper, Austrian society was organised by Nazi ideology.

Asperger had managed to further his career under the Nazi regime due to the opportunities created by political upheavals. In 1931 Asperger had joined the Vienna University children's clinic, which at the time was headed by Franz Hamburger, a fervent Nazi. In 1935 Asperger took charge of the Heilpädagogik ward in the clinic, even though he had not yet obtained his specialist qualification in paediatrics and had published only a single work. Asperger had got the job in preference to the more experienced Jewish doctor, George Frankl. We will come back to Dr Frankl later in this story.

Austrian universities at this time were sites of virulent anti-Jewish agitation, and Jewish doctors faced increasing difficulties in securing university positions. With Hamburger's appointment as chair in 1930, the children's clinic in Vienna became a flagship of anti-Jewish policies long before the Nazi takeover after Austria's annexation to Germany in 1938. Although Asperger did not join the Nazi Party, he shared ideological common ground with Hamburger and his network, allowing him to blend in without apparent friction.

Historian Edith Sheffer, drawing on records discovered by

Austrian researcher Herwig Czech, found that Asperger wrote wholly damning descriptions of at least forty-two of his patients, transferring them to the notorious Am Spiegelgrund clinic, where almost eight hundred children were deliberately euthanised. Asperger also endorsed forced sterilisation laws, believing that some people were a burden on the community and considered to have 'a life not worth living'.[4]

One of Asperger's tasks as a paediatrician in the children's clinic was to sift out potentially educable children to prevent them from becoming victims of the euthanasia programme at Am Spiegelgrund. The four young people described in his 1944 paper as having 'autistic psychopathology' were potentially educable, he believed, and, therefore, could be spared from being sent to the death hospital. Asperger's paper would later form the basis for expanding autism beyond Kanner's narrow definition and into the broader autistic spectrum disorder. Thus, the creation of an autism spectrum owes its origins to a gruesome period of history where the dominant preoccupation is whether troubled children might be euthanised for having 'a life not worth living' or not.

In 1937, two years after Asperger's promotion, George Frankl emigrated to the US. Once there, he was introduced to Leo Kanner, who, as a Jew, had also escaped from Europe several years earlier. In 1938, Frankl began to work with Kanner at Johns Hopkins Hospital. Frankl's merits were immediately recognised by Kanner, who wrote that 'I have become very much interested in what Dr Frankl calls the affective contact of children . . . in that it opens a new approach to the observation and understanding of the mental life of the child',[5] paving the way for Kanner's classic 1943 paper, 'Autistic Disturbances of Affective Contact'.

It seems likely that Frankl brought with him ideas circulating in Austrian society and medical circles of the time and is maybe more important in the development of Kanner's and Asperger's definitions of autism than has been recognised.[6] It also suggests that autism, as a concept, emerges from a society increasingly preoccupied with human typologies and hierarchical classification of people.

Kanner maintained an open mind about causation. Writing with

Leon Eisenberg in 1956, they concluded that it was unhelpful to try and tie autism solely to biological or environmental causes, suggesting that arguments that counter-pose 'hereditary' versus 'environmental' causation were unhelpful.[7] By the 1960s Kanner's diagnosis of 'infantile autism' had become a recognised diagnosis for what was considered a rare disorder primarily found in children with moderate to severe intellectual impairments.

Infantile autism becomes autistic spectrum disorder (ASD)

Asperger's work was publicised in the English-speaking world by British autism researcher and psychiatrist Lorna Wing in the early 1980s. Wing saw a similarity in some people she was seeing and those described by Asperger. In her influential 1981 paper proposing the 'Asperger syndrome' diagnosis, Wing describes six case histories that appear to have little in common with the four cases Asperger described in his 1944 paper, beyond sharing a lack of social reciprocity.[8] Four of Wing's cases were adults, whereas all of Asperger's were children; two had some degree of learning disability, whereas none of Asperger's did; most of Wing's cases learned to speak late, whereas most of Asperger's spoke early; most of Wing's cases were described as having little capacity for analytical thought, whereas Asperger's cases were described as highly analytical; and none of Wing's cases were described as manipulative, malicious, nasty, aggressive, cheeky, confrontational, liars or vindictive (terms Asperger used about his cases).

Pre-eminent British child psychiatrist Michael Rutter, in his much-quoted 1978 paper, had earlier concluded that autism likely exists on a spectrum with a strong genetic contribution to its expression.[9] He proposed that autism is characterised by the triad of symptoms of impaired communication, impaired social skills and a restricted imagination leading to narrow interests.

Wing's and Rutter's papers began the process of expanding autism away from a rare diagnosis and into the spectrum that now dominates practice. There were no new scientific discoveries about the bodies and brains of those thought to have an autism that could be expanded, just a new set of definitions.

Because autism started as a rare diagnosis given to children, most of whom are likely neurologically compromised (for example, having high rates of learning difficulties, epilepsy and genetic syndromes), the association between autism and brain-based abnormalities became entrenched.

The soil for this way of thinking to grow was becoming more fertile, with cultural events such as the film *Rain Man** and controversial global news stories linking autism to the MMR vaccine because of what we now know to be a fraudulent piece of research. More people started talking about this 'thing' called autism. Soon there were courses, assessment tools, research, services, documentaries, experts and institutions all dedicated to furthering our knowledge and understanding of autism, its causes, and how to identify, treat or prevent it. Autism became a fact of culture. As infantile autism (prevalence 0.04 per cent of the population) morphed into ASD (prevalence now close to 3 per cent and rising), the idea that autism is a genetically predetermined, lifelong, neurodevelopmental disorder persisted and would soon rival ADHD as a popular consumable product.

In the late 1990s the term 'neurodiversity' was coined by Judy Singer, an Australian disability rights activist. Singer argued that neurological differences should be viewed as a natural variation in human experience, rather than a medical problem. She contended that individuals with neurological differences should be accepted and supported, rather than pathologised and stigmatised.[10]

I have met, corresponded with and debated via email, meetings, conferences and in person with some neurodiversity activists. I admire what they have done and set out to do, which is to move autism from the sphere of disorder into one of a human difference. I think many people have been helped by this, particularly those who saw themselves in a negative light and were burdened by self-criticisms. However, taking something that is defined as a medical condition, often characterised as resulting in a lack of empathy,

---

* A film about an autistic savant that starred Tom Cruise and Dustin Hoffman.

brings along dangers when expanded rather than challenged as a notion. The sense of not being good enough is so ubiquitous in this hyper-individualised culture that an individualised explanation (having a neurodiversity that causes you to be 'not good enough') may reinforce rather than challenge or change cultural and economic systems encouraging that.

Neurodiversity activists started writing books and articles proposing that autism should be seen as a different but equally valid way of viewing and interacting with the world, because of different neurological wiring. Tensions have sometimes emerged between these neurodiversity activists and those (often parents) who were struggling to cope with the behaviours of diagnosed children and felt the disorder side of things. Autism became a visible and lively topic for conversation, debate and often heated antagonism between the disorder versus difference perspective. The difference activists asserted that they are autistic, not people with autism, and criticised the medical profession for viewing autism as a medical condition. Those (including parents) who considered autism a disease/disorder campaigned for better recognition, prevention, treatment and support.[11]

What unites both sides of this acrimonious disagreement is that they believe there is a real tangible identifiable brain-based thing called autism (or ASD). No one was asking the obvious and fundamental question: on what evidential basis can you conclude that autism represents a natural category that can be differentiated from other natural categories, whether disorder or difference? Furthermore, what evidence is there that this natural category is 'neuro'-based? I will examine that basic question in the next chapter.

Autism now

According to the US-based Autism and Developmental Disabilities Monitoring (ADDM), during the past two decades, ASD prevalence estimates for children aged eight years have increased markedly, from 0.7 per cent in 2000 to 2.3 per cent in 2018 and to 2.8 per cent (approximately 4 per cent of boys and 1 per cent of girls) in 2020. In 2020, for the first time, the prevalence of ASD was lower among white children than among other racial and ethnic groups.[12] These figures are for eight-year-olds. Given the rapid expansion in the number of people getting the diagnosis for the first time as adults, autism is on a steep and rising trajectory.

In the UK there was a 787 per cent exponential increase in recorded incidence of autism diagnoses between 1998 and 2018, with the increase in diagnoses being greater for females than males and with the greatest rises in diagnostic incidence being among adults.[13] As with ADHD, there have been rising numbers of women seeking and getting a diagnosis of autism, many of them being celebrities who have declared that they have been diagnosed with it.[14]

Published in November 2021 under the title, 'The celebs who have bravely opened up about being diagnosed with autism as adults', an article in the *Mirror* discussed how several, like Christine McGuinness, revealed 'I have been confirmed as autistic. It's strange, but I've noticed there are little hints throughout my life.' She recounts how she discovered she was autistic. 'Patrick [her husband Paddy McGuinness] and I were invited to meet with expert Sir Simon Baron-Cohen at Cambridge University. We filled out what's called an AQ questionnaire. It tests for symptoms of autism . . . While my husband was bang-on average, mine was 36, which is high . . . Sir Simon quickly put me out of my misery and confirmed I'm autistic.'[15]

TV presenter Melanie Sykes announced that she has been diagnosed at fifty-one years old. She took to social media to explain how the diagnosis was 'life-changing', 'finally, so many things made sense. I now have a deeper understanding of myself, my life, and the things I have endured.' She went on to discuss the difficulties she faced while working in television due to her sensitivities and memory problems. As with ADHD, I can understand and sympathise with why any individual who feels they are struggling might seek such a diagnosis, given how widely advertised it is nowadays.

The upshot is that, as with ADHD, we have a list of successful people explaining how liberated they feel, now it's been confirmed that they have some sort of brain-based condition that made it hard for them to feel part of the environments in which they lived. Trying to reconcile the pain of being bullied by concluding there was something wrong/different *in you* is the one I struggle with most.

What are these tests (a medical procedure leading to a diagnosis) that enable autism to be recognised in an adult? I googled 'adult autism test' and did the online test for the first website listed.[16] I scored 19 out of 30 and it said, 'You experience many typical signs of autism.'

I then asked my wife to do the AQ10[17] autism screening questionnaire with me and about me. 'Autism: recognition, referral, diagnosis and management of adults on the autism spectrum' is the NICE recommended screening test in the UK (NICE clinical guideline CG142).[18] Here are the questions (for each question you choose one of four possible answers: definitely agree, slightly agree, slightly disagree, definitely disagree):

1. I often notice small sounds when others do not.
2. I usually concentrate more on the whole picture, rather than the small details.
3. I find it easy to do more than one thing at once.
4. If there is an interruption, I can switch back to what I was doing very quickly.
5. I find it easy to 'read between the lines' when someone is talking to me.
6. I know how to tell if someone listening to me is getting bored.
7. When I'm reading a story, I find it difficult to work out the characters' intentions.
8. I like to collect information about categories of things (e.g. types of car, types of bird, types of train, types of plant, etc.).
9. I find it easy to work out what someone is thinking or feeling just by looking at their face.
10. I find it difficult to work out people's intentions.

You score 1 point for definitely or slightly agree on each of items 1, 7, 8, and 10, and score 1 point for definitely or slightly disagree on each of items 2, 3, 4, 5, 6, and 9. If you score more than 6 out of the possible 10, then the advice is to consider a specialist diagnostic assessment. I scored 6, but half the time I didn't know what to make of the question – maybe because I'm autistic – but, then again, neither did my wife.

This problem of interpretation is impossible to escape. Notice how devoid of context the questions are, all assuming that they relate to internal functioning. For example, 'I find it difficult to work out people's intentions.' Well, do I? If I replied that I don't, how do I know that? Doesn't that depend on the person I'm trying to figure out? Should it be more problematic to think you know someone's intentions than being honest that none of us can really tell what another human being is thinking, feeling or intending? How about the question 'I often notice small sounds when others do not'? What is often? What is a small sound? How do you know if others notice it or not?

OK, so you might argue that these are just screening questionnaires, not the actual test. In the next chapter I discuss an actual test used for diagnosing young people and show that the above problems are simply magnified rather than resolved. When all you essentially have are a set of subjective questions that cannot tap into anything objective and you've entered an assessment interview having already been influenced by the result of your screening test, well, what do you think is going to happen?

What is behind the diagnosis being mainly in boys when they are young, but there is now a new cohort of adult women who are getting the diagnosis?

The American magazine *ADDitude* asks: why do women find it hard to get an ADHD or autism diagnosis? 'The reasons are similar: Women are socialised to mask their autistic traits.'[19] According to the UK National Autistic Society:

> To 'mask' or to 'camouflage' means to hide or disguise parts of oneself in order to better fit in with those around you . . . Masking may involve suppressing certain behaviours we find soothing but that others think are 'weird'. It can also mean mimicking the behaviour of those around us, such as copying non-verbal behaviours, and developing complex social scripts to get by in social situations . . . I was

twenty-three when I received my autism diagnosis, and it was only through learning more about masking that I realised how my diagnosis had been hidden for so long. It wasn't that my autistic traits weren't there, they'd just been in disguise for so long.[20]

So 'masking' provided the necessary link to open autism to the main adult mental health customer base – women. This means that the observational element that is used to diagnose children now more or less disappears and we are just left with ruminations on an internal state born out of a 'who am I' introspection. This is counter to much of the purpose of introspection in collectivist cultures where the spiritual element orientates a person away from a self-focus and towards a sense of connection with the wider universe, in order to diminish not feed ego knowledge. It also creates a weird scenario where symptoms no longer matter. So, you don't have symptoms because you mask them, which means that you do have symptoms, just that no one else will see them. Even though you don't have the symptoms you do have them. Not even symptoms are relevant – just how you feel.

How did ASD become so popular?

In previous articles and books, I, along with colleagues, have speculated about the possible cultural drivers leading us to problematise and pathologise human socialisation as being something to do with individual brains.[21] Of course, the overarching theme of this book is that autism operates as a consumable brand and so is a product of capitalist marketisation, which creates consumerist individualism as the primary model of human consciousness and activity. But what made autism such a popular and growing brand? What is it helping commodify?

Here are some speculations.

As educational and psychological authorities were developed during the last century to meet the changing demands for social adjustment, the boundaries between what was considered normal and 'pathological' were created and gradually expanded. Psychologists, psychiatrists and paediatricians became increasingly involved in 'discovering' apparent indicators of an ever-increasing range of disorders among the children they surveyed and created age-based expectations of development. Systems of developmental surveillance and intervention came into being and became enlarged.

With the demise of welfarism in the post-Thatcher/Reagan politics of the 1980s and the growth of a more aggressively competitive free market ideology, modern Western governments promoted the idea of the 'free' individual able to compete in the marketplace for the best jobs. Societal-wide protections diminished, social solidarity was seen as suspect, and a narrative took hold that our communities were made of two main classes of people: the strivers and the skivers. This reflected a belief in a meritocratic hierarchy where the well-off have worked hard to get there and the rest are work-shy whose poverty is a reflection of their lack of application, ambition or talent.

The individualising with stories of shaming and/or valorising has meant that policing no longer just involves the army, law and prisons. There is a greater emphasis in systems that rule by consent in getting people to police themselves.[22]

These days much of the work on defining who does and doesn't fit into our social standards is done by the individuals themselves. The practice of self-examination causes a cult of self-awareness. In doing so it creates inner qualities, including whatever passes for personal growth, with every day one seeking to make oneself a better product – new, improved, best and brightest yet. This internal monitoring can become as draconian as the secret police. You monitor yourself, find yourself inadequate in some way, and so keep consuming to fill whatever hole you feel you have found.

With the goal of self-fulfilment and gratification being so hard to sustain, and the competitive mistrust of our personal relationships being promoted by consumer culture, it's not difficult to see why more and more of the population become concerned about their psychological state and/or their children's.

French philosopher Jean Baudrillard, writing in the early 1980s, many years before the ubiquity of the internet, social media and smartphones, suggested that we were reaching an age where consciousness would find it difficult to distinguish reality from a simulation of reality, the image from the object.[23] This creates a heightened awareness of appearance and style. The invasion of images from media and advertising, particularly with the spread of social media use, creates a dream world, a virtual reality to fantasise about, as commercials sell us images of ideal lifestyles that they attach to their products. Our culture has become so consumed by this perpetual imagery that we can now take off one identity and slip on another just as we change our clothes, make-up and shoes. We are so seduced into becoming concerned with our surface identities that we submit ourselves to long surgical procedures to change the shape and appearance of our bodies.

It is within the ideology that creates such fractured, superficial identities that we discover the same superficial labelling acting as an escape from this torment, reimagining we are made whole again by the latest consumable we're encouraged to identify with. But this creates communities who are brought together because of something they believe about themselves and which excludes those who are not like them. Binaries that you are either 'neurodiverse' or 'neurotypical' are created, but also disassembled to create sub-products as found in the dizzying numbers of gender identities on offer. This is a turn away from the sort of comradeship you get with social movements or religious communities who are tied by beliefs that allow them to have faith in something bigger than the individual.[24]

The decline in the manufacturing sectors and the growth of the service industry eroded embedded working communities, such as those around mining and heavy industry. The socialisation opportunities a trade union or working people's clubs provided become replaced by workplace stress and staff well-being services.

Companies have traded job security, stability and a unionised workforce for employee well-being services, mindfulness classes and mental health days. Anxiety, stress, depression are things that happen to the worker that our enlightened approach to mental health can now treat, so you can return to the insecure jobs we offer without the employer having to change working practices. This new world of pseudo-emotionally aware language of mental health with the requirement of having strong people skills in the workforce means that there is now a greater political and personal demand for everyone having the sort of enhanced social and emotional flexibility they didn't previously need.

In relation to autism this leads to an interesting paradox. One of the core features of the diagnosis implies a lack of empathy. However, improving the 'emotional intelligence' of the workforce is for the purpose of using empathy to successfully exploit and manipulate your customers and workforce into doing what you wish for your own personal (and company) gain. It seems strange that people who find it difficult to understand emotional nuances but who can be compassionate are pathologised, yet those who can use an understanding of others' emotional state to manipulate them for selfish ends are rewarded.

There seems to have been a confluence of several factors that allowed autism to develop into a popular brand. The professionalising of child-rearing and child development, anxiety about children's well-being, changes in family structure and time, concern with the welfare of the individual over the collective, a change in the economy as it moves from the factory to consumer-facing services, identity becoming important as we become branded, topped off with the attraction of a fix through medical technology. Autism becomes popularised and spreads out beyond a rare childhood condition affecting mainly male children, to a lifelong difference which includes women who were being missed because of masking.

While autism is undoubtedly a 'culture-bound' syndrome invented in and for Western populations, as with many other Western cultural products from Hollywood films to McDonald's and Starbucks, this brand had been growing in appeal and was ready for export.

Autism goes global

In his 2007 book *Unstrange Minds*, anthropology professor Roy Grinker examines the rise in autism diagnoses and argues that there is no autism epidemic, but that the higher prevalence rates are a sign of progress in identifying and helping children with developmental disorders and disabilities.[25] He concludes that the new and, in his opinion, more accurate statistics on autism are a sign that we are finally seeing and appreciating a kind of human difference that we once turned away from and that many other cultures still hide away in homes or institutions or denigrate as bizarre. Surprisingly for an anthropologist, he dismisses the role of cultural norms and describes the experiences of parents of children with autism in South Korea, India and South Africa by viewing those societies through the lens of stigma (i.e. in need of educating and civilising).

Professor Grinker then heads a research team to evaluate the prevalence of autism in South Korea. They screen 55,266, seven- to twelve-year-old children using the autism spectrum screening questionnaire. Parents of children who screened positive were then offered comprehensive assessments using 'standardised diagnostic procedures'. Published in 2011, the research concludes that 2.64 per cent of the children had ASD, the majority of whom were in mainstream schools and had no psychiatric diagnoses or extra help.[26] To me this is ethically problematic. To take a large number of children who thus far have had no labels attached to them, are not seen by school or parents as having any extra needs, and to conclude that they have a disorder that no one has previously recognised, has the hallmarks of a type of Western colonial superiority, where non-Westerners are viewed as in need of saving from their primitive ignorance.

The prevalence rate they found was twice that recorded in the US at the time. Did no one stop and think about cultural traditions and their implication for so-called symptoms? For example, holding eye contact while speaking to an elder in South Korean culture is considered disrespectful or disobedient, and children are taught to avoid this from a young age. In autism diagnosis, lack of eye contact is considered a symptom.

Several studies using different criteria are registering global increases in rates of autism diagnosis, including in areas such as Eastern Europe and many African countries where such a diagnosis was hardly, if ever, used. In 2013 the World Health Organization, in response to global advocacy, produced a report that called for a move from awareness towards capacity building in the area of autism, thus sowing the seeds for an 'official' initiative to globalise ASD.[27]

A 2022 review of international prevalence studies confirmed that across the world rates of autism diagnoses were rising. Pooling the results from seventy-one studies, researchers concluded that globally the median prevalence was 1 per cent (with a range from 0.01 per cent to 4.36 per cent). The median male/female ratio was 2:1, and the median percentage of autism cases with co-occurring intellectual disability was 33 per cent. The previous systematic review conducted in 2012 found that the median prevalence of ASD was 0.62 per cent, confirming a rapid rise in rates across the world. Most of the data came from high-income countries, which remained the countries with the highest rates of diagnosis (the 4.36 per cent coming from a study in Australia).[28]

What happened to Oscar?

Reading and listening to today's media, you'd be forgiven for thinking that getting an autism diagnosis leads to a better understanding of a person, and as a result knowing what specific treatments and targeted supports should be offered. The main challenge is imagined to be that of stigma, lack of acceptance by society and the need for more funding of services.

For many it is far more complicated than societal prejudice and better financial support. At the start of this chapter I introduced you to Oscar, who felt that having autism was a life sentence. He was close to his mother, estranged from his father, felt hopeless about his future and trapped by his autism diagnosis. What might happen if instead of shaping the treatment around his diagnosis (as autism advocates say we should do), it was put to one side and the specific challenges, fears and contexts were engaged with instead?

Over the next few sessions, I had an opportunity to talk to Oscar about what he understood autism to be. What it was that led to him feeling so trapped by it. He felt autism was something in his brain that was fixed and made it difficult for him to mix with others and do the things he wanted to do in his life. I discussed with him and his mother, Sue, the tremendous level of empathy, insight and emotional intelligence he shows to her. Oscar, it seemed to me, was quite an emotionally aware and sensitive person. We talked about how many things about him (like his finely tuned empathy) didn't fit the stereotyped picture of autism. Perhaps there was a lot more to him than the diagnosis.

We talked about his growing-up years, what had happened during that time and how he had dealt with the many changes, including his father leaving. I asked Sue how Oscar had changed during those years. He was different now to when he was younger and there was no reason to believe he wouldn't be different again as he grew older. The idea that he had a condition that fixes you in some way for life is mistaken.

We talked about his strengths, surviving all the difficult years, and yet still maintaining such a sensitivity towards his mother, to the point that Sue described him as her 'rock'. Perhaps what he calls autism might also be a strength — a capacity to sometimes see the world differently, and in a unique way, compared to others. We spoke about his interest in computers and what an amazing thing it was to be able to teach yourself computer code. This really showed that he didn't just have a good brain but an amazing one. It demonstrated that he could be self-directed and so was capable of a lot more than he believed he was.

We talked about his fear of turning out like his father, Peter, and Sue pointed out how different Oscar was to Peter. Perhaps it was talking about his father and a curiosity to find out what he was like now that led to Oscar contacting him.

Oscar met up with his father for the first time in nearly six years. Peter now lived with a new partner, and they had a one-year-old daughter. After Oscar's first meeting with his father I arranged for a joint session with Peter and Oscar. Peter tried to explain that there were two sides to each story. He'd wanted to stay in touch with Oscar, but Oscar's mother had prevented him. I'm pretty sure Oscar didn't buy his father's version. Nonetheless, they were now talking and seeing each other. The imagined monster of a father Oscar had created was dissolving into a real, rather flawed, but at least available one.

He started seeing his father intermittently once he was satisfied Sue didn't mind him doing that. He found he was awkward around Peter, but liked his new partner Emma and adored his newly discovered baby sister Stephanie. Oscar had a new family as part of his social support network. The narrow, barren world he had been inhabiting was widening, creating new anxieties, but new possibilities too.

Oscar managed to go to college, and despite the inevitable ups and downs, he made some new friends, started to enjoy his studies, got a part-time job, and really turned his life around. By the time he was discharged, autism was no longer mentioned as being of any relevance to his life story.

8.   Is autism an evidence-based construct?

'The more you know, the more you know you don't know.'

Aristotle

In 2017, I, along with thirteen other attendees, went on a two-day training in the Autism Diagnostic Observation Schedule (ADOS). ADOS is promoted as 'a standardised diagnostic test for diagnosing and assessing autism' and considered to be the 'gold standard' for diagnosing ASD. The protocol consists of a series of structured and semi-structured tasks that involve social interaction between the 'examiner' and the person under assessment. A potential diagnosis is based on whether the quantitative scoring used goes beyond a predetermined threshold. This is the most widely used 'diagnostic tool' for diagnosing autism in children and young people. As it has a large observational component, it could be argued that it has more objectivity than the questionnaires used for diagnosing adults.

I attended the ADOS training as part of a group of four, including three autism activists involved with the University of Exeter project Exploring Diagnosis: Autism and the Neurodiversity Movement.[1] We wrote a paper together summarising each of our different critiques of ADOS.[2]

When anyone talks about their child getting a 'test' for autism, they are likely referring to having an ADOS assessment or one of the other similar ones that have become available. ADOS was developed by a group of prominent autism researchers (including Professor Michael Rutter mentioned in the last chapter) and first published in 1989. It has had several updates since then. The core of the training involved watching videotaped sessions of ADOS assessments where we had to make our own ratings based on the observational schedule we were given. After each video the course facilitator discussed the ratings and showed us how to arrive at the 'correct' conclusion.

The ADOS assessment involves an interviewer (whom I shall refer to as the 'examiner') and a subject (whom I shall refer to as the 'patient'). The examiner presents a series of tasks for the patient to complete in a limited time and then removes each task at the end of this time and moves on to the next one. The whole process is meant to take a standardised forty to sixty minutes. The behaviour of the patient is observed and given empirical ratings. The examiner is not allowed to change their approach in response to the patient's behaviour, including the requirement to produce all the tasks in sequence. Tasks include free play; describing a picture-book story; play with miniature figures; completing a puzzle; and, with older patients, questions about their social life, understanding of relationships, and hopes for the future. Throughout the assessment the examiner is looking for the presence of certain 'symptoms' or the absence of 'normal' behaviour.

The quasi-autistic rigidity of seeing only 'real' internal qualities in the patients was a recurrent theme. Most of the questions I asked during the course stemmed from genuine puzzlement as to how certain patient behaviours in the videos could be ascribed as solely the consequence of symptoms in the patient. The course facilitator would insist that what was being observed could only be understood as being the manifestations of ASD spilling out into the assessment session, due to the expertise of the examiner in conducting a 'standardised' assessment. Thus, as the facilitator guided us through the scoring, they kept referring to the 'fact' that this or that symptom occurred.

The philosophy of ADOS assumes that context, relational or otherwise, is irrelevant. In one example, the course facilitator discussed how ASD can manifest by recounting a story told to her by a parent of a child brought to the clinic she worked in. This parent had asked her child, 'Why do you never look at me?' The child then started to look at her. The parent now complained, 'Why do you stare at me?' The confused boy now decided maybe he should learn to look at her and then away from her. His mother now complained,

'Why do you move your eyes from one place to another?' According to this story, the boy eventually developed a complex formula for how long to look at her and away from her. In recounting this tale, the facilitator made no comment about the parent's role in this developing relational discomfort – it was all the result of this child's (at the time undiagnosed) ASD.

No allowance was made for the gender or cultural relevance of the activities/questions in the ADOS. The illusion of objectivity starts dissolving when you see the wording of what you are being asked to rate. For example, for rating 'stereotyped/idiosyncratic use of words or phrases', a mark of 2 (indicating high degree of abnormality) is given if 'often uses stereotyped utterances or odd words or phrases, with some other language'. A mark of 1 (indicating some level of abnormality) is 'use of words or phrases tends to be more repetitive than that of most individuals at the same level of expressive language, but not obviously odd'. For 'quality of social overtures', 1 is 'slightly unusual quality of some social overtures', 2 is 'significant minority (or more) of inappropriate overtures; many overtures lack integration into context and/or social quality'.

All the 'symptoms' in the schedule are of this manner. Remember how it was impossible to escape subjectivity in the adult autism questionnaires? In this supposedly more 'objective' observational approach, we run straight into the same problems of vague subjectivity. What do the words 'often', 'unusual', 'quality', 'some', 'significant', and so on, cropping up all over the place, mean? You cannot establish objective facts when all the ratings are shrouded in subjectivity.

Reliance on the interpretive bias of the examiner was regularly revealed. For example, in one of the video assessments, I saw the child regularly smiling, but the facilitator said this was not smiling but the symptom of 'smirking'. Even if it was 'smirking', it's difficult to understand why that should be considered a medical 'symptom'. Other behaviour rated included: 'unusual' use of words; quality of the child's attempt to initiate interaction; whether the patient requests things from the examiner; not spontaneously giving toys or other objects back to the examiner; not showing toys or other objects (e.g. by holding them up) to the examiner; lack of flexible, creative use of objects (e.g. a doll) in a representational manner; unusual sensory interests; and so on, all open to interpretive variation. The ratings bring up questions of where notions of appropriate/inappropriate, normal/abnormal, healthy/ symptomatic, etc., are derived from.

My genuine interpretations using the ADOS scoring systems were quite different from what the facilitator explained were the correct 'objective' scores. After the first video of the assessment of a five-year-old child was shown, I was convinced this was being shown to illustrate an assessment of a 'normal' child so they can be contrasted with someone who 'has' ASD. In the end it turned out that every video showed someone who had been given an autism label.

We could comment on and then code the patient's behaviour but were not allowed to interpret the patient's possible affect (their feelings/emotions) or the relational/contextual nature of interactions. It seemed to me that this 'test' of social communication was done through setting up a deliberately provocative environment and expecting these young patients to acquiesce to the examiner's unusual demands.

Thus, in the videos, ADOS looks more like a test of social conformity to a bossy adult's constantly shifting demands. In one video, early in the session, after the examiner removes the toys the seven-year-old patient was enjoying playing with, the child stands with his back to the examiner and says, 'You're not my friend.' The rest of the assessment then plays out a complex interaction, part, at times, hilarious rebellion by the young patient, part engagement, and part distressing-to-watch pressuring and cold detachment by the examiner.

In the videos of older children, they get asked questions that I'm not sure how the younger me would have answered, like, 'What does a friend mean to you?', 'Do you ever think about a long-term relationship or getting married?', 'Do you take care of your own money?', 'Do you have plans or dreams for the future?' According to our rating scales there are normal and pathological ways to answer these questions.

I came away from the course feeling that ADOS is not a diagnostic tool but a diagnostic trap. The two-day training costs around

£600 per delegate and a pack of 50 scoring booklets (10 for each different age bracket), which you'll need to carry out an ADOS, costs around £3,000.

There is something autistic about the ADOS itself. It attempts to identify relational 'deficits' while demonstrating the instruments' own lack of awareness about the nature of relationships. It relentlessly seeks to uncover evidence of abnormalities and creates a context where the examiner can readily find it. It is a system that catches many in its net, from young kids who won't do as the examiner instructs and in the way the examiner believes they should to older ones who have an interesting turn of phrase. It constructs how the culture-, gender- and sexuality-neutral person should and shouldn't function. It's promoted and sold around the world, subjecting ever more children and young people to its normalising/pathologising agenda.

What is or isn't autism or ASD?

It's easy to get confused about the different terms that get used. 'Diagnostic' criteria are different in different systems and have changed over the years, widening beyond infantile autism to include terms like Asperger syndrome, atypical autism, high functioning autism, and, more recently, a term that doesn't appear in any diagnostic manual – pathological demand avoidance. The umbrella term autistic spectrum disorder is meant to cover all these suggested variations and is nowadays used interchangeably with just autism.

To confuse things further, autism itself is sometimes classified as part of the broader construct of pervasive developmental disorders, which includes a couple of rare conditions: Rett's disorder and childhood disintegrative disorder. Both describe a gradual loss of functioning in early childhood and are therefore highly likely to include a significant neurological component.

ASD is said to be characterised by three core deficits: impaired communication; impaired reciprocal social interaction; and restricted, repetitive and stereotyped patterns of behaviours or interests.

But it keeps changing. The latest version of the *American Diagnostic Statistical Manual* (*DSM-5*) defines autism by referring to only two core 'symptoms': 1) persistent deficits in social communication and social interaction across multiple contexts; 2) restricted, repetitive patterns of behaviour, interests or activities.[3] The authors have basically merged the first two of the supposed three core symptoms into one, giving us a two-dimensional model. I discussed a similar set of changes in the ADHD triad of symptoms in Chapter 6 – going from three separate lists of symptoms to one, and most recently (like ASD) to two lists in the *DSM-5*.

What are these social and communication difficulties and repetitive behaviour issues meant to look like? Here's the UK National Autistic Society explanation:

> Some autistic people are unable to speak or have limited speech while other autistic people have very good language skills but struggle to understand sarcasm or tone of voice. Other challenges include: taking things literally and not understanding abstract concepts, needing extra time to process information or answer questions ... Autistic people often have difficulty 'reading' other people – recognising or understanding others' feelings and intentions – and expressing their own emotions ... Autistic people may: appear to be insensitive, seek out time alone when overloaded by other people, not seek comfort from other people, appear to behave 'strangely' or in a way thought to be socially inappropriate, find it hard to form friendships ... they often prefer to have routines so that they know what is going to happen. They may want to travel the same way to and from school or work, wear the same clothes or eat exactly the same food for breakfast. Autistic people may also repeat movements such as hand flapping, rocking or the repetitive use of an object such as twirling a pen or opening and closing a door. [They] engage in these behaviours to help calm themselves when they are stressed or anxious, but many autistic people do it because they find it enjoyable.[4]

OK, so that's what autism is like: some language difficulties including understanding sarcasm, finding it hard to read their own or others' emotional states, and they like routines and predictability.

Sounds vague and I can't see how these are signs of a 'disorder' but maybe I'll get my head round it. However, just when you think you might be beginning to get it, an expert or an autistic person will tell you that you haven't.

In their 2022 'Myth Busting Autism' webinar, Drs Ozsivadjian and Murin explain several of what they call 'myths' about autism.[5] The myths include that autistic people are: not able to socialise, have little empathy, have limited imagination, cannot understand metaphor, and have difficulties in communication. They conclude that autistic people, just like anyone else, have strengths and difficulties and, therefore, defy stereotyping of any kind. They explain that the way any feature presents varies considerably. For example, some autistic people are highly verbal, and others hardly use any language; therefore, you cannot assume any therapeutic strategy will work for everyone. They also explain how many of the 'diagnostic tools' don't pick up females with autism because they usually present with anxiety and depression, as 'masking' is a significant issue.

Are you getting more and more confused as to what autism *really* is? All the symptoms could also be the basis for myth-making stereotypes and so you can't go by 'symptoms' to make a diagnosis; what you need is an 'expert' who knows what's lurking underneath the surface to 'see' the autism in there. In addition, you can't use the diagnosis as a basis for understanding what sort of help and support an autistic person may need. This reminds me of being at a conference where a consultant was talking about the first hundred people they had diagnosed in their new adult autism assessment service. 'If I put all hundred in a room together and you went to meet them all, you'd struggle to find anything in common with each other beyond their diagnosis. If you know one person with autism, you know one person with autism.' So, what's the point of a diagnosis?

These days the same behaviourally defined syndrome (autism) is applied to residents of institutions with little hope of living independently and a long list of the great and the good such as Mozart, Van Gogh, Edison, Darwin, Einstein – all of whom, along with many others, have been retrospectively diagnosed as having an autism (just type 'famous people with autism' into Google and see what comes up). From an impairment perspective, this is the entire human spectrum. Are people who support the idea that autism is a recognisable condition seriously saying that what might be helpful for these cultural icons is the same as for residents of institutions with little functioning language?

This problem of having a vast repertoire of presenting behaviours and levels of functioning that can lead to a diagnosis is referred to as the problem of 'heterogeneity' (defined as the quality or state of being diverse in character or content). Not only do the supposedly 'core' features such as difficulties in social communication have a large crossover with people who would not consider themselves as having a disorder, but what are considered as autism symptoms are also commonly listed in a variety of mental health diagnoses from ADHD to depression and anxiety to psychosis.

Wherever you look, heterogeneity is evident, along with a lack of conceptual clarity about what autism is. In the criteria for 'conduct disorders' (CD) you can find 'inability to form bonds with peers and egocentrism, which is shown by a readiness to manipulate others for favours without any effort to reciprocate, together with a general lack of feelings for others'. This description bears (arguably) a closer resemblance to the descriptions of the cases Hans Asperger wrote about than Lorna Wing's cases (discussed in the last chapter). One of the core features of autism is meant to be a lack of empathy, a lack that is supposed to cause enduring difficulties in social interactions. How is this type of 'lack of empathy' to be differentiated from the lack of empathy found in CD or indeed those considered to have a 'sociopathic personality disorder'? Other 'disorders', such as 'attachment disorder', also describe children who lack empathy and have what is referred to as 'dysfunctional patterns of social interaction'.

Attachment disorder is described as often associated with some form of neglect, abuse or trauma. However, in the absence of robust evidence on what causes attachment disorder or autism, making the distinction between 'social dysfunction' in the context of conduct disorder and attachment disorder or autism becomes little more than a matter of the semantics carried by the subjective opinion of the person making the diagnosis.

Lack of empathy can also appear because of a lack of self-confidence in social situations. In fact, if you think about it, any experience connected to a preoccupation with your own problems tends to reduce your interest in other people's lives and interests. The extent to which you can feign interest in all subjects or empathise with all predicaments is limited. As expectations for social empathy (e.g. in school and in the workplace) increase, so more may appear to lack this capacity.

How about the 'symptom' of 'restricted and repetitive behaviours'? You will find versions of this in obsessive compulsive disorder, obsessional personality disorder, schizoid personality disorder, ADHD, major depressive disorder (morbid preoccupation with negative aspects of life), eating disorders (fixation with food and/or weight), and so on. Away from manuals and medicalised symptoms you can also find this with: many men (e.g. with football!), sportsmen and women (with their sport and training regimes), and humanity in general, as an obsessive interest in a restricted sphere is characteristic not only of a depressed state of mind, but also of the application needed for discovery and exploration. Most high achievers thus have the capacity to fixate on their area of interest/expertise. In an astonishing circularity of reasoning, this then becomes the motivation for labelling the long list of great achievers mentioned earlier as having autism.

Thus, what are considered primary symptoms of autism, like 'social communication difficulties', 'lack of empathy' and 'restricted and repetitive behaviours', cannot be thought of as isolated individual pathologies/differences without an understanding of the context in which they appear. When you start to dig around the undergrowth that constructs our idea of autism, it becomes apparent that it is so shallow that nothing can realistically take hold there.

Autism, therefore, doesn't even work well as a descriptive classification, as it's what narrative therapists (a type of psychotherapy that explores how we construct stories about our life) would call a 'thin description' because it leaves out all sorts of other things that might be important to understand that person's life (family, social environment, school, cultural differences, bullying, etc.) as well as their skills, abilities and things they do well in.

This deconstruction suggests we are about to encounter the same problems of defining a case for research or clinical purposes that I discussed with ADHD. The 'case-ness' issue predicts that disproving the null hypothesis (that autism is a category of nature that is genetic and neurodevelopmental) will be problematic.

Let's see.

Has the null hypothesis been disproven for autism genetics?

As previously discussed, the correct scientific stance is to assume that what we are characterising as autism/ASD does not exist as a natural category until we can demonstrate that this null hypothesis can't be true.

The argument that autism is a strongly genetic condition rests primarily upon twin studies. I explained in Chapter 6 why estimating genetic heritability using the twin method does not help you in distinguishing environmental from genetic causes. The only reliable way to establish the relevance of the genetic component is through molecular genetic studies, of which there is a growing database involving whole genome scans of thousands of children with the autism/ASD label.

No specific, characteristic, rare or common genes for autism have been discovered, but not for want of looking. Various candidate genes, linkage studies, genome scans and chromosome studies have all failed to produce and reliably replicate any genes associated specifically with autism. The more failures pile up, the more proponents of the genetic explanation talk about how autism genetics is 'complex' and that there must be some sort of mysterious polygenetic interaction that accounts for the 'missing heritability'.[6] The most likely explanation for this finding, or rather lack of finding, is that there is no such thing as genes that cause autism.

The continuing failure to identify specifics seems to have resulted in the majority of the human chromosomes being identified as potentially harbouring autism genes, with major expert reviews typically concluding: 'Many research teams have searched for genes that may be involved. They haven't turned up any prime candidates yet, only dozens, maybe hundreds of bit players';[7] and 'With the advent of next generation sequencing techniques, the number of genes found that are associated with ASD is increasing to over 800 genes; consequently, it is becoming even more challenging to find unified explanations and functional associations between the genes involved.'[8]

As with ADHD we are now in the era of 'big data', where multiple research teams come together in the hope that this can reveal tiny associations by pooling data on tens of thousands of individuals' genes for comparison. It's hard to face the possibility that this mass of research money has led to a wasted endeavour; instead, they carry on getting the lion's share of research money because 'Sequencing technology quickly confirmed that the aetiology of ASD was multigenic and highly heterogeneous, with very few of the same pathogenic variants present in a significant percentage of afflicted individuals' and so 'It may take many more decades of research before the scientific community has an accurate picture of how these modulators contribute to the aetiology of ASD'.[9]

This 2021 review aptly sums up where autism genetic research has got to: 'Despite the many insights provided by recent ASD gene discovery, even a preliminary answer for one of the most striking and obvious aspects of ASD pathology remains obscure.'[10]

As regards genetics then, the cupboard is empty, and the null hypothesis stands: there is no characteristic identifiable genetic abnormality/profile associated with autism.

Has the null hypothesis been disproven for autism brain imaging?

Before discussing the autism neuroimaging literature, it should be mentioned that even if significant differences were found compared to non-autistic individuals, it doesn't necessarily mean these are the consequence of internal biology rather than environment. An important consideration to take into account is that of 'neuroplasticity'. This refers to the remarkable ability of the nervous system (particularly in children) to grow and change in response to environmental stimuli. The amazing plasticity of the human brain makes it difficult to determine precise cause and effect when individuals with different life experiences subsequently show what appear to be differences in neurological structure or functioning.

We see this neuroplasticity at play in all sorts of ways, from the ability that children have to compensate over time for brain injuries to the findings that London cab drivers have larger volumes than almost anyone else in brain areas that are highly involved in navigating and spatial awareness.[11] Thus, any brain differences found could be the result of environmental factors affecting brain development (like psychological trauma), differences in the rates that maturation takes place (for example, we know that, on average, girls develop a little faster than boys), and variations resulting from other features in the research subjects (for example, their intellectual ability). It means that we can't assume any differences we find are the result of a pre-existing biological cause. After all, the brain is the body organ, one of whose functions is that of enabling the organism to adapt to the environment. It would be surprising if the brain was not influenced by the experiences the organism has.

I mention the importance of neuroplasticity because it is often assumed that there is something lifelong and fixed in an autistic person's neurology, but this is not how the nervous system develops and works.

The biggest problem for autism studies, as with ADHD, comes from the lack of consistently replicated findings. This consistent inconsistency plagues autism research. For example, studies focusing on an area of the brain called the cerebellum have documented an increase in cerebellar volume among children diagnosed with ASD, while others have found smaller than average cerebellar volumes, yet others have reported no significant differences between children with ASD and non-ASD subjects.[12] Similarly, studies on another area of the brain called the amygdala have found wide inconsistencies, including some finding significant differences in volume and others finding no differences.[13] With clockwork regularity, a team of researchers announce their latest finding: 'the connections between the two halves of the brain are smaller in autism, suggesting ASD is a disorder of brain connectivity', and this then goes around the world media, but then we never hear of the subsequent research teams who can't replicate these findings.

Some prominent researchers started waking up to the idea that maybe biologically based autism research will lead nowhere. A 2016 paper entitled 'ASD validity', which includes the renowned autism researcher Professor Christopher Gillberg among its authors, concluded, 'The findings reviewed indicate that the ASD diagnosis lacks biological and construct validity,' and recommended disbanding ASD diagnosis as a basis for research.[14]

However, the industry is too big to fail. The Autism Brain Imaging Data Exchange is an international research collaboration that pools brain-imaging data from studies across the world.[15] Not surprisingly, despite the vast research effort, it has made no progress in understanding autistic brains. As I discussed with ADHD brain-imaging research, there are numerous technical issues involved when comparing data from different scanners using different technology and where issues such as age, gender and IQ need to be carefully controlled for.[16]

An alternative to anatomical brain imaging is functional brain imaging (such as functional magnetic resonance imaging – fMRI). This is where the person is carrying out some task, while their brain is being scanned for levels of activity in different regions (such as tracking blood flow or glucose uptake patterns). Unfortunately, 'converging evidence is demonstrating poor reliability of task-fMRI measures . . . Collectively, these findings demonstrate that common task-fMRI measures are not currently suitable for brain biomarker discovery or for individual-differences research.'[17] Another dead end.

These problems that bedevil autism neuroimaging research have meant that the likelihood of identifying any reliable or valid brain biomarkers for autism is close to zero. Here too then the cupboard is also empty. No one has come near to finding a characteristic abnormality and as a result there is no biological marker or brain scan used to diagnose autism. The null hypothesis stands – there is no characteristic brain abnormality or difference associated with autism.

Autistic outcomes

It has been harder to critique autism than labels like ADHD, as autism has no specific pharmaceutical treatments attached to it and hence the conflict-of-interest issue is not as easily apparent. However, when such dramatic diagnostic expansion takes place, this should make you suspicious that we are not dealing with a diagnosis, but rather a branded commodity with market appeal. This renders it vulnerable to the 'elastic band effect' I've mentioned before, where the boundaries can be stretched almost endlessly.

But at what cost do we continue to widen and widen the autism net? Who has looked at the data of what happens to those caught in this net? Where is the evidence that a diagnosis improves the real-world outcomes for those diagnosed? How many are warned about the potential negative outcomes associated with a diagnosis? Why are we not researching these important questions? Labels do carry associations and stereotypes. Most research on adult outcomes for those with an ASD label indicate very limited social integration, poor job prospects and high rates of mental health problems,[18] with only an estimated 20 per cent rated as having a good outcome.[19]

I understand that there are many who have found the act of naming helpful. Parents may be enabled to have a new sympathy for their child and adults may feel something about their life now makes sense. But at what price? How long do these initial feelings of relief last? What goes missing from that person's narrative when a label that cannot explain is used to explain? I worry about the potential for a subtle kind of violence that can be inflicted on someone thus labelled, which may limit their own, their families' and a whole host of people's beliefs about what they can and can't do, what they need protection from and don't. I'm concerned that having the label of autism provides a cruel kind of hope. Parents may feel that something is now understood, so experts will know what to do to help. As the days, months and years accrue with matters not improving, what does that do to parents' feelings about their 'disordered' child? These are the types of dilemmas I regularly see in my consulting room.

An autism diagnosis can disempower parents and teachers by accident because there is an assumption that they don't have the expertise to know how to intervene and to know what the right way to support the child is. Ordinary things can fly out the window, and so I've seen families where the power dynamics have switched because of parents' concern that if they intervene in any way in their young person's life, they might make things worse. So they end up walking on eggshells around them, at the same time as panicking about their future. This makes for a very tense household. It paralyses parents and others, leaving them feeling deskilled and waiting for more qualified professionals to advise them or, even better, provide the right therapy for their autistic child.

I've seen parents so paralysed by the autism diagnosis in their child that they were no longer able to say 'no'. I have seen young people lose weight and get close to death's door because their parents were given the advice not to make demands on their autistic children. Faddy eating and fear of certain foods took root and all that was needed to help reverse this dangerous consequence was to give parents' permission to take control and explain to the child (often to the child's relief) that their job now was to let go and pass control back to their parents.

Autism has become the new catch-all for young patients who don't follow the increasingly narrow boundaries of expected behaviours, and to such an extent that we overlook histories that would obviously have an impact on their presentations. It keeps coming up as a 'maybe they have autism' by referrers, parents, teachers, in meetings and clinical reviews, as if that's going to provide an explanation for behaviours that concern, frustrate or infuriate.

Autism, like any other psychiatric diagnosis, is not a diagnosis but a brand as confused and unstable as the culture that created it and the lives it was meant to liberate.

9. Start them young

'Schools serve the same social functions as prisons and mental institutions – to define, classify, control and regulate people.'

Michel Foucault

Twelve-year-old Molly was one of the most withdrawn people I had ever met. She was admitted to a paediatric ward complaining of stomach pains and nausea and had stopped eating and drinking. After medical investigations, the ward consultant concluded that her presentation was not physical and asked me to assess her. When I came to meet her in a side room off the main ward, I first encountered her worried father who sat at her bedside with a dazed look on his face. Molly was lying curled up in a tight ball with her arms around her legs, and her face buried in her knees. She was not answering to anyone or anything.

The medical team had concluded that this was a mental health problem and they wanted me to make a diagnosis, prescribe some medication, advise the ward staff on her management and get her moved to a psychiatric hospital as soon as possible. When I first qualified as a consultant it was common to work jointly with paediatricians, but over the last decade or so there has been a growing tendency to hand over patients they consider as primarily having a mental health problem to mental health services, alongside requests to get the patient moved out of their ward. If there are any challenges for a ward in managing a patient, the tendency now is to request that the patient is placed under a section of the Mental Health Act and for mental health services to then employ staff trained in 'restraint' to watch over the patient – a situation that often leads to escalating behavioural challenges.

There is little doubt that the spread of the mental health industrial complex into childhood has meant a growing pressure to come up with treatment plans that include providing a diagnosis and prescribing medication (which the physicians will refer to as 'pharmacotherapy'). You may, understandably, feel that with presentations like Molly's, such a process is indeed needed. Twenty years ago there seemed more opportunity to discuss patients with a ward paediatrician and nursing staff without pressure to use medication, diagnosis or the Mental Health Act. Is this a sign of progress? Is there a way to manage even extreme presentations like Molly's without doing this? I will return to Molly's story at the end of this chapter.

McDonaldisation of mental health

Earlier in this book I explained why mental health in general and psychiatric diagnoses in particular, because of the inescapable subjectivity involved, defy attempts to make them function in the same manner as physical health diagnoses. I explained how this made psychiatric diagnoses vulnerable to continuous expansion of its boundaries in tandem with growing media discussion, sometimes in an alarmist manner, of the importance of mental health. In the last four chapters, using ADHD and autism as examples, I illustrated how these developments are affecting larger cohorts and spilling out into everyday culture. In this chapter I want to further interrogate the impact on young people, who are of particular concern.

When I was training in child psychiatry back in the early to mid-1990s, childhood depression was seen as rare, different to adult depression, the consequence of more extreme adversity, and not amenable to treatment with medication. The commercial success of marketing Prozac as an 'antidepressant' spurred other pharmaceutical companies to manufacture copycat drugs and open new markets for their lucrative products, including selling the idea of childhood depression to create a demand for prescriptions to juveniles. Use of stimulants for ADHD was already accelerating and, with 'antidepressants' being added, a rise in prescribing of all classes of psychiatric medications to children was taking place. The systemic thinking that used to dominate mental health ideology in child and adolescent services that I described in Chapter 1 was giving way to diagnostic pathway-based protocols that introduced mechanistic 'corrective' therapies and a flourishing of individualised approaches.[1]

As the numbers of those considered to have mental disorders rose, the media began talking about epidemics of mental disorders in the young and lack of services for them. Governments saw this as a funding priority and together with the media this made schools a prominent site of concern as mental health problems were said to start early in life, thus targeting intervention at people in their early years was perceived as an important mental disorder prevention strategy.

In tandem, campaigns to combat stigma and for greater mental health awareness found their way into classrooms and teachers' staffrooms. Far from leading to enlightened progress, because we don't know what we're talking about when it comes to mental health, it inadvertently set young people on a path towards alienation from, and suspicion of, not just each other, but their emotional lives too. Young people were encouraged to turn varieties of suffering from something to be understood and at times tolerated, into meaningless torture that needed eliminating. Consequently, there has never been a generation of young people as pathologised as this current generation.

With the widespread application of medical and other technical approaches to managing children's behaviour and emotional states, we have achieved the 'McDonaldisation' of children's mental health. The diagnostic pathway-driven practice is like fast-food consumerism in several ways:

a) it comes from the most aggressively consumerist society (US)
b) it promotes global industrial over local production
c) it feeds on the desire for instant satisfaction
d) it fits into consumers' busy lifestyles
e) it requires little engagement with the product from the consumer

f) it only needs superficial training, knowledge and understanding to produce
g) it de-skills people by providing an easy way out (thereby reducing resilience)
h) it creates potentially lifelong consumers for the product
i) it has the potential to produce long-term damage to both the individuals who consume these products as well as public health more generally[2]

Reported rates of mental health problems among the young have increased at the same time as the amount of psychiatric medication and mental health treatments and services aimed at young people. Many behaviours and experiences previously deemed ordinary and/or understandable are now viewed as possible mental health problems that require professional expertise that teachers and parents believe they lack.

A research project in which nineteen UK-based experienced secondary school teachers were interviewed about their beliefs and practices in relation to the mental health of their students found that the teachers believed that ideology and practice had changed dramatically. All the teachers interviewed felt that awareness of mental health and disorder had increased in the preceding five to ten years, and that this had led to an expansion in the numbers of students thought to have mental health problems.[3]

While there had been a substantial increase in mental health provision both within and outside the school system, teachers felt these services were still woefully inadequate. They identified many behaviours and experiences they would previously have thought of as ordinary and/or understandable, as likely mental health problems that required professional knowledge which they lacked. They were now discouraged from even ordinary interactions like spending time talking to a distressed student, as the student could be developing a mental disorder and they didn't have the expertise to know what the right thing to do would be.

Many teachers were unsure where the boundaries for mental disorders lay and how to differentiate those from 'unruly' behaviours or 'putting it on' to get some extra perceived benefits. Most teachers when asked about causes of mental health problems referred to everyday challenges such as exam stress, relationships, family, social media and bullying. Even though teachers were oriented towards these environmental models of causation, when it came to how best to help young people, teachers subscribed to a more medical model view that relied on 'trained experts' who could diagnose and treat the resulting disorders.

This is the backdrop that creates more referrals, and despite external services expansion, these services then have trouble dealing with the number of new patients wanting help, leading to access problems and media coverage of a 'crisis' in services.

In Chapter 4 I mentioned a 2019 survey in the UK of one thousand young people, which found that 68 per cent thought they'd had or were currently experiencing a mental health problem. Of those, 62 per cent thought that 'de-stigmatisation' campaigns helped them identify it. It also found that there had been a 45 per cent increase in mental health referrals of under eighteens in the previous two years.[4] These numbers are not that far off a 2019 academic paper that, using a child self-report questionnaire methodology, came up with a prevalence figure for mental health problems in eleven- to fifteen-year-olds of 42 per cent.[5] A 2020 study from New Zealand reported that 86 per cent of people will be eligible for a psychiatric diagnosis by the time they're forty-five, with about half of the population having met the criteria for a 'disorder' by the age of eighteen.[6]

This has real-world implications in terms of levels of suffering. Mental health-related paediatric emergency department (ED) visits in the US increased from 4.8 million (7.7 per cent of all paediatric ED visits) in 2011 to 7.5 million (13.1 per cent of all ED visits) in 2020. While all types of mental health-related visits significantly increased, suicide-related visits demonstrated the greatest increase from 0.9 per cent to 4.2 per cent of all paediatric ED visits.[7] Is it possible that our framing of distress in diagnostic, mental health technology terms adds to the burden of suffering?

Could the pathological disease-based mystification of mental distress contribute to transforming into illness the challenges, confusions, intensity and changes that happen as we grow and develop, particularly in our adolescent years? Are our young being encouraged to identify and consume psychiatric brands, along with simplistic remedies that they may wish to take, intermittently or continuously, for the rest of their lives? Will the crumbs of comfort they get by identifying with this or that label open the door to a potential lifelong struggle with the consequences of this consumption? What does it mean to the potential future of possibility and change to be shackled by a fixed abstraction (a psychiatric diagnosis) as a prism (or prison) through which meaning will be filtered and created?

This expansion is reaching our youngest children. Anecdotes from conversations at the primary school gates tell of parents who discuss their concerns about how their child may have autism or ADHD or may be depressed. Nursery schools carry out 'professional' mental health assessments on two- and three-year-olds, particularly if a child is deemed 'aggressive'.

Schools now employ counsellors who make referrals after the young person they are seeing is not feeling better. My service receives referrals where a counsellor may state that they think the young person they're seeing has a 'personality disorder', or 'autism', or is 'bipolar', or has 'depression', or 'needs medication'. I've even seen one saying an eleven-year-old child has 'psychopathic traits'. Technical language like 'dysregulated', 'overthinking' and 'traumatised' litter these referrals.

Mental health awareness goes on the rampage

In Chapter 4, I discussed 'social looping' and 'concept creep' as two theories that explain the social and cultural mechanisms that encourage expansion of psychiatric diagnoses and mental health concepts more generally. Psychologists Lucy Foulkes and Jack Andrews argue that the increase in mental health problems in young people may be directly caused by greater awareness of mental health ideology creating mental health problems that would otherwise not have existed due to the power of labelling. They write: 'We propose that awareness efforts are leading some individuals to interpret and report milder forms of distress as mental health problems. We propose that this then leads some individuals to experience a genuine increase in symptoms because labelling distress as a mental health problem can affect an individual's self-concept and behaviour in a way that is ultimately self-fulfilling.'[8]

Name it, and it exists. The dangers of the apparently innocent or well-intentioned 'labelling' are not always understood or recognised. A reinforcing loop of 'moral panic' about youth mental health (later expanded to encompass mental well-being) causes problems to inflate themselves. Young people, their parents and teachers are exposed to this, so they start noticing their emotions and behaviours in a new way, searching for signs of this epidemic, having been sensitised to its existence and the importance of early intervention.

According to Canadian research published in 2023, kids – especially teenage girls – are presenting with self-described Tourette's, eating disorders, autism, dissociative identity disorder and other mental disorders in exponentially increasing numbers. This is happening suddenly, and in a way that doesn't match how these diagnoses have previously been identified. In other words, Canadian youngsters are experiencing sudden mass outbreaks of even apparently rare conditions. The authors conclude that identifying with and glamorising certain 'disorders' has become a way for some teenage girls to express negative emotions in a way that, rather than stigmatising them, makes them feel part of a community and even unique and special.[9]

With this type of social contagion what often happens is young people (particularly girls) watch videos (particularly on TikTok) by content creators who self-identify as having these various 'illnesses' (like ADHD). Videos show and describe how the symptoms manifest during everyday activities and how it is an important part of the creator's identity that makes them unique. Then, these youngsters present with the outward symptoms, just as described by the content creator, thus producing sudden outbreaks of a particular condition, or increases of those considered more common (such as ADHD).

I often wonder if we are aware of how our understanding of children, childhood, child development, family life and education has changed as we have succumbed to the 'McDonaldised' notion that the challenges and uncertainties connected with growing up can be placed into neat categories of things 'wrong' with individual children, which can then be fixed with simple, one-size-fits-all interventions.

Children are ultimately dependent on adults to make most decisions on their behalf. But now we have professionalised the process of growing up to such a degree that many parents and other adults in caring positions (such as teachers) are afraid of actively intervening to guide children in their care. They may feel they need that 'expert' to best understand the right thing to do. Others feel judged and embarrassed by their children's behaviour, as parents (particularly mothers) are often blamed for poor parenting with 'tut-tuts' and raised eyebrows, but rarely praised for good parenting. Yet others have been forced to work long hours, leaving little time to be with their family, and often with little support because of diminishing local community and extended family connections.

It's hard to be a 'normal' parent these days. If you are judged too close to your children, you are enmeshed; too distant, you are too cold and don't know how to love your children in the right way. Of course, abuse and harm do happen and being a parent has always been full of worries and conundrums. Whether deliberate or accidental, the anxiety-provoking experience of being a parent has gone through the roof, with much confusion and often little emotional and practical support, particularly for mothers who continue to carry the majority burden for bringing up kids. There is much money to be made from exploiting this anxiety and the inevitable desire parents have to make things better for their kids, as well as to soothe the anxieties they feel.

Children meanwhile are measured, tested, ranked and commented on in schools, sports, social media, and so on, such that they, from a young age, learn that they get value from how they do compared to their peers. Like living in an ongoing *X Factor* contest, they may feel scrutinised for how they perform as individuals, more than how they contribute to the common good or being part of the family and community around them. They may have full timetables and then plenty of distractions such as TV, smartphones, junk food and an array of colourful toys.

It's hard to be a 'normal' kid these days. If you're judged too lively, you're 'hyperactive'; too quiet, you may be 'depressed'; a bit shy, you're probably 'autistic'. Of course, kids do suffer abuse and trauma and communicate this through their behaviour, but, in many Western societies, to be a kid these days is to be closely monitored and scrutinised for your level of performance. When things are judged 'not right' by someone, you can then become exposed to a variety of assessments and procedures to determine what's wrong, broken and dysfunctional in you.

Childhood after the Second World War

Before the onset of the Second World War, Western society tended to view relations between parents and children primarily in terms of discipline and authority. This behavioural approach stressed the importance of forming habits and 'good' behaviours needed for a productive life. After the Second World War, there was concern about the impact on children of discipline and authority. A debate on what caused the nightmare society of Nazi Germany, influenced by the growing respect for psychoanalytic theory, suggested that authoritarian behavioural approaches could cause a person to become aggressive, hostile and murderous.[10]

Professional and scholarly opinions, which spoke about the child as an individual and favoured a more democratic approach to child-rearing, started to percolate. A movement away from harsh towards more humane forms of discipline, through guidance and understanding, gradually became more popular in political circles and everyday culture. In addition, while the pre-war model prepared children for the workplace within a society of limited resources, the post-war years of economic boom meant that children were growing up in a society where pleasure-seeking consumerism was soon to become the new 'normal'.[11]

The post-war 'permissiveness' model saw parent–child relations increasingly in terms of pleasure and play rather than obedience and respect. Parents now had to relinquish traditional authority so that children could develop their own capacity for making choices and to support their sense of self-worth.[12] This cultural shift also meant that, as these post-war children became parents themselves, they too had less of an emphasis on parental duty and responsibility, and wanted opportunities for fuller expression for themselves. Parental obligations were paving the way for the cultural expectation of fun and permissiveness for all.

Changing economic structures also led to important changes in the organisation of family life. More mothers were entering the workforce and a renegotiation of power within the family was taking place. The growth of new suburban communities and the demands of market economies were resulting in greater mobility, less time for the family, and a reduction in geographically connected extended families rooted in community networks. Many families (particularly those headed by young women) became isolated from traditional sources of child-rearing support and information. As a result, various child-rearing guides increased in importance, and child-rearing advice started migrating from being primarily the domain of extended communities and older generations to the professional classes.

The backlash against what was perceived as the culture of permissiveness took place during the 1980s and 90s in the West. It continued to put the individual at the centre, and state support, particularly for children and families, was cut, resulting in widespread child poverty, a situation that was to be replayed after the 2008 financial crash. With this growing sense of insecurity about how best to raise children, parenting advice and interventions became big business. Cloaked in the language of science, ownership of knowledge on how to be a 'good' parent was acquired by the professional classes. There was now a right way to love your child, standards by which children were judged to be correctly developing, and a set of (primarily white Western middle-class) rules that parents, teachers and other adults had to adhere to in order to avoid 'damaging' children. The injunction that childhood should be free from strife and full of fun remained but became harder to achieve. Books and classes on parenting abound and multiple methods for surveillance of our young populations have become institutionalised. In the world of smaller families, less community and extended family support, two working parents – often stressed with keeping a secure source of income – and a high demand on parents to ensure their children have fun, it's not surprising that the professionalisation of parenting results in many parents deciding that engagement with the pains of growing up should be left to experts.[13]

The political and economic self-interest of the medical profession, the pharmaceutical industry, psychologists, therapists and a ragbag of opinion givers have found an ideal set of social preconditions that could be used to promote an ahistorical, culture-blind, individualised, biomedical interpretation of childhood unhappiness and dissatisfaction. This now brings relatively common growing-up experiences previously regarded as ordinary, which children themselves, or their parents, would deal with, into the sphere of medical problems requiring a medical opinion and possibly a medical procedure known as 'treatment'.

Most cultures understand emotional suffering to be part and parcel of what it means to live and develop as human beings. Suffering has the potential to inform and deepen our connection, experience and understanding of human life and resilience. Suffering is thus not something we should assume to be of no value and that we have to find a way to remove.[14] For Buddhists, suffering is understood as a necessary part of the process of enlightenment. In this way, a person cannot escape the confines of their ego without the experience of the mental pain involved in loosening our egoist attachments and egocentric view of the world. But there is money to be made in the infantile fantasy that we can live our lives without suffering.

Just as we socially construct what we consider to be a normal healthy individual and, by implication, what we consider a disordered one looks like, we also socially construct childhood, growing up and what we believe to be good parenting. As with how we construct the self, the choice of construct we use has consequences in what we notice, how we notice and what we then do.

Mental health awareness teaching in schools

For a couple of decades, some sociologists and educationalists have been raising the alarm about the impulse towards what they term 'therapeutic education'.[15] This literature critiques the rise of 'emotional well-being' programmes, teaching about emotions, self-care and resilience in school curricula.[16] Although the focus is more broadly on emotional well-being of all students, rather than those thought to have a mental health problem, teaching about emotions in schools provides a potential backdrop that begins to influence pupils', parents' and teachers' understanding and responses to distress, discomfort and how their pupils 'feel'.

This development has been fuelled by a transition in the view of the self, which detaches the experience of an individual from life events and relational contexts, towards internal issues like how to regulate emotions and develop resilience. Far from such a turn proving to be a liberating one, there is much evidence to suggest it is having the opposite effect.[17]

You cannot detach policy and ideological developments from the nature of, and unwritten rules in, the society that gives birth to it. Whatever benevolent and compassionate impulses it grew out of, it can only generalise and become incorporated into policy if it provides little threat to established power structures. As I have been arguing in this book, the concern with emotions and emotional well-being, when it takes place in a society that has marketised subjectivity, eventually opens up new avenues for commodification (the act of turning something into an item that can be bought and sold).

It should not surprise anyone, therefore, that mental health awareness, mental resilience training and mental health education programmes have been spreading their tentacles throughout the educational sector. Evidence of effectiveness or evaluation of potential harms becomes irrelevant once a product has sufficient brand awareness and enthusiasm and corresponds with the prevailing zeitgeist.

The first large-scale trial to compare a focused classroom-based cognitive behavioural therapy (CBT) programme with usual school provision found no evidence that the intervention reduced depressive symptoms in adolescents considered at high risk of depression. Instead, they found that it may have a harmful effect, with higher rates of depressive symptoms (according to self-rating questionnaires) a year after the intervention.[18] A 2022 review of school-based, CBT-informed, preventive interventions for mental health concluded that they have limited/no efficacy in improving symptoms of anxiety and depression.[19]

In a British study published in 2022 and involving over 8,000 pupils, a school-based mindfulness training (MT) course resulted in worse scores on risk of depression and well-being in students considered at risk of mental health problems, both at post intervention and one year follow-up, compared to those who did not attend the training. The more you received the MT intervention the worse the social, emotional and behavioural functioning was post intervention.[20] Reviews have concluded that there is no evidence that MT improves the mental health of young people, implying that enthusiasm for MT has run ahead of the evidence.[21]

A 2023 published study of over a thousand Australian teenagers found that those who participated in a dialectical behaviour therapy (DBT) group skills training programme at school reported more depression, anxiety, difficulty managing their emotions and worse relationships with their parents than those who didn't.[22] Yet another study, published in 2023, which included over 2,500 Australian teenagers, also found that a CBT-based mental health programme resulted in more distress among the attendees from participating schools than non-participating ones.[23]

Universal prevention of depression and anxiety through school programmes has reached a dead end as the research can't find any positive public health impact.[24]

The enthusiasm for spreading awareness and accompanying services has reached universities in the UK who have ramped up mental health support in response to media pressure and reports of increased student suicide post-Covid. What sort of support do they mean? Anecdotally I've been hearing from friends' children, my children's friends, colleagues' children and emails from therapists aghast at what is happening. There is an influx of students getting ADHD and autism diagnoses, and I feel like having a John McEnroe moment and shouting 'you cannot be serious' for all the good that would do.

The STAR*D trial discussed in Chapter 3 was the largest real-world trial (meaning people already attending medical care) of treatment for depression, where patients could receive between one and four successive treatment steps. If you recall, the STAR*D investigators triumphantly reported that the remission rate was 67 per cent, but reanalysis concluded that the actual figure for those who had enrolled, remitted and then stayed well for one year (the target of the intervention) was 6 per cent.

In this real-world sample, the first episode occurred before the age of eighteen in 37 per cent of cases. Is it possible that creating the idea that young people have a condition called depression, which is the cause of their low mood and which needs treatment (often with medication), leads to this 'depression' becoming chronic?

I think we have put in place all the structures needed to create (not discover) the mental health crisis in the young, and have provided them with an induction period into becoming potential long-term mental health consumers.

What happened to Molly?

This chapter started with an introduction to Molly, who first presented as a twelve-year-old admitted to a paediatric ward after she had stopped eating and drinking. She was withdrawn and closed off from all communication. I mentioned how practice in paediatrics with potential mental health patients has shifted away from open discussion without assumptions towards an expectation that mental health services will take the lead and provide a diagnosis and medication, and, if there is any hint of non-compliance, place the patient under a Mental Health Act to enable involuntary treatment and, if necessary, restraint.

Molly managed to avoid being placed on a Mental Health Act order as I encouraged the staff to proceed with putting her on a drip for dehydration initially and using her father's consent. Molly did not resist. After a couple of days of not eating, I suggested she had a nasogastric tube to allow food to be delivered directly to her stomach. When a nurse explained to Molly that she either has to eat or the nasogastric tube will be passed through her nose and into her stomach, Molly said she would eat. Over the next couple of weeks, she gradually increased the amounts she ate. While still communicating minimally, at least she was now cooperating and regaining her physical health. I did not, then or since, at any time prescribe any medication for her.

The years after that first admission were really difficult for Molly, her family and the professionals involved. When she was finally discharged from hospital, she went to live with her father. Her parents were separated, and she refused to see her mother. Her father, understandably desperate, tried some private therapy for Molly, as well as the ongoing sessions with our service. She continued to be withdrawn, still not attending education, prone to angry outbursts and barely communicated in our sessions beyond occasional nods of the head. Then something changed. It's hard to pinpoint what, or even why, but Molly started talking. In fact, now she wanted to see me on her own.

It was four years since I'd first met her. Molly sat upright in her chair looking to one side. She was ready to explain what had happened. She paused, looked down, then, her fingers nervously playing with each other, began to recount her story.

She told me that things were really unpleasant when she was living at home with both her parents. They used to argue and she would stay out of the way in her bedroom listening to them night after night. Then, one day, her dad just left with little warning. Her mum was distraught, and would tell Molly how unhappy she was. Then her mum tried to kill herself. Molly remembered her drunk mum crying and stuffing a load of pills into her mouth right in front of her.

Molly grabbed the bottle of pills and sat by her bed that night, worrying about what she might do next.

A few weeks after that incident, Molly started feeling stomach pains. She now thinks this was probably because she hadn't eaten for a couple of days with worry that her mum was going to try to kill herself again. The pain got so bad that her mum took her to hospital. Once she was in hospital Molly didn't want to leave. She felt safe and away from the awful situation at home. She did not want to get better. She tried to stay in hospital as long as she could. She refused to go back to living with her mother. Eventually she agreed to move to her dad's house. While she was glad to be with her dad again, she was also angry at him for abandoning her. For the next few years, she oscillated between being angry at him and afraid he would get sick of her and abandon her again. She had not wanted to see her mum until recently when she decided she was ready to make contact. Her mother had been messaging and writing to her, begging to see her throughout the four years.

I asked Molly what had changed, what had made things ease up for her to feel ready now to talk and to re-engage with the social world.

Molly explained that she just got tired of being angry all the time. A few months back there was a particular day when she woke up after a horrible day of anger, her room was a mess, she hadn't washed for a couple of weeks, she felt terrible, had a headache, and said to herself, 'I don't want to go on like this. I don't want this to be my life any more.'

It seems it was as simple as that. A moment in time where, for whatever reason, an emotional switch happened. Something in her mental state just shifted. I saw Molly on and off for another year. By then she was attending an educational establishment, catching up with missed academic work, had a part-time job, had made some friends, was seeing her mum regularly, and was getting on with her life. Her father dropped me a line a couple of years later to tell me that Molly had made it to university. He felt very proud.

I've met many Mollys over the years. People who get stuck in mental health services with therapy, medication, hospital admissions and then, at some point, for some reason, something shifts in their mental outlook. They are ready to recover. Ready to move on. I've never been able to work out when or what the trigger might be that enables them to come out of their mental trap.

Molly taught me the importance of being patient, maintaining hope and being on the lookout for that moment where something is ready to shift. The worst thing you could do is prematurely label someone as having a 'treatment-resistant' or 'chronic' condition and start piling on more diagnoses (things wrong in them) and more aggressive treatments.

10. Conveyor-belt therapy

'The ruling ideas of each age have been the ideas of its ruling class.'

Karl Marx

It took a long and convoluted journey of discovery for me to eventually realise that the research on mental health treatment outcomes pretty much confirms that the active ingredients in successful therapeutic encounters take place in the negotiated space between the person and the therapist/practitioner. One person's definition of trauma is another's normal. There is always potential for hidden misunderstandings and divergent meanings when confronting 'otherness'.

Like many people who decide to work in mental health, I was drawn towards this branch of medicine because of personal historical issues and insecurities, although I wasn't aware at the time how much these may have influenced my choice. I do remember feeling shocked when my therapist used the word 'traumatic' to describe some of my experiences. I had never thought of them in that manner as, to me, they were just my normal. I don't think my therapist realised how perturbing that was.

During my years of training in psychiatry, I was exposed to a variety of psychological and biological explanatory models for what I understood to be mental illness. Yet in my daily practice I could see that the treatments given and services I worked for helped very few people get better and stay better.

After years of trying to find the correct evidence-based model, I eventually came to the realisation that (except for some aspects of psychoanalytic and systemic models) most psychotherapeutic models were just systematised versions of Western 'folk psychology':

variants with a few rules and turns of language to create an aura of cleverness, professionalism and science. From challenging your dysfunctional thinking to facing your fears, from creating a space for unconditional positive regard to dialogical listening, these are all, when put in simpler everyday terms, things we would recognise in everyday culture.

My long search for the holy grail of therapeutic approaches eventually led me to a literature that was never touched upon in all my years of training. I still find it shocking that in my psychiatry and most of my psychotherapy training, this scientific/empirical body of knowledge was hardly ever mentioned. I discovered that there was an ongoing and lively debate in the psychotherapy research literature between the model-specific approaches and the 'common factors' paradigm. The common factors literature emphasises that the ingredients of change are in factors common to all therapy modalities (such as a trusting therapeutic relationship), rather than in the specific psychotherapeutic technique you use.

The first headline from the common factors literature is that the extra-therapeutic aspects – in other words, factors that have little or nothing to do with what directly happens within a therapy session – have a much bigger influence on outcomes than those within treatment. This is the whole range of things that the person walks into the consulting room with. From their personal history to their social, financial, employment, relationship circumstances and beliefs about therapy/treatment. Within therapy, the therapeutic alliance (the quality of the relationship between patient and therapist as judged by the patient) is king/queen.[1]

This means that the models we use need to find a way to connect meaningfully with the people we see. The implications of these findings are that the relationship between treatment models and outcome is not that you should choose the model by the way you categorise the presenting problem, but that the models you construct are the ones that lead to a productive alliance.

Every meeting with a person in therapy is a creative and negotiated encounter with expected and unexpected turns, where curiosity, dealing with your own anxiety as a therapist and being careful not to impose your saviour/hero fantasy onto your patient is important. The therapeutic encounter relies on creating a physical and mental space where you can sit with discomfort and pain. This doesn't mean sessions have to be all doom and gloom. Some of the most effective interventions seem to have been when I am not trying to solve emotional pain, but helping people stay with, accept and, therefore, see aspects of their life beyond the pain they experience. Industrialised therapy seems to me at risk of mechanising emotions by trying to reason and appeal to the patient's rational side. When this doesn't work there is a risk that the patient will, often unintentionally, be blamed for being too stupid/uncooperative/bloody-minded/ill.

In 2007 I attended training with two American psychologists/psychotherapists (Barry Duncan and Scott Miller) who have developed creative ways of building on the common factors perspective.[2] Following this, I, with some local colleagues, developed a project in our child and adolescent mental health service that used a systemic orientation and was built around a therapeutic feedback model rather than diagnostic treatment pathways. For a number of years, we ran a successful service developed around the common factors perspective, which won a number of national awards. We wrote up some of our experiences in an article[3] and a book.[4]

In April 2016 our project came to an end after a new national model for child and adolescent mental health was implemented in services across England and Wales. The new model took us back down the diagnosis route through the requirement for services to implement 'treatment pathways'. If you are diagnosed with 'depression', for example, you go onto the depression pathway which starts with cognitive behaviour therapy, and if the patient doesn't improve you add in an antidepressant, and so on.

A report on the outcomes from the nine pilot sites for this new national model was published in October 2015. The report is seventy-seven pages long and outlines all sorts of wonderful achievements from reducing the number of days between referral and assessment to the number who had been trained in the recommended therapy modalities. On page 57, there is a table showing rates of improvement in the different treatment pathways. According to children's ratings, these ranged from the highest being 31 per cent of patients (for depression) to the lowest being 10 per cent (for separation anxiety). Parents' ratings of improvement in their child ranged from 20 per cent (for social phobia) to 6 per cent (for separation anxiety).[5]

So often it seems policymakers are determined to design services around the ideology of those with power rather than the evidence.

For the few, not the many

Many critiques of mental health models tend to draw a distinction between treatment with medication and treatment with psychotherapy, where I often hear the cliché medication is bad, psychotherapy is good. In this way of thinking, the demand is to reduce reliance on medication and increase the provision of therapy. The complaint to authorities is that they are not funding enough therapy services and, as a result, patients get medication instead of the therapy they need. In this book I have argued that the problems are more foundational. Any model that imagines it has a technical method for correcting/curing/ameliorating 'symptoms' and uses a psychiatric diagnosis as its starting point will share the problems I have outlined thus far. In this chapter I explain why the critiques I am giving extend into the therapy realm too.

As I have discussed, replication of findings is one of the defining hallmarks of the scientific methodology. This process protects against what is known as 'false positives', which is when researchers announce a result that other research teams cannot repeat, suggesting the original finding is unlikely to be a true. Media excitement about this or that study is full of false-positive reports and empty of reporting on studies that fail to replicate the enticing new finding.

Like psychiatry, psychology faces a replication crisis. Many studies in psychology – including famous and highly cited ones – cannot adequately replicate. According to a wide-ranging review, only about a third of the psychological studies in premier psychology journals replicate.[6] One of the issues psychological research encounters is the bias in populations studied. Nearly all psychology research takes place in the developed world of European, North American or Australasian continents. Even in these locations, certain captive populations such as university students account disproportionately for the subjects recruited.

This study population bias means that what we refer to as 'psychology' is, really, the psychology of Western societies and largely Western-educated society. The psychology of those living in a poor Rio de Janeiro slum will have important differences to those living in a predominantly white middle-class suburb of London, who will also have significant differences to those in another London neighbourhood with a large number of Pakistani immigrants.

Psychology is rooted in subjectivity and cannot escape it. While there are several aspects that are more mechanical, such as reflexes, perception and motor control, and thus potentially more amenable to a natural sciences investigative approach, most of our psyche exists in a subjective space that we are not able to tap into by purely objective methods. The research that tries to establish elusive psychological laws is of less interest to me than that which acknowledges and investigates our differences. These differences arise from the multiple sources of subjectivity that may affect us, such as our personal histories, the cultural beliefs we are exposed to and the nature of the socio-economic system we must interact with.

One important differentiator that sociologists and anthropologists point to is the different orientations to self and relationships that collectivist versus individualist positionings encourage. Some classic research touched on broad differences in the way Japanese and Americans tend to perceive the world, including the observation that when American and Japanese participants are asked to take a photo of a person, the Americans most frequently take a close-up, showing all the facial features, while the Japanese were more likely to take a picture that showed the person in his or her environment with the human figure much smaller.[7] This may reflect that Americans are more inclined to attend to some focal object, analysing its attributes and categorising it, whereas Japanese participants are more likely to attend to a broad perceptual and conceptual field, noticing relationships and grouping objects based on family resemblance rather than category membership. Of course, such studies can only show a snap-shot in time (literally!). In this globalised era, cultural influences are in constant motion and, therefore, so is our psychology.

Hence, most of psychology is not reducible to easily quantifiable universals that can be measured with a neutral objective eye. All we can really measure by empirical methods are inputs to the person (various environmental associations that sociologists might study) and outputs from the person (levels of functioning in various spheres). What happens between the input and the output is not revealed through empiricism. You cannot get a proper handle on what is happening in the mind by clever neuroimaging or giving people complicated puzzles to solve. The story of the TV series *Breaking Bad* will not reveal itself by examining the TV hardware for patterns of electric current activity. We cannot measure meaning. Psychology is but one branch of philosophy expounding a particular Western-centric view of the mind.

Emperor of the brands

There are more than five hundred different forms of therapy documented and every year new ones come on stream. Not only has this proliferation of models not resulted in improved outcomes, but studies show that psychotherapy is less effective for those who are poor, have minority status, or are on antidepressants.[8]

The field has been troubled not so much with a replicability crisis, but rather the repeated finding of a lack of progress. Nothing in therapy seems to be getting better. Controlled trials that test efficacy of therapies started using the sort of methodologies we regularly use in research in the 1970s. Studies carried out since then with different therapeutic modalities have not shown improved rates of recovery from treatment. Some comparisons even suggest outcomes from therapy in controlled trials have got slightly worse over time.[9]

Technically, then, as with physical treatments, there is no evidence that the proliferation of psychological techniques to treat mental disorders has resulted in improved outcomes for patients. In most healthcare fields it's possible to see a gradual, and sometimes sudden, improvement in outcomes. Survival rates after heart attacks have been increasing, thanks to better understanding of the physiology, leading to better treatments. Average cancer survival years have improved for most cancers, and vaccination programmes have reduced the prevalence and lethality of many diseases. That's what happens when the technical aspects of care are central to outcomes. As I've discussed, this is because it's possible to build a base of technical knowledge, as 'case-ness' has empirical anchors.

Therapies have hung on the coattails of psychiatric paradigms selling themselves as specific treatments for particular diagnoses. But, as already mentioned, this 'battle of the brands' has not revealed any psychotherapy to be superior to others, with the common factors being far more important than specific therapy ingredients.

This hasn't stopped claims of brand superiority.

Cognitive behavioural therapy (CBT) has emerged as the grand emperor of the psychotherapies. It's regularly touted as the treatment of choice for many conditions and gets top billing in most psychological treatment pathways. Yet when properly controlled studies are done comparing it to other brands of therapy (such as psychodynamic or interpersonal therapy), it fares no better or worse. On top of this, several studies have shown that most of the specific techniques of CBT can be dispensed with, without that affecting the outcomes. In other words, if you take out any one feature of the standard CBT model (for example, a requirement to do certain types of homework), you get the same outcomes as if you had included them.[10]

Its popularity comes from the 'I've got a bigger one than yours' phenomenon that is related to the volume of publications, professional and media attention, and training courses. This has given CBT high visibility as a brand. CBT started gaining ascendancy in the 1970s, when it began displacing the, up until then, more favoured and established psychoanalytic approach to psychotherapy. With its emphasis on thinking patterns, it was easier to research (using questionnaires), and the early CBT researchers developed many of the symptom-based questionnaires for investigating psychiatric conditions' response to treatment that are still in use today. CBT is the ruling psychotherapy brand because of brand profile, not science.

According to a 2022 'umbrella review' of outcome research across psychiatric presentations, after more than half a century of research and thousands of therapy trials, the degree of improvement from psychotherapies and pharmacotherapies for mental disorders are limited, suggesting what the authors call 'a ceiling effect' for treatment. Nothing is better than anything else, nothing is improving over time, and the real-world effects of treatment remain disappointingly small.[11]

Although some studies have found that outcomes for therapy in some clinical settings are comparable to those found in research projects, most have not. Those who have examined outcomes for patients who are accessing treatments from standard community mental health services, who will thus be subject to all the medicalising tendencies I have discussed, have found their outcomes to be very poor indeed. The unacceptable picture that emerges when we look at patients attending such services is that only 15–25 per cent report ongoing clinical improvement.[12]

In child and adolescent mental health some evidence suggests even larger differences in outcomes between research and clinical practice, with some studies finding that there isn't even a short-term difference between those with a similar level of distress (according to a rating questionnaire) who attend a service and those who don't. Other studies suggest that those who stay with the service longer may have worse outcomes than those who don't.[13]

The paradigm of diagnosis followed by a standardised 'treatment pathway' simply replicates and embeds the belief that we have a technology that accurately categorises patients' complaints and that this will lead to knowing what specific corrective will work. It is this surgical model that dominates and renders people passive recipients of a fantasy of skilled expert intervention. By surgical I mean that the human factors, like a good alliance between patient and therapist, are the anaesthetic to render the patient under your spell, so that you can 'get in there' with the right therapy brand and excise or manipulate the malfunctioning thoughts or feelings. This type of disempowerment often creates long-term patients.

Industrialised therapy

In response to this idea of needing to supply more therapy provision in order to improve mental health outcomes, some governments have set out to scale up the delivery of psychotherapy services.

In 2007, the UK government embarked on such a project, to provide better support for people with conditions such as anxiety and depression. The project, called Improving Access to Psychological Therapies (IAPT), planned to dramatically increase access to talking therapies with the aim of decreasing waiting times and allowing more people with common mental health problems to recover. IAPT (now rebranded as the 'NHS Talking Therapies Programme') has gone from strength to strength, expanding year after year from around 880,000 referrals in 2011 to 1.8 million in 2023.[14] However, from the start, IAPT has come with considerable baggage in terms of both ideology and results. Its mixed reputation has not dented its continued expansion, though.

IAPT makes the same mistake of valorising the technical aspects over the human ones. Thus, certain therapies, particularly CBT, are fetishised and make up the bulk of what is delivered by IAPT using a standard diagnostic treatment pathway, mainly for 'depression' and 'anxiety'.

IAPT's origins are political. The economist Lord Layard was commissioned to produce a report on how mental health affects the economy. He concluded that common conditions such as anxiety and depression result in significant loss of productivity through days lost by sickness. Layard believed that scaling up treatments for these conditions would lead to more people returning to work resulting in increased national productivity, thereby more than paying back the government's considerable investment in a treatment service.

In this way, some of the problems of the economy can be magicked away by treating ill people as if anxiety and depression were just like other diseases and could be tackled by applying the correct treatment. Whatever the social origins of many people's mental distress (for example, poor housing or chronic job insecurity) now becomes an individual illness to be remedied by manipulating the diseased mind.

You can see why the alert politician would like this. It shows care and sympathy, at the same time as changing the focus from social change to individual rehabilitation. It shifts policy from the sociopolitical space (where it is a public and collective problem) to a mental space (a private and individualised problem).[15]

The result is an upside-down strategy to improving well-being where Lord Layard opined that in Britain mental illness has now taken over from unemployment as our greatest social problem. To great fanfare, IAPT was commissioned and Britain boasted that it was the first country in the world to take the idea of widespread and free public access to talking therapies seriously.

The NHS set a target recovery rate of 50 per cent for those who engage in treatment, and miraculously the average recovery rate in 2021/22 was 50.2 per cent (although according to their own figures, recovery from the lowest 10 per cent income group was 42 per cent).

These figures don't tell the full story. The first independent evaluation of the initial IAPT pilot sites found little difference between the IAPT sites and comparator services, but IAPT treatments had cost more per patient than those provided in neighbouring boroughs.[16] The published recovery rates also hide low staff morale, low patient satisfaction, aggressive target-driven management and high dropout rates.[17] But it may be even worse than that.

A paper published in 2018 described a detailed evaluation of ninety patients who had been discharged after being seen by IAPT, allowing comparison of IAPT's data for these patients with other indicators. IAPT's data claimed 44 per cent of these patients were 'moving to recovery'. Local GP data revealed a recovery rate of 23 per cent in this group, whereas the authors' own study found that only 9.2 per cent of these post-IAPT clients could be regarded as recovered when using a more in-depth standardised semi-structured interview. The researcher also documented the patients' accounts of their interaction with IAPT, which supported the impression that the treatments they were offered made little real-world difference to their problems.[18]

Like other mainstream mental health services, IAPT fails to improve outcomes.

But perhaps IAPT has helped reduce use of medication by providing improved access to talking therapies? Again, the answer is 'it hasn't'. Prescriptions for antidepressants have continued to rise with little evidence that introducing IAPT has had any meaningful impact on these trajectories. In the years since IAPT's national implementation, prescriptions for antidepressants have risen steadily. Access to IAPT is not associated with the extent of antidepressant prescribing, with availability of IAPT services having no impact on the continuous increase in antidepressant prescribing rates.[19] Between 2016 and 2022 antidepressant prescribing increased by 34.8 per cent, with 14.7 per cent of the population in England receiving at least one antidepressant prescription in 2022.[20] It's likely that many of those referred to IAPT end up being prescribed an antidepressant after getting minimal benefit, meaning that one outcome of IAPT may simply be the enlargement of the pool of those considered to have a mental disorder.

The children and young people's version of IAPT, introduced to child and adolescent mental health services in England and Wales in 2016, fared no better,[21] despite understandable attempts by the developers to argue otherwise.[22] Scaling up the provision of psychotherapy for the 'masses' becomes just another cog in the expanding MHIC.

Western folk psychology

The most commonly used therapies are simply versions of Western folk psychology.

Take the emperor of the therapies, CBT. Google CBT and you get something fancy-sounding, like CBT helps make the links between thoughts, emotions and behaviour, or how it helps patients to develop more adaptive cognitions and behaviours, or sometimes the more enticing-sounding 'reprogramming' the way you think and therefore feel and behave. CBT basically focuses on thinking patterns and patients are encouraged to analyse how their thinking affects their feelings and then behaviour. It looks for examples of 'dysfunctional' thoughts that result in the patient feeling worse and then behaving in a way that doesn't help them feel better. If you're depressed, you think about how bad things are and notice things that go wrong and interpret most things in the negative, which confirms how bad you feel, and so you feel hopeless, and because you feel hopeless you don't do things that might make you feel better, like going out and meeting friends.

Take away all the scientific-sounding language and rituals, and it boils down to 'stop focusing on the negatives'. More than that, it views emotions as something suspect, promoting a rational/logical approach to controlling and managing them. Improving your thinking and logic is how you regain control of those pesky irrational emotions. This logic-over-emotions framework is central to a dominant strand in Western post-enlightenment philosophy. It also has a managerial flavour to it, with the idea of analysing the components of the problem (the thoughts) and using logic to apply a better thought to the situation.

Now there is nothing wrong per se with CBT. Like I said, the evidence shows that it fares no better or worse than other therapies. But there is nothing more to it than a 'tarted up' form of Western common sense, particularly managerial common sense.

Take another popular example – behaviour therapy (BT). Like CBT, versions of it exist for most psychiatric conditions. If you have a phobia of dogs, for example, then two forms of BT could be used. One is called 'graded desensitisation' and involves exposing the person to things to do with dogs in gradual steps. You could start perhaps with images, then toy dogs, then looking at a dog at a distance, then closer, until you first stroke a small placid dog, etc. Each step in the treatment gets closer and closer to the feared object, so that you gradually acclimatise. The other approach is called 'flooding'. In flooding you essentially go for it all in one go, exposing the person to the feared object (in this case, a dog) and supporting them to stay around the dog for as long as it takes for their fear level to come down. BT, in a nutshell, is a treatment that is no deeper than the common phrase 'face your fears'.

Counselling involves empathic listening. Many therapies have an idea of catharsis — an extension of the confessional. I'm sure most readers will be aware of another common expression, 'a problem shared is a problem halved'. I fully appreciate the value of having someone external to your social circle to talk to, but there is no great technical innovation behind that. Stripped down to their essentials, our most used therapies contain nothing special. It's therefore not surprising that in these days of mass therapy we are seeing no breakthroughs that radically change outcomes.

This brings me to mindfulness. Mindfulness is everywhere now — in schools, therapies, mental health services, at gyms, in workplace mental well-being projects, and so on. Many assume this to be an example of a psychotherapeutic approach that comes from Eastern not Western philosophy. In mindfulness the person is encouraged to focus on fully attending to the here and now and to put some brakes on thinking. It is claimed, by its advocates, to have been researched and found to be effective and revolutionary.

Anything that offers success in our unjust society without trying to change it is not revolutionary. It may help some people to cope, but it could also accidentally make things worse for others (as I discussed in the last chapter in relation to schoolchildren). Mindfulness implicitly says the causes of suffering are disproportionately inside us and so joins the market of mind fixers, feeding the beast that implores us to accept that we are dysfunctional in the way we react to our circumstances.

It isn't that mindfulness practice can't help some. Tuning out of mental rumination can help reduce stress and allow people to feel calmer and potentially kinder. However, in mindfulness we see what happens when ideas that come from another culture are expropriated. Mindfulness is derived from Eastern spiritual practice and Buddhism in particular. It has, however, been stripped of the teachings on ethics, philosophy and spirituality. The original aim of Eastern spiritual practice is dissolving attachment to a false sense of self and gaining awareness of the unity and interconnectedness of all things. Meditation is but one component of a set of practices that aims to diminish the ego and decentre the importance of the individual. It teaches humility, not self-love.

In its Western therapeutic form, mindfulness has been extracted from its origins, given a label to enable branding, and packaged into a discreet easily digestible 'McDonaldised' form. It then becomes a marketised commodity promising the individual consumer that this will make them feel better. In this form it's consumed to nourish the ego and enhance the individual's self-care.

By practising mindfulness, individual freedom is supposedly found within 'pure awareness', undistracted by external corrupting influences. All we need to do is close our eyes and watch our breath. With the retreat to the private sphere, mindfulness becomes a religion of the self. Rather than the holistic ideal of expanding our sense of connection to the world we are embedded in, the Western version perpetuates a Western folk psychology paradigm by focusing on the free-standing individual in a depoliticised world.

The term 'McMindfulness' was coined by Miles Neale, a Buddhist teacher and therapist, who described a feeding frenzy of spiritual practices that provide immediate nutrition but no long-term sustenance. The individualistic spirituality it promotes links nicely to the capitalist agenda of privatisation, especially when masked by the exclusive and mystical language used in the mindfulness literature. Mindfulness then becomes a tool for domesticating unhappy workers and convincing them that their suffering is coming from within and not from an external context and system that produces suffering.[23]

According to research, is mindfulness any better than other therapies, or does it improve outcomes when added as a component of other therapies (such as CBT)? No and no.[24]

Psychiatry and psychology are branches of philosophy

Philosophy is defined as the study of general and fundamental questions about existence, knowledge, values, reason, mind and language. Is that not a reasonable definition of what those of us who work in the mental health field engage in when we encounter a person experiencing mental distress or behavioural change? Given that we have no technical advances that enable us to see the mechanics of the mind at work and so we cannot empirically capture anything that happens between input (environmental stimuli) and output (behaviour and functioning), then all we have is interpretation. All we have are meaning-making frameworks. Therefore, the most appropriate way to think about what we do as mental health practitioners is, in my opinion, that we act as philosophical guides.

The common philosophical systems we use like CBT, medical model and mindfulness are derivations of Western folk psychologies loaded with that philosophy's assumptions, such as individualisation, rationalisation, suspicion of emotions and the need to control emotions. These approaches shape the research conducted and the therapies we provide. They are seamlessly incorporated into a commodity-driven market economy.

I am referring to most psychotherapies. Not all of the philosophical systems we use therapeutically conform to the McDonaldised versions I've described.

Psychoanalytic approaches have delved into the human psyche exposing the great dramas at play in the universe beyond our everyday consciousness. Psychoanalytic thinking has influenced our culture, sensitising us to layers of meaning that can develop as our animal instinctive selves clash with the restraints imposed by our civilisations, often through the medium of our caregivers, giving rise to internal conflicts and tensions.

These deeper layers of meaning are revealed through the language we use, the night and day dreams we have, and the slips of the tongue we make. Our early relationships and our personal interpretation of these early relationships create a 'blueprint' that sits beyond our daily consciousness, but subsequently structure our feelings towards others and thus our thoughts and behaviours. Therapy involves a deep awareness of how these interpersonal dramas present from infancy, keep repeating themselves in subsequent relationships, including the relationship with the therapist. As a philosophical model the work is slow, possibly punctuated by epiphanies (many can be false epiphanies), involving a 'working through' of these conflicts to develop a better insight that allows you to have more sustaining relationships. Where I might fall out with some psychoanalysts is that, like everyone else, they have no special access to the inner workings of the mind. It is a philosophy like any other, albeit a more interesting one than the Western folk psychology versions.

The other area of theory that has gone beyond folk psychology is systemic philosophy. Starting in the late 1950s and influenced by anthropology, systemic theories placed the human subject in a nexus of surrounding relationships in families, communities and societies. Influenced by several philosophical positions including social constructionism, Marxism and postmodernism, it spurred on several therapy models that considered the influence of power, gender, race, sexuality and politics more broadly.

It suggested that the systems of knowledge we use are relative and arise from those who have the power in any society to influence the common social narratives. It understood that our consciousness and even 'common sense' are products of our social and personal circumstances, from our family to wider community histories and practices. This means we have finite ways of making sense of our experiences, through using the stories our families and broader culture provide as meaning-making vehicles.

Such a philosophical stance resonates strongly for me, with my understanding of the evidence and an ethic that seems humane and capable of sitting with difference. In this way of imagining, treatment may involve helping patients look beyond a consumerist model of care or cure that may inadvertently trap them in patient-hood. It also sensitises practitioners to helping patients locate the ills as being external to them and encourages the involvement of a social network to help support improvement.

I have no evidence to suggest any of my preferred philosophies improve outcomes more than others. Unfortunately, systemic theory has itself been branded into 'family therapy' or 'systemic therapy' and particular trainings that produce 'family therapists' who then set up family therapy clinics. Patients then get offered family therapy as a brand in the same way they might be offered CBT. Branded 'family therapy' does no better or worse in research than other branded therapies.

A market economy requires ongoing selling to sustain itself. It needs consumers to feel a bit better, but not in a sustained way, so that they keep coming back for more. Western folk therapies do this function well. The market in medications, psychotherapies and wellness products continues to expand without evidence of population-wide mental health improvements as a result. This is perfect for profit extraction. It is the territory of MHIC.

11. The mental health industrial complex (MHIC)

> 'I'm running low on serotonin. Chemical imbalance got me twisting things. Stabilize with medicine.'
>
> From 'Serotonin', song by Girl in Red

Here's a snapshot of the sort of conversations happening in clinics these days that I cannot recall ever happening in my early years of being a child and adolescent psychiatrist.

Fourteen-year-old Sam's mother: 'I think Sam needs medication. I'm pretty sure he has some sort of chemical imbalance. I take an antidepressant and so does Sam's dad, it's probably genetic and that's what he needs.'

Fourteen-year-old Sam: 'Yes, I can literally feel the chemicals in my head going down. I know when I'm starting to get depressed again.'

Sixteen-year-old Lucy's mother: 'She needs to get her moods under control – one minute she's as high as a kite laughing and joking around, then minutes later she'll crash, go to her bedroom and will be moody the rest of the day.'

Sixteen-year-old Lucy: 'I've looked this up. I'm pretty sure I've got bipolar disorder and need a "mood stabiliser" to help me. My friends are on medication, and they're surprised when they hear I haven't been prescribed anything.'

Fifteen-year-old Jack's father: 'What we want to work out is whether his checking behaviours are because of his autism or because he has OCD, or is it just because he's stressed?'

★

Seventeen-year-old Jade's mother: 'I know she has autism, ADHD, depression and anxiety, but I don't think that's all that's wrong with her. There's something more. Something deeper. Maybe she has some sort of personality disorder.'

Common team case discussion scenario: 'He was quite hard to engage. I think he may have some neurodiversity, maybe autistic traits or perhaps even autism.'

At a teaching session with GPs, I ask what they say to people when they're thinking of prescribing an antidepressant. Most respond by saying they explain to patients that they have low serotonin, and the medication will boost this and so make them feel better. None said they would mention that antidepressants can be dependency-forming. In teaching with psychiatric trainees, I find a similar response.

An immigrant doctor who completed their training outside the UK was referred to the regional trainee support service after he failed the first of the Royal College of Psychiatrists membership exams on several occasions. He was given a 'specific learning difficulty' diagnosis. I later hear of other doctors who get a similar label and an increasing number of doctors being diagnosed with ADHD and who should be considered 'neurodivergent'.

A patient information leaflet on 'antidepressants' produced by a British NHS mental health trust, and passed anonymously to me, includes in the blurb: 'It can sometimes take weeks, months or even years, to get the right medicine at the right dose for you. Think of it as a bit like dating. Some make you feel sick or sleepy; some are great to start with but wear off; others may not be much to start with but after a while grow on you. Then you might have found the one that makes you feel good long-term. So don't lose hope if the first one doesn't work.'

A Google search on what causes depression finds that most websites, particularly American ones, allude to neurotransmitters and brain differences and suggest that antidepressants act by improving abnormally low chemicals: 'Low levels of serotonin are linked to depression. The most commonly used antidepressants, the selective serotonin reuptake inhibitors (SSRIs) and serotonin and norepinephrine reuptake inhibitors (SNRIs), work by increasing serotonin levels in the brain.'[1]

I am writing these paragraphs in 2024. The chemical imbalance theory and belief in a chemical cure is alive and thriving.

We are now dabbling more seriously in the slimy swamps of our political systems. We've seen how little evidence exists to support the dominant ways in which mental health and illness are discussed in our societies, so it's time to 'get down and dirty' and wrestle with the forces that shape our understanding of mental life and its relation to how an economy should operate. In the next few chapters, I will deal with mental health as part of an economic system, the role mental health plays in shifting political discourse towards identity and culture wars, the capitalist model of what it means to be human, and the racist and colonial nature of MHIC. In this chapter, I will discuss some of the social drivers (such as the myth of the chemical imbalance) that allowed the dominant ideas we have about what mental disorder/illness is to spread and become popularised.

The myth of the chemical imbalance

In her 2007 book *The Myth of the Chemical Cure*, professor of psychiatry Joanna Moncrieff examines the rise in popularity of psychiatric medications. Moncrieff reviews available research, describing how flawed science and aggressive marketing has resulted in a marked increase in psychiatric drug prescribing, despite the absence of evidence that this has led to sustained benefits. One mechanism that enables this rise is the creation and subsequent popularisation of the idea that psychiatric drugs work by correcting a chemical imbalance – the creation of the 'myth of the chemical cure'.[2]

Moncrieff contrasts two frameworks for making sense of the

actions of psychiatric drugs. In the first, the 'disease-centred' model, the medication is assumed to work by targeting an underlying disease or abnormality – in other words by correcting an assumed chemical imbalance – and therefore restoring normal function. This is the model that has been popularised. Calling the chemicals we use antidepressants, antipsychotics, mood stabilisers, and so on, assumes that they work in a disease-specific corrective manner.

Moncrieff carefully sifts through the evidence and concludes that there is no evidence to support that depression, anxiety, any of the other common psychiatric presentations, or even psychosis, are associated with any specific lack or excess of a neurotransmitter. Psychiatric medications therefore cannot correct a non-existent imbalance. But they clearly do something and affect how people feel. All of them can produce physiological withdrawal symptoms if a person stops abruptly once they have been taking them for long enough, therefore they are influencing the nervous system in some way.

The second framework, and the one that accords with the evidence, she labels as the 'drug-centred' model. This is what happens with all substances that effect neurotransmitters in the brain, whether prescribed by a doctor or bought for recreational purposes. They exert generic psychoactive (mind-altering) effects in everyone regardless of whether or not they have a psychiatric diagnosis. These effects can interact with experiences of mental distress. For example, so-called antipsychotic drugs dampen down thinking processes and emotions because they have a generalised inhibiting effect on the nervous system. This is what appears to reduce psychotic symptoms, not the targeted reversal of underlying chemical imbalances.

Just as alcohol can cause some social disinhibition whether you are socially anxious or not, antidepressants can produce a low level of emotional blunting (a kind of 'I don't care' feeling) in whoever takes them regardless of diagnosis. Calling drugs antipsychotics or antidepressants is a marketing not a scientific/therapeutic term. Antipsychotics should be called 'neuroleptics' (inhibiting the nervous system) and antidepressants by their subcategory action (such as selective serotonin reuptake inhibitors or serotonin and norepinephrine reuptake inhibitors).

But in everyday life we refer to them as antidepressants, or antipsychotics, or mood stabilisers, or anxiolytics, or anti-ADHD medication. This is a sure sign that marketing not science is dictating the concepts used in practice and in the language that has since leaked out into culture. Psychiatric brands are ripe for exploitation and profit extraction, and the chemical imbalance story is ideal for medicalisation of mood, distress, difference, and the sort of widespread insecurities so many feel these days.

The serotonin story

In surveys, 85 to 90 per cent of people in Western countries report believing that depression is caused by a chemical imbalance.[3] This rests on the hypothesis that depression is caused by a lack of the neurotransmitter serotonin in the brain.

The SSRI class of 'antidepressants' have been massive profit-makers for pharmaceutical companies. They are marketed as correctives – a bit like insulin for diabetes – replenishing the brain of its deficiency in serotonin. The theory is even compatible with psychosocial causation, by arguing that stress causes the brain to use up serotonin, leading to depression.

In textbooks and journal articles, the idea of low serotonin is widespread and remains so.[4] The American Psychiatric Association continues to tell the public that 'differences in certain chemicals in the brain may contribute to symptoms of depression'.[5]

Moncrieff re-enters our chemical imbalance story in 2022. Together with several colleagues, she authors an important paper entitled 'The serotonin theory of depression: a systematic umbrella review of the evidence'. This review of all the research ever published on the link between serotonin levels in the brain and depression, concludes that there is 'no consistent evidence of there being an association between serotonin and depression, and no support for the hypothesis that depression is caused by lowered serotonin activity or concentrations. Some evidence was consistent with the possibility that long-term antidepressant use reduces serotonin concentration'.[6]

In other words, after decades of research, there is only evidence that serotonin imbalance can be caused, not corrected, by antidepressants.

This paper caused an uproar. Within a few months of publication, it became one of the most cited research papers in history, in the top 200 out of over 23 million. Pundits on various talk shows and podcasts responded with phrases like 'this has blown my mind'. So deep was the assumption that depression is caused by a chemical imbalance that can be treated with drugs that this finding seemed extraordinary.

The mainstream psychiatric establishment was rattled. One expert after another, many of them with long-standing ties to the pharmaceutical industry, came out with a variety of often contradictory critiques, essentially shrugging off the finding by saying things like 'I don't think I've ever met any serious scientists or psychiatrists who think that all cases of depression are caused by a simple chemical imbalance of serotonin', and arguing for more complex biological theories that are impossible to test. Others complained that it was premature to give up on the serotonin theory.[7]

Moncrieff and her co-authors responded comprehensively to the wave of establishment criticisms.[8] The psychiatrists who dismissed the paper had complained that this could lead to people rejecting an important treatment. However, there is a potential negative impact on patients of spreading the chemical imbalance myth. This narrative encourages people to take antidepressants, because why wouldn't they if they've been told it reverses an underlying chemical problem?

According to research, believing that one's depression is caused by a chemical imbalance tends to make people more pessimistic about recovery, leads them to believe they have less ability to deal with their moods, and to believe that medication is a more credible solution than therapy.[9] Those who believe this disease theory of depression also have poorer recovery rates than those who don't.[10] In all countries where antidepressant prescriptions are rising, there is a simultaneous rise in numbers receiving some type of disability allowance due to a mental health problem.[11] It was 2011 in the UK when disability benefits for mental health problems overtook all other reasons (which were declining), with depression being the most common reason within the mental health category.[12]

One legitimate argument is that it doesn't matter whether or not antidepressants correct a chemical imbalance, if they work. Unfortunately, the evidence to support that is weak. When you look at all the trials together, they show that antidepressants are a tiny bit better than a placebo (an inactive sugar pill), but not by much.[13] In fact, it's not even certain that this tiny difference is related to antidepressant superiority, because there are methodological problems with most studies that may explain this small difference between drugs and placebos.[14] In one trial in which all the patients were given an antidepressant, but half were told that it was a placebo and half told the truth (that it was an antidepressant), those who were told that they had received the antidepressant showed twice the change in anxiety and depression scores compared to those who believed they had received the placebo. Expectations have powerful effects on outcomes.[15] Furthermore, a review of 131 randomised placebo-controlled trials concluded that antidepressants increase the response by 12 per cent compared with placebo, but also increase the risk of serious adverse events by 37 per cent, suggesting an unfavourable benefit to harm ratio.[16]

Antidepressants are widely recognised to cause some numbing of emotions; not just sadness and anxiety but all emotions, including happiness and joy.[17] Numbing emotions is also likely to reduce depression scores on questionnaires, and it may be experienced as useful by someone with distress. But it may also lead to neglecting important tasks (like paying the bills) and the motivation to do certain things that might otherwise help with feeling more connected to others and engaged with the world around you.

Most trials are conducted by drug companies, and it has long been established that drug company-funded trials report more favourable results for their drug than non-industry-sponsored trials. They often use methodology and reporting that favour a medication effect.

Australian child psychiatrist Jon Jureidini has been investigating this topic for many years. Back in 2004, he, with colleagues, first noticed that careful reading of the published trials claiming that antidepressants were effective and safe in young people didn't quite stack up.[18] They found that young people prescribed an antidepressant were twice as likely to experience suicidal feelings as those taking a placebo and did not show significant improvements in their depression questionnaire scores compared to the placebo. Despite this now well-known finding, prescribing rates for the young continued to rise.[19]

In 2013 Peter Doshi and colleagues set up the Restoring Invisible and Abandoned Trials (RIAT) initiative.[20] They invited researchers to reanalyse published trials or restore abandoned or unpublished trials (it's common for drug companies to simply abandon or not publish unfavourable trials if they can't spin the results).

One of the first RIAT publications, which included Dr Jureidini as one of the co-authors, was on a study by SmithKline Beecham on the efficacy and safety of the SSRI antidepressant paroxetine for adolescents with depression. The original study had concluded that paroxetine was both safe and effective. This was one of those key early studies that convinced the medical community and public that SSRI antidepressants could be used in the under eighteens. Jureidini and colleagues managed to get hold of about 77,000 pages of de-identified individual case report forms and all the associated data from the original trial. Their reanalysis found a very different picture to those in the published articles. They concluded that paroxetine had no benefits over placebo, and there was an increase in harms, including suicidal ideation and behaviour.[21]

Many years before RIAT got going as a concept, Dr Jureidini had approached me to ask if I wanted to join a team reanalysing some data they had from another of those early influential studies that encouraged the prescribing of antidepressants to the young – the Treatment of Adolescents with Depression Study (TADS).[22] The data we had was difficult to organise and interpret, but we were also lacking some key documents, such as the original study reports. Original documents used in a study enable you to match the scoring made by the investigators to what was said in the actual interviews with patients by the researchers. We couldn't make any progress with a meaningful analysis based on what we had at this stage.

After the publication of their RIAT trial of paroxetine discussed above, Jureidini approached me again to say the team were going to have another go at reanalysing TADS. We particularly wanted to examine the reporting on harms, which remained unclear despite more than thirty publications by the TADS team. Jureidini and colleagues kept trying to get the original data set, but the TADS author group dragged their feet, giving one reason after another as to why they couldn't release the original data. Jureidini and a colleague wrote a paper about their experience of trying, unsuccessfully, to complete a RIAT study on TADS, concluding: 'our unsuccessful efforts to obtain more detailed side and adverse effects data from TADS' data custodians, highlights several problematic blocks to comprehensive safety reporting'.[23]

RIAT for antidepressants in youth wasn't finished with just yet, though. In 2022 two prominent medical researchers, Peter Gøtzsche and David Healy, published a RIAT study on the SSRI fluoxetine in young people. They reanalysed the first two studies on SSRIs in under eighteens, which was with fluoxetine (the drug with the commonly known brand name of Prozac). These formed the basis for the first approval of an SSRI for depression in children and adolescents. Fluoxetine remains the one (antidepressant) that is said to be safe and effective in young people, even in countries that are more cautious about using SSRIs in this age group. Gøtzsche and Healy drew different conclusions to the original papers: 'Our reanalysis of the two pivotal trials showed that fluoxetine is unsafe and ineffective.' Suicidality or violence occurred more often on fluoxetine than on placebo. Fluoxetine was also found to be associated with reduced height and weight over nineteen weeks by 1cm and 1.1kg respectively, and to have prolonged the QT interval on heart tracings (this can cause fainting or even seizures).[24]

Every aspect of the chemical imbalance story unravels when properly scrutinised. It is another remarkable example of the marketing and propaganda power of MHIC.

The firm

I first met Professor Peter Gøtzsche in March 2015 when we both spoke in favour of the motion 'This house believes that the long-term use of psychiatric medications is causing more harm than good', at the 52nd Maudsley Debate in London.[25]

Gøtzsche was one of the co-founding members of the Cochrane Collaboration, formed in 1993 to organise medical research findings and facilitate evidence-based choices about health interventions. It quickly became one of the most important innovations in evidence-based medicine and Gøtzsche one of its most productive members. Something of a celebrity in the world of medical statistics and analysis, he has published in all the leading medical journals, and found himself on the front page of papers such as the *New York Times* with his work on mammography. He became a byword for the importance of rigorous methodology and a fierce crusader against medical practices that failed to demonstrate adequate evidence of benefits over harms. This would soon earn him many enemies among pharmaceutical companies, some senior academics, and eventually even in the hierarchy of Cochrane.

In his award-winning 2013 book *Deadly Medicines and Organised Crime: How Big Pharma Has Corrupted Healthcare*, Gøtzsche argues that the way drug companies operate is akin to organised crime syndicates. He shows how major pharmaceutical companies have been repeatedly convicted of marketing harmful (often fatal) drugs, price manipulation and concealment of evidence.[26] The billions of dollars in fines levied against them for these offences pale in comparison to the profits they continue to make, so for them these convictions are just part of the realities of doing business. His book describes substantial flaws in the way that medical evidence is produced, and how it has become worse over recent decades because of more commercially oriented drug-approval policies implemented with the intent of reducing delay in drugs coming on the market.

In this book, Gøtzsche begins a critique of psychiatric drugs that would soon earn him the ire of the psychiatric establishment and the eventually successful campaign to get him removed from the organisation he helped create – the Cochrane Collaboration (now renamed as 'Cochrane').[27] He shows how psychiatry has developed into what he characterises as an unscientific drug-pushing branch of medicine, using drugs with poor evidence of effectiveness while ignoring side effects and the difficulties patients have in withdrawing from them.

In his next book, *Deadly Psychiatry and Organised Denial*, published in 2015, Gøtzsche turns his critical eye on the psychiatric establishment. He critiques the rise of the chemical imbalance theory and argues that psychiatry has created a world full of erroneous ideas based on poor science and pseudoscience.[28]

Partners of the firm

In their 2015 book *Psychiatry Under the Influence*, Robert Whitaker and Lisa Cosgrove document how institutional self-interest in the form of conflicts of interest and the influence of big money from big pharma, decisively and irreversibly compromised the ability of the American Psychiatric Association (APA) to support and promote the health and well-being of patients.[29] Without the willing support of the APA, the promotion of psychiatric drugs, encouraged by the drug companies, could not have succeeded.

Whitaker and Cosgrove emphasise how contextual and systemic explanations, rather than bad actors and characters, play a decisive role. This is not a conspiracy theory but a description of how mutual interests, with money and cultural power, work together and, in doing so, create a system that perpetuates and enhances those interests. The APA working in tandem with pharmaceutical companies selects research and researchers and promotes those who go on to become regarded as 'opinion leaders'. Opinion leaders, through acting as consultants to drug companies, find that their portfolio of publications grows, enabling them to apply for the top university academic posts. Not only do they get substantial income directly from the drug companies, but they also bring income to the universities through attracting grants, research money and donations from these companies. What do the drug companies get in return? The best marketing campaigns they could wish for, fronted by an expert who has the aura of science and the prestige that comes from their high academic status.

As Gøtzsche's work shows, drug companies' pernicious influence on health care is not limited to psychiatry. Psychiatry, however, is particularly vulnerable. As I have described earlier in this book, in most other medical specialties, the majority of diagnoses have empirical anchors to help define case-ness. This means that treatment outcomes can be more easily quantified. Does a treatment reduce the size of a tumour, lower blood pressure, decrease blood sugar or resolve inflammation? In psychiatry, though, we don't know how to identify case-ness using any biological markers and so rely on the subjectivity of both the patient and the person providing the diagnosis. Manipulating data is much easier when the end points you are measuring are essentially consumer questionnaires. And when that doesn't deliver, you also have the power to shape what gets heard and what doesn't.

For example, Whitaker and Cosgrove discuss how thirty-one studies for four drugs (Celexa, Paxil, Prozac and Zoloft) were registered with the regulators in the US – the Food and Drug Administration (FDA). Only fourteen of the studies produced a positive result in favour of the drugs. However, the published literature related to those thirty-one studies told of nineteen positive outcomes (positive results can lead to more than one article published about the same study) and two negative ones. This is just the tip of the iceberg. Ghostwritten papers from post-marketing studies fill psychiatric journals, regularly telling of a drug's efficacy.[30] A merry-go-round of personnel moving employment from drug companies to the regulators and vice versa, an industry of journals set up to create more opportunities to publish papers, and pharmaceutical companies sponsoring scientific symposia all add to the marketing machine.

Before drugs are brought to market they undergo clinical trials, in which psychiatrists are lead authors. These researchers receive generous grants from public bodies and drug companies. The resulting articles are published in medical journals, sometimes in drug-industry-funded ones. After publication, opinion leader psychiatrists hold news conferences, and appear on the front page of *The Times* or the cover of *Newsweek* extolling the merits of the new 'wonder' drug. Others conduct continuing education programmes about this medication and give lectures at conferences. Drug reps provide free samples to physicians. Drug advertising floods the airwaves. Drawbacks, harms and efficacy blemishes are hidden or minimised, and the drug's supposed potency becomes fact.

Now the latest miracle drug has found its way onto the doctor's prescription pad. The doctor on the front line doesn't really know the efficacy and safety profile, just what they've heard from the drug rep or from the lecture they've just attended by a leading academic expert. Patients read articles, see news reports or direct-to-consumer advertising, and ask their doctor for the latest 'breakthrough' drug. To expand the market for this new drug an educational effort is made to increase 'awareness' of some unheard-of diagnosis or to insist that well-known ones are being under-diagnosed and under-treated.

Drug companies are big players in the stocks and shares market, and thus important in maintaining the structural edifice of financial institutions. The lobbying power this gives them, together with the ease with which 'mental health' can be incorporated as part of a government 'caring' agenda, has combined to give them enormous political and, therefore, cultural power too.

Once a moneymaking ecosystem is created and embedded, mechanisms to sidestep inconvenient scientific findings are in place. Layer by layer, institutional psychiatry and drug companies have built a powerful arrangement that became woven into the socio-political fabric of capitalist societies. The myth of the chemical cure became part of mainstream culture in the US, then spread to the rest of the advanced Western economies, and finally, like most US cultural products, across the world.

Without the linchpin belief in psychiatric diagnosis, such an expansion would have been so much harder. How did all that start and what is the science behind its origins?

How to create a new service industry: the origin story

James Davies is an anthropologist and psychotherapist with a long-standing interest in the historical and cultural drivers for modern-day psychiatric diagnostic practices. His interest led to him interviewing members of the panel that drew up the third edition of the *Diagnostic Statistical Manual* (*DSM-III*) published in 1980,[31] and to dig through the abundant archival material housed at the American Psychiatric Association.[32] *DSM-III* marked a major shift in how psychiatric conditions were categorised. Subsequent editions have been an evolution of the approach used by *DSM-III*.

Psychiatry was experiencing one of the many challenges to its legitimacy during the 1970s. Critics like psychiatrists Thomas Szasz and Ronald Laing, philosophers like Michel Foucault and sociologists like Erving Goffman were complaining that many treatments were more damaging than helpful to patients, highlighting the poor reliability or validity of psychiatric diagnoses, and painting psychiatric hospitals as cruel, degrading and anti-therapeutic. There was also widespread critique of coercive practices tethered to the belief that psychiatry had become an agent of state control.

In 1973 a study by psychologist David Rosenhan, a Stanford University professor at the time, was published under the title 'On Being Sane in Insane Places'. Rosenhan, along with eight other people, presented themselves to twelve psychiatric hospitals (some presented to more than one hospital) in the US, complaining they were hearing a voice saying 'thud', 'empty' and 'dull' (the only falsehood they should report). If admitted, they were to abandon their symptoms and simply behave as they normally would. None of these pseudo-patients had any actual symptoms or history of mental disorders. In all twelve instances, the pseudo-patients were diagnosed with a mental disorder and hospitalised. They were kept as inpatients between eight and fifty-two days. In no instance was any diagnosis removed during hospitalisation. Hospital notes on the pseudo-patients seemed to confirm that once they were categorised as patients, their behaviours were viewed through a pathological lens.

The way to get discharged was to agree with the staff that the treatments they were getting (medication) was helping them get better. These findings led to the claim that psychiatrists couldn't differentiate between real and non-patients.[33]

The psychiatric establishment protested. They complained that the study was unfair as they don't usually deal with patients who are malingering (faking symptoms). One hospital challenged Rosenhan to send pseudo-patients, claiming they would spot them if they knew they were coming. They identified 41 (21.24 per cent) of the next 193 patients as potential pseudo-patients. In fact, Rosenhan had sent none.[34]

Something had to be done to rehabilitate psychiatry's growing reputation as a field lacking in science or humanity. Up until *DSM-III*, psychiatric diagnosis was descriptive. The much smaller *DSM-II* gave broad descriptions, had fewer diagnostic categories and was about a third of the size of *DSM-III*. *DSM-III* was published to great fanfare, claiming that the reliability problem had been solved and the basis for scientific progress had been made by shifting from descriptive to operationalised definitions.

An operational definition of mental disorders means having 'well-defined' inclusion criteria that allows the reliable identification of a case. For *DSM-III* this meant producing a 'tick list' of 'symptoms' for each diagnosis and some criteria for how a diagnosis was made. For example, for major depressive disorder there had to be at least five symptoms from a list of symptoms present continuously for at least two weeks, and one of those symptoms must be 'low mood'. Making a diagnosis then follows a standardised process as quasi-mathematical counting replaces the more interpretive descriptive approach.

Or at least that was the theory. We have already seen in the earlier chapters how this symptom tick-list approach cannot solve the problem of case-ness. Careful analysis showed that *DSM-III* had not solved it either,[35] and, if anything, reliability has got worse in subsequent *DSM* editions.[36]

So how did *DSM-III* come into being? In 1974, Robert Spitzer, professor of psychiatry at Columbia University, became the chair of the American Psychiatric Association's task force for the third edition of *DSM*. At its height the task force comprised fifteen white, middle-class Americans all, bar one, from the disciplines of psychiatry and psychology. There was no representation from non-white, non-American or non-middle-class groups, and no intellectual presence from the social sciences or humanities. As the work of the task force developed, stung by the publicity around Rosenhan's study, Spitzer's vision for *DSM-III* was that it should reverse the descriptive approach and instead create criteria sets for each disorder.

The process for creating these criteria (evolutions of which still make up the criteria we use today) was centred around consensus. Task-force consensus could, therefore, overrule that attained by any advisory committee or lobbying faction or group, a privilege extensively exercised since the demands of different groups would so often be at variance. According to interviews conducted by James Davies:

> We thrashed it out, basically. We had a three-hour argument. There would be about twelve people sitting down at the table, usually there was a chairperson and there was somebody taking notes. And at the end of each meeting there would be a distribution of events. And at the next meeting some would agree with the inclusion, and the others would continue arguing. If people were still divided, the matter would be eventually decided by a vote . . . that is how it went.[37]

This was the process that led to the most influential book on psychiatric diagnosis, often referred to as the psychiatrists' bible. In one of many examples recounted by Davies, he describes a forty-minute conversation that took place between Spitzer and two psychiatrists from Saint Elizabeths Hospital, in Washington DC, where they decide that 'hysterical psychoses' should be divided into two disorders. Short episodes of delusion and hallucination would be labelled 'brief reactive psychosis', and the tendency to show up in an emergency room without authentic cause would be called 'factitious disorder'. 'Then Bob asked for a typewriter,' recalled Peele, one of the Saint Elizabeths' psychiatrists. 'He banged out criteria sets for factitious disorder and for brief reactive psychosis, and it struck me that this was a productive fellow! He comes in to talk about an issue and walks away with diagnostic criteria for two different mental disorders!'

Davies's work gives us a flavour of the origin story for how the psychiatric diagnoses we are so familiar with came into being. There was no science, no new medical breakthroughs, just a few people representing the interests of a class under threat, who went on to create arguably one of the most influential books of the last five decades.

The spread of mental health propaganda

The role the profit-motive plays is an obvious starting point for understanding the power of MHIC. But one might be mistaken in imagining that pernicious marketisation is solely caused by an industry exploiting weak definitions and poor regulatory standards. This is not a case of medication bad, therapy good. If the concepts produced initially by psychiatry were not valuable to a neoliberal culture, an excellent way to extract profits and valuable to the political classes, we would not have seen the extraordinary proliferation into so many social and cultural spaces. Under the guise of anti-stigma, prevention, self-help, employee support, suicide prevention and education, mental health ideology, and its sibling the wellness industry, found favour and expanded markets this way and that.

In 2021, 42 million adults in the United States sought mental health care of one form or another, up from 27 million in 2002. Increasingly, Americans have bought into the idea that therapy is one way they can reliably reach significantly better lives.[38] In the last chapter I outlined the growth of therapy in the UK and the paucity of evidence that this has been accompanied by an improvement in people's mental health at the population level.

Workplace mental health has become a standard part of health and safety policies, and wellness workshops and events provided by employers are now numerous. This is a convenient way to leave the workplace causes of the distress unexamined. Common practices include mental health training for some staff and formalised processes for identifying mental health problems in staff members, which may then result in a referral to a mental health professional or primary care doctor.

Mental Health First Aid (MHFA) courses have spread like wildfire and a plethora of organisations have sprung up in the UK offering online and face-to-face courses that lead to qualifications. Employers can get their MHFA-approved badge to show that they've taken the mental health of their workforce seriously and know how to look out for crises, help people and demonstrate how much they care about the well-being of their workforce. This new moneymaker is, predictably, yet to demonstrate that their graduates improve the mental health of the people they work with.[39]

In his 2022 book *Sedated*, James Davies describes going on one of these MHFA courses.[40] He meets attendees from HR departments of corporations and university staff who enthusiastically take in the course material and feel that, thanks to trainings like MHFA, we are finally moving away from the 'stiff upper lip' culture and towards openness and acceptance of mental health problems. So, what did the course say you should do if you found out that someone was struggling with their mental health? Advise them to consult their GP. How would you spot that someone might be struggling? By course facilitators outlining the 'symptoms' of mental disorders. Davies found nothing in the course about empowering workers to challenge organisational culture, or empowering managers to make workplace changes.

I have had similar experiences at recent trainings discussing burn-out, work–life balance and supporting staff 'wellness' – it's about you as an individual improving your lifestyle or seeing a professional for treatment if you're struggling. I learned that burnout is a syndrome to be dealt with by recognising it and doing something about it, such as seeking help because it could turn into an anxiety disorder or depression. You don't deal with it by changing institutional demands that have become overwhelming. Of course, if you do admit to 'burnout' and must take time off, it's on your record. Not all employers will be sympathetic to this whatever legislation is in place. The employer side of the equation that contributes to 'burnout' is 'burnt out' of causative and reparative factors. MHIC facilitates this societal move away from solidarity (through a unionised workforce for example) and towards individualised pathologies.

I know someone who works for a global bank that has initiated a mental health and wellness support programme. This includes regular time put aside within working hours where the employee can go to the gym or attend a mindfulness class (for example). At the same time this employer is renowned for its ruthlessness, where once a month at least one employee who is considered the least well performing is sacked. But at least you can cure your anxiety about losing your job by going to a mindfulness class.

Suicide prevention programmes get periodic media coverage and policy development that usually equates suicide with mental illness and so emphasises the necessity of early identification and treatment. This line of argument suggests that solving the suicide problem is through investing in more mental health services. People are (rightly) encouraged to talk about how they feel, so that suicidal feelings can be identified, but then what? You need to identify the mental disorder that's causing them to feel suicidal so that they can access the correct treatment.

We have known for a while that unemployment, indebtedness, precarious working conditions, inequalities, lack of social connectedness and housing instability emerge as the main factors associated with increased likelihood of suicide, particularly for working-aged men. Will turning these factors into a mental disorder needing treatment change austerity measures, disenfranchisement and lack of supportive welfare systems? Or will it let these socio-political factors off the hook?[41]

More young Australians are taking antidepressants, and more young Australians are killing themselves and self-harming, often by intentionally overdosing on the very substances that are supposed to help them. Suicide Prevention Australia (SPA) is badged as 'the national peak body for the suicide prevention sector'. It has received substantial funding from successive Australian governments to provide guidance on suicide prevention. It advocates for identifying and treating youth depression as a suicide prevention strategy including using SSRIs (which as I have explained do not improve outcomes over placebos and can increase suicidal feelings). Despite its long record of poor outcomes in tackling suicide, SPA continues to get funding and support of a few notable 'key opinion' leaders, who have become the government's go-to people for mental health policy advice.[42]

Then, finally, there are mental health apps. We now have an app for everything and with proliferation of social media leading to Generation TikTok, of course MHIC has entered the app world.

Mental health apps are promoted as helping users circumvent barriers associated with traditional treatment methods, including issues of poor availability, accessibility and acceptability. For some, rather than seeking mental health support in face-to-face settings that require individuals to identify themselves, they may access support via apps anonymously and remotely, thus evading any fears about social judgements.

But what do these apps promote? Who has oversight on the development of the apps? What are the consequences of the ever-expanding range of new and easily accessible apps? How do they talk about mental health and mental health problems, and what sort of framework do they encourage for how we understand our emotional lives? While they clearly make money, do they improve mental health outcomes as they claim to do? The largest study thus far synthesised results from 145 trials and 47,940 participants. It failed to find convincing evidence that *any* mobile app intervention improved outcomes related to people's anxiety, depression, smoking, drinking, thoughts of suicide, or feelings of well-being.[43]

Now that the MHIC is so widely and unquestioningly embedded, we inevitably get a parade of celebrity ambassadors from royals to Hollywood stars talking publicly about their depression, ADHD, eating disorders, neurodiversity, you name it. Mental health charities and promotional campaigns have become socially valued and an easy way for those with political, economic or cultural power to shift the experience of mental distress, alienation and not fitting in, into workforce efficiency demands and individualised technological fixes.

MHIC may have its biggest drivers in the profit motive, but its tentacles go deeper and wider and connect with the commodification of emotions, the growth of therapies, the wellness industries, workplace promotions, apps, media personalities, and so on. Nowhere is now free of mental health propaganda. Emotions are no longer something to be experienced, tolerated and engaged with, but suppressed, managed, controlled or mechanically expressed. MHIC promises to cleanse us of unruly emotions to help us adapt and survive in the customer-facing service economy.

MHIC started its journey in boardrooms where a few American men met to write *DSM-III*. They provided the tools that first the pharmaceutical industry and subsequently all manner of professionals, businesses and politicians jumped on, as the gravy train took MHIC to the heart of our social and cultural lives. Now it was ready to go beyond commodifying distress. Now it was ready to create identities.

12. Neurodiversity, gender and new human typologies

'I cannot teach anybody anything, I can only make them think.'

Socrates

As part of my involvement with the Autism and Neurodiversity: Exploring Diagnosis project at the University of Exeter in the UK, in the summer of 2016 I had an email debate with Damian Milton, a passionate autism advocate and sociologist, who describes himself as 'autistic'. After we agreed to it, our exchange was written up and copied on the project website.[1]

The email thread had gone on for over 13,000 words by the time we relented! I have had many similar debates with others before and since then. There are two issues that come up again and again and where, thus far, an agreeable resolution has not been possible. I can understand why people who have an emotional connection to the idea that they are neurodivergent feel so strongly about such a grouping being questioned. After all, many of them have experienced stigma, discrimination and being seen as having something wrong in them. I share the desire of neurodiversity advocates for all to be freed from the problematising of their personhood. I do, however, believe it is legitimate to question whether popularising the concept of neurodiversity will achieve this.

The first theme we've got stuck on is the nature of 'neuro' in neurodiversity. In chapters 5 to 8 I have already analysed the lack of scientific support for there being anything specifically and characteristically different about the brains and bodies of those with the common neurodivergent diagnoses of ADHD and autism. In my debate with Damian, he accepts that there is no tangible evidence that categorically separates a group who could be considered 'neurodivergent' from one that is 'neurotypical' and therefore that these concepts are 'social constructs'.* However, Damian does not accept that this is only a social construct, as he refers throughout our exchange to concepts like 'dispositional tendencies', 'monotropism' and 'embodied differences'. He concedes that he believes these characteristics are likely to have a biological component that results in neurodivergent people having something essential and biological in common that marks them out as different.

The second theme that comes up in this exchange is the one that's the focus of this chapter: the viewing of neurodiversity through the political lens, and in particular the idea that neurodivergent people are a specific social community with identities that should be recognised as having something unique that gives them a common bond.

Political neurodiversity

In our exchange, Damien regularly references issues such as 'neoliberal norms', 'feminism' and 'gay rights'. He argues that there is a particular social grouping that arises from some sort of 'dispositional' tendency differences, which has been and is being discriminated against in the same way as other minority groups are. He sees autistic culture (for example) as a subculture that has developed in reaction to being so labelled and so becomes a cultural identity marker. He compares this to other cultural groupings such as being gay or a 'punk'. For me there is obviously something different for autism cultures/communities when compared with being gay or a punk. The latter are more easily self-identified (sexual preference or music preference, which then develop various cultures, e.g. around dress or lifestyle), do not need to posit a biological disposition (whether there is or not), and do not need a medical professional to identify and allow potential entry into their communities.

---

* An idea that has been created and accepted by people in a society, rather than a fact of nature.

What I have realised through this exchange, and others since, is that neurodiversity as a concept has developed in tandem with broader political trends in Western society – towards identity politics and the culture wars, reflecting the increasing role a politicised hyper-individualism plays.

The intersection between mental health and politics has always been there, whether it's the accusation that people are labelled mentally ill to suppress their political voice (as is alleged to have happened with Soviet psychiatry) or the disproportionate labelling of young black men with a psychosis (that Western psychiatry is accused of). In the emergence of the neurodiversity movement, we find the modern iteration of the political in mental health ideology. From rare diagnoses given to kids with significant learning difficulties or active and mischievous boys, autism and ADHD follow an impressive developmental trajectory out of the confines of child guidance clinics and into the belly of mass culture. Women have become important consumers and private services have taken up the invitation to make profits from them. Transformed, autism and ADHD emerge visible and emboldened as identity consumables. They are assumed to have a 'neurodevelopmental' basis (i.e. in the brain) and so still require the gaze of medical and other healthcare professionals to identify them.

But under the neurodiversity banner a political flag of a 'difference' is waved. A difference that needs recognising rather than treating away. Society needs to adjust. Confusion soon follows. 'Is it a difference or disorder' keeps a certain helpful fog for those who profit from the new identity brand. If it's a disorder it needs diagnosis and treatment. If it's a difference it needs acceptance and inclusion (but still needs diagnosing). Is there a bit of cake and eating going on? Is that what makes it perfect as a commodity, human rights issue and object with cultural power all at once?

The neurodiversity movement takes us from the expanding MHIC in the health arena into the political one, as it fuses with the increasingly influential identity politics. Inevitably, the concept of self-identification rather than getting a formal diagnosis enters the lexicon of some campaigners. Autism and ADHD are no longer disorders, they are an essential part of an identity, of who you are. You are autistic, not a person with autism or, even worse, a person diagnosed with autism. Language can now be used to detach the person from biological reality and allow them to enter the sociopolitical realm as if they are some kind of 'natural' grouping.

The move to identity politics, and the desire to be seen in the culture wars, is a feature of much of today's left politics. Establishing visibility and entryism into the capitalist order for a smorgasbord of minorities becomes the focus. Neurodiversity campaigners could now show their revolutionary prowess by shaking their fists against neoliberal, white, heterosexual, ableist men, and they could now add neurotypical to that list.

Diversity issues are indeed important political ones, but in the cancel culture that is coming from both right and left we see a weaponisation of identity politics, an easy labelling of those who express a contrary opinion as 'fascists' or 'extremists', and a succession of clichéd tropes. But, as I have demonstrated, there is no 'neuro' to neurodiversity. If you take the 'neuro' bit out from 'neurodiverse' or 'neurotypical', what are you left with? Diverse and typical. Seriously, some people are diverse and others typical?

In his books, the American academic Walter Benn Michaels argues that there is a major disconnect between the dominant political forms purportedly dedicated to the equality of various identities and the economic inequality produced by capitalism.[2] What we see is a politics of difference so that what becomes central is not the inequality produced by economic structures but the equality of differing subjective positions. It is more concerned with how we feel about ourselves and our contexts than the material inequalities and class relationships that structure them. It becomes a politics concerned with appearances as opposed to its material consequences.

Racialising difference takes our attention away from class difference and then gets us to imagine that inequality is a consequence of our prejudices. If we can stop thinking of the poor as people who have too little money and start thinking of them instead as people who have too little respect, then it's our attitude towards the poor, not their poverty, that becomes the problem to be solved, and we can focus our efforts not on getting rid of classes but on getting rid of what we might call classism. Diversity then becomes the left's way of doing neoliberalism and by moving away from socioeconomic realities becomes in effect a contributor to enhancing market efficiency. This does not ignore the scourge of racism, merely the convenient distraction it provides from changing the economic structures that would do more for people of colour all over the world than having more black CEOs.

A further problem arises as identity politics assumes centre stage. We start to treat economic differences as if they were cultural differences. Capitalism is left unscathed. What we end up with is a world where individuals are either oppressors or victims, not because of property and capital ownership, but because of their surface signifiers. I can be an oppressor when I am described as a white Western middle-class man, but a victim if I'm identified with my ethnic minority status (coming from Iraq).

While there has been growing criticism of neoliberal/capitalist politics, particularly among young people, identarian politics has provided a convenient way of keeping the field of debate in non-economically based social groupings. As material circumstances continue to be eroded and inequalities widen, one consequence has been cynicism and passivity in the face of pessimism about change. Much of the population is not particularly enthused by fighting for this group and that group's rights and what you then get is low voter turnouts, a focus on day-to-day financial survival, and a lack of trust in politicians. Accepted protest then gravitates towards low-cost, high-noise signals, from the economically comfortable (like me) as a substitute for genuine reform. Those with power inside institutions love splashy progressive gestures across social media and in the press because they help preserve their power.

In June 2020, the US company that makes Doritos tortilla chips announced that it had joined the Black Lives Matter movement and was committed to amplifying black voices with its new 'Do you hear us now?' campaign. The company declared it was donating $650,000 worth of outdoor advertising, including billboards and murals, for the initiative to #AmplifyBlackVoices.[3] At the height of the uprising against the murder of George Floyd, protesters arrived at Brooklyn's Barclays Center in New York to find slogans painted in massive white letters across an entirely black three-storey building. The slogans included '#Black Lives Matter' and '#Amplify Black Voices'. Near the bottom was the Doritos logo. Corporate identity politics has learned that 'social justice'-type messaging is good for brand image and sales, particularly among young people.

BlackRock is an American multinational investment company. It's the world's largest asset manager, with nearly $9 trillion worth of assets.[4] BlackRock invests the funds of its clients in numerous publicly traded companies, and because of its size the company is among the top shareholders in the world. BlackRock has been one of the world's largest investors in coal-fired power stations and has substantial investments in the arms industry. It wields enormous economic power. It has not been slow in jumping on the 'sustainability' and 'diversity' bandwagons. It claims to now pursue 'an environmental sustainability strategy that is focused on reducing GHG emissions and increasing the efficiency and resiliency of its operations by utilizing low-carbon energy solutions'.[5] It also claims, 'Our philosophy of working as One BlackRock is at the core of our commitment to diversity, equity, and inclusion (DEI) across every level of our firm and within every region and country we operate – At BlackRock, DEI is a business imperative.'[6]

In February 2023 an event for Washington lobbyists titled '#DiversityAcrosstheAisle', featuring a dozen sitting members of Congress, was held. Lobbyists representing a range of interests, including Walmart, Reynolds American, Eli Lilly and Pfizer to name a few, attended. In a message to clients sent after the event, Ferox (a lobby group representing several companies) bragged about using diversity as a way to ingratiate its corporate clients with Democratic leaders. 'Ferox clients Walmart, Alexion, and Waste Management joined a who's who of corporate sponsors to generously celebrate the most diverse Congress ever,' the message noted. The invitation for the event included the LGBT Congressional Staff Association, the Black Women's Congressional Alliance, the Congressional Asian Pacific

American Staff Association and other identity-based professional societies for Capitol Hill staff.[7]

Corporate identity politics is well funded. Many corporations and political establishments, along with the liberal corporate media and academia, are attempting to present themselves as leading voices in the fight against climate injustice, racism, sexism, homophobia, and other oppressions. American Express rolled out a $1 billion plan to promote racial equity. Pepsi spent $400 million to 'dismantle the systemic racial barriers that block social and economic progress for Black people'. Apple devoted $100 million to a racial justice equity initiative.[8]

These dollars are not being spent because of the caring nature of shareholders, CEOs and company owners. These amounts would not be spent unless they believed doing so will help with their profitability. Identity politics is profitable. What it won't do is change the systemic injustices in housing, jobs, health care, education, policing, criminal justice, debt, and so on. What you don't see is corporate support for groups fighting for working-class rights and against economic injustice. Privilege based on class tends not to be a feature of DEI trainings.

The shortest ever rule of a UK prime minister was for Liz Truss, who reigned for forty-nine days. She was the third female UK prime minister. Under her the UK had the most diverse Cabinet to date. Of the four leading roles, including that of the prime minister, two were held by women, and three (before the sacking of the chancellor Kwasi Kwarteng) by people of colour, while the post of deputy prime minister was also held by a woman. For the first time in British history, none of the most senior ministerial positions was occupied by a white male. However, it was also one of the most socially exclusive, with nearly all of the new Cabinet educated at fee-paying schools. Following Truss's resignation, the UK got its first British prime minister of Asian descent in Rishi Sunak, a multimillionaire with a billionaire wife. Diversity alone does little for class or economic justice.

The concept of intersectionality in academia has been an important development, reminding us that class alone cannot account for the specific structural oppressions that certain groups experience in addition to those based on class. Intersectionality refers to the interconnected nature of social categorisations such as race, class and gender as they apply to a given individual or group. This results in overlapping and interdependent systems of discrimination or disadvantage. Women all over the world experience horrendous sexual violence. They are also disproportionately found in both the unpaid and (poorly) paid care sectors. Racism is woven into colonial and imperialist ideology and has been used recurrently by ruling elites to justify their right to rule over those cast as uncivilised. The criminalisation of homosexuality blighted for millions the chances of finding love, dignity and living a happy life. Putting economic injustice at the centre of the striving for social justice does not mean ignoring these discriminations, but making identarian injustice the primary concern allows the system that creates class privilege to strengthen its hold rather than weaken it.

Perhaps the most divisive of identity politics issues has been trans rights. It is with some trepidation that I write about this controversial issue, but in discussing the intersection of mental health and politics it's just not possible to avoid it.

Tavistock and the two Bells

When journalist Hannah Barnes carried out an exposé on the Tavistock and Portman NHS Trust in London for the BBC programme *Newsnight* in 2019, she was so shocked at what was uncovered that she wrote a book about her findings, *Time to Think: The Inside Story of the Collapse of the Tavistock's Gender Service for Children*.[9]

The Gender Identity Development Service (GIDS) was set up in 1989 after a perceived need for a clinic that focused on gender identity issues in children. The clinic initially operated out of a small office at the Tavistock. Although the numbers were minuscule, the work was difficult. For many years it ran quietly in the background, trying to help, using psychological approaches, the few children who came there. Concerns about the treatment provided to gender-distressed children were first raised in 2005.[10] This resulted in a report that made some specific recommendations (such as better management processes and the make-up of the type of staff employed), but as it was not considered important by management at the time, it was largely ignored.[11]

In the pre-Covid decade, numbers referred to GIDS grew exponentially. The demographics also changed as there came reports of an unexplained rise of teenage girls presenting at clinics with gender-related distress (males had previously been the largest proportion of the paediatric cohort). Close to three-quarters of those had been bullied before they came to think about their gender identity, and three-quarters had been or were currently attending child and adolescent psychiatric clinics for reasons other than gender distress.

As a result of the growth in numbers, GIDS rapidly became a lucrative aspect of services at the Tavistock (which had been operating at a financial deficit for many years). GIDS's income was 5.9 per cent of the Tavistock total in 2015/16, 10.4 per cent a year later, and then, in the draft operational plan for 2020/21, gender services for children and adults were said to make up 28 per cent of the Tavistock's funding.

Dr David Bell, consultant psychiatrist and the most senior psychoanalyst at the Tavistock at the time, submitted a complaint about GIDS in 2018. He was rebuked by a colleague who said that the Tavistock would 'go down' if GIDS closed. Ten members (about a third) of GIDS staff had brought their worries to him unsolicited. The Tavistock trust hierarchy, far from being grateful to him for alerting it to a potentially dangerous situation, tried to silence him and instituted proceedings against him. The trust told the *Observer* newspaper that it was proud of the GIDS service and that the claims made by Dr Bell were historical and dealt with following proper processes at the time. It also stated that it had a duty to safeguard its staff, who had faced intense, personalised and upsetting harassment. Bell was forced to find a lawyer to defend himself.[12]

Among the concerns brought to Bell were the fact that children attending GIDS often seemed to be rehearsed and sometimes did not share their parents' sense of urgency; that some senior staff spoke of 'straightforward cases' who then went straight onto puberty blockers; that some were recommended for treatment after just two appointments; and that clinicians who'd spoken of homophobia in the unit were told they had 'personal issues'. A few years later Dr Bell's concerns would be vindicated when a different Bell took the Tavistock to court.

In July 2019, Dr Kirsty Entwistle, a psychologist who worked at the Leeds GIDS site, published an open letter to the GIDS director at the time, expressing her concerns about the difficult backgrounds of many cases, and how children who were 'sexually abused and have witnessed and/or been subjected to domestic violence' were referred for puberty blockers without acknowledgement of the complexity of their needs.[13]

In a bid to obtain some clinical evidence for the medicalisation of children's gender identities, a study had been commissioned by GIDS in 2011 to examine the outcomes of puberty blockers on children. Puberty blockers stop sexual development, meaning the adolescent doesn't experience a full sexual awakening.

The first results emerged early in 2016. By then puberty blockers had become an established treatment at GIDS. The youngest child to have started on puberty blockers was just ten. Apart from one, every child on puberty blockers subsequently moved on to cross-sex hormones. Puberty blockers turned out to be the first step in a medicalised identity, and rather than offering the opportunity to reflect, blockers effectively locked children into a medicalised treatment pathway.

The results of the study, finally published in 2021, were not good by most standards. They had followed up forty-four patients aged twelve to fifteen with 'gender dysphoria (GD)'.* They were followed up for at least one year and some for two and three years. The authors concluded: 'Overall patient experience of changes on GnRHa [puberty blockers] treatment was positive.' In other words, the participants who wanted to undertake puberty blockers and then (all but one of the forty-four) cross-sex hormones were happy with

---

* GD is defined as a sense of unease because of a mismatch between a person's biological sex and their gender identity.

that treatment. But wasn't the treatment meant to 'treat' 'dysphoria' (a profound sense of unease or dissatisfaction) too? The young patients' distress was based on clinical measures of things like self-harm, suicidal ideation, psychiatric symptoms and body image. All had either plateaued or worsened. Moreover, they found a statistically significant increase in those answering the statement 'I deliberately try to hurt or kill myself' as well as a significant increase in behavioural and emotional problems for natal girls (meaning female at birth).[14]

Keira Bell (no relation of Dr David Bell) was the second Bell to raise the alarm, this time from a patient's perspective. In December 2020, three judges from the High Court in London weighed the evidence provided by Mrs A, the parent of a gender-distressed child, and Keira Bell.

In a blog outlining her journey Keira Bell described herself as being a classic tomboy. She liked typical boy clothing, was athletic, and preferred to play with boys. Her parents divorced when she was five years old and her mother, whom she lived with, subsequently struggled with alcoholism and mental health problems.[15]

Puberty was difficult for Keira. She hated how her hips and breasts were growing, periods were often painful and disabling, but particularly difficult was that she could no longer pass as 'one of the boys', and so lost most of her male friends. Her mother's alcoholism had become so bad that she didn't want to bring friends home and so became increasingly solitary and isolated. By '14, I was severely depressed and had given up: I stopped going to school; I stopped going outside. I just stayed in my room, avoiding my mother, playing video games, getting lost in my favourite music, and surfing the internet.'

She also started to become attracted to girls. All of this made Keira wonder if there was something inherently wrong with her. She found some websites about females transitioning to male. One day her mother asked if she wanted to be a boy, which got Keira thinking more about this as a possibility. Later, after she moved in with her father and his then partner, she told them that she realised she was really a boy and wanted to transition to become one.

At fifteen years old, Keira was referred to GIDS at the Tavistock. She was diagnosed with GD and at sixteen was put on puberty blockers. A year later, she was receiving testosterone shots. When she reached twenty, she had a double mastectomy. By then, she had a masculinised body, a man's voice, a beard, and had changed her name to Quincy.

However, all was not well for Keira. She recalls how after surgery, she started asking herself deeper, more existential questions, trying to make sense of what had happened to her. 'What makes me a man?' she wondered. At some point she remembers realising that she wasn't a man, and never would be. She began to understand that her 'gender dysphoria was a symptom of my overall misery, not its cause'. She worried about the effect her transition might have on her ability to find a sexual/romantic partner.

Five years after beginning her transition to becoming male, she began the process of de-transitioning. After coming to this decision, she found an online community forum for de-transitioners. The number of people on it was rising, with many young women having come to the same realisation as her. She felt that there was a medical scandal going on.

For Keira the consequences of what happened to her were profound: possible infertility, loss of her breasts, atrophied genitals, a permanently changed voice and facial hair. De-transitioning cannot reverse these changes. She felt let down by the professionals she saw at the Tavistock who hadn't enquired about what may have contributed psychologically to her wish to become male, and instead just affirmed 'my naive hope that everything could be solved with hormones and surgery'.

Keira decided to initiate legal action, enabling a judicial-review case against the Tavistock to consider whether youths under treatment at the clinic could meaningfully consent to the medical interventions they were providing. The three judges expressed serious doubts that the clinic's young patients could understand the implications of what amounted to experimental treatment with life-altering outcomes. They noted the lack of evidence for putting children on drugs to block puberty, a treatment that is almost universally followed by cross-sex hormones and which must be taken for life to maintain the transition. They ruled that it was unlikely that under sixteens could give informed consent to treatment with puberty blockers.

In January 2020 the Care Quality Commission (the independent regulator of health and social care in England) published their report on GIDS at the Tavistock and rated the service 'inadequate', the lowest possible safety rating. In March 2022, Dr Hilary Cass's independent interim report on GIDS was published and concluded that the clinic was not a safe option for the long-term treatment of gender-related distress in children,[16] and her final report, published two years later, upheld this finding.[17] In July 2022, seventeen years after concerns were first raised, NHS England announced that GIDS at the Tavistock would be closed and replaced by regional centres with a greater focus on mental health.

Trans transformations

There are parallels with neurodiversity in the developmental trajectory of GD in clinical settings, its subsequent ballooning out into identity politics, and the profitability of gender-affirming care. My clinical experience matches the statistics. The rise in ADHD starts in the mid to late 1990s, some five to ten years later autism begins its meteoric rise, and a few years after that, young people who, in addition to low mood or anxiety, are saying that they believe they are 'trans' start appearing at my clinic and steadily become more numerous.

Those referred to GIDS in the UK went up from 138 in 2010–11 to 3,585 in 2021–22. By then, two-thirds were teenage girls with no prior history of gender dysphoria before puberty and complex mental health histories prior to referral. A decade earlier it was largely boys who experienced GD from early childhood. .[18] Same-sex attraction was particularly common among natal females, with only 8.5 per cent of those referred to the GIDS describing themselves as primarily attracted to boys.[19]

In Sweden, in 2001 there were a total of twelve people younger than twenty-five with GD in specialised outpatient care; in 2022 there were 2,077 people.[20] A study of referrals to a gender identity unit in Valencia, Spain, found that the number of referrals increased tenfold, from eighteen in 2012 to 189 in 2021. The increase was significantly greater for those who were female at birth.[21] In 2021, about 42,000 children and teens in the US received a diagnosis of GD, nearly triple the number in 2017.[22] In 2020, 1.4 per cent of those aged thirteen to seventeen in the US identified as transgender. These youths are comprising a larger share of this population than previously, at 18 per cent of the transgender-identified population up from 10 per cent in 2017.[23] A 2022 US survey found that 5.1 per cent of adults younger than thirty identify as trans or non-binary, including 2 per cent who identify as a trans man or trans woman and 3 per cent who are non-binary – meaning they identify as neither a man nor a woman.[24]

Within a few years of launching GD services for under eighteens in 2011, Finnish researchers noticed a sharp rise in the number of patients referred. Most of these patients were teenage girls with no history of GD in childhood, and some 68 per cent had a history of significant psychological problems prior to the emergence of their gender-related distress. Together with colleagues, Dr Riittakerttu Kaltiala, a leading researcher in this area, examined the numbers of referrals per year between 2011 and 2017 in Denmark, Finland, Norway, Sweden and the UK. They found a similar pattern of increase in referral rates across all countries. In adolescents they found a preponderance of those who were female at birth wishing to transition.[25]

A 2021 study from Australia found high levels of distress, suicidal ideation (41.8 per cent), self-harm (16.3 per cent), suicide attempts (10.1 per cent), anxiety (63.3 per cent), depression (62.0 per cent), behavioural problems (35.4 per cent) and autism (13.9 per cent) in those attending a GD clinic. The developmental stories told by the children and their families also showed high rates of adverse childhood experiences, with family conflict (65.8 per cent), parental mental illness (63.3 per cent), loss of important figures via separation

(59.5 per cent) and bullying (54.4 per cent) being most common. A history of childhood maltreatment was also common (39.2 per cent).[26]

Those with an autism diagnosis are significantly more likely to be over-represented in GD clinics,[27] and prevalence of other mental health problems is elevated in both individuals diagnosed with autism and with GD.[28]

According to Kaltiala, evidence from a combined twelve studies demonstrates that when children with cross-gender or gender-variant behaviour are left to develop naturally, the vast majority, 'four out of five', come to terms with their bodies and learn to accept their sex. When they are socially transitioned earlier in childhood, virtually none do.[29]

A 2019 review of the evidence base for gender-affirming hormone treatments in children and adolescents described the large number of unanswered questions that include the age at start, reversibility, adverse events, long-term effects on mental health, quality of life, bone mineral density, osteoporosis in later life and cognition. The available evidence base was unable to evaluate the long-term safety profile. The authors concluded that the available evidence base did not support informed decision-making and safe practice in children.[30] On 12 June 2023, NHS England came to the same conclusion: 'Puberty suppressing hormones will not be prescribed to under 18s for gender dysphoria, except in exceptional circumstances, because of a lack of evidence to support their safety or clinical effectiveness.'[31]

Systematic reviews of evidence conducted by public health authorities in Finland, Sweden and England similarly concluded that the risk/benefit ratio of youth gender transition ranges from unknown to unfavourable. As a result, there has been a shift from 'gender-affirmative care', which prioritises access to medical interventions, to a more conservative approach that addresses other psychological problems and psychotherapeutically explores the development of the trans identity. The conclusions of these systematic reviews are consistent with long-term adult studies, which fail to show credible improvements in mental health and find a pattern of treatment-associated harms.[32]

Despite claims of the lifesaving nature of gender transition for adults, none of the many studies convincingly demonstrated enduring psychological benefits, and it remains unclear whether gender transition leads to lasting benefits to their mental health.[33]

In a follow-up study of seventy-nine young people who attended a GD clinic in Australia, four to nine years post-presentation from their first appointment, 90 per cent had persisted with their hormone treatments (60/66) and 88 per cent reported significant ongoing mental health concerns.[34]

According to a study that examined the records from the US Military Healthcare System between 2009 and 2018, around 30 per cent of those who undergo treatment to change sex may wish to de-transition. The study sample included 627 trans men and 325 trans women with an average age of nineteen. The four-year gender-affirming hormone continuation rate was 70.2 per cent. Trans women had a higher continuation rate than trans men of 81.0 per cent versus 64.4 per cent.[35]

The emerging voices of de-transitioners have identified several concerns. Some have reported that they had come to believe that gender-affirming medical treatment would alleviate their feelings of dysphoria, but it had not. Some have highlighted the potential for adverse outcomes, particularly in relation to interventions whose effects cannot be reversed (such as the effects of some cross-sex hormones and gender-affirming surgery). Some have reported that, in hindsight, because of their age or mental health concerns, they were not fit to give consent. Some express regret about making decisions related to their sexuality before that sexuality, and an understanding of that sexuality, fully developed. Some feel that they were misguided in focusing exclusively on their gender dysphoria and that they should also have considered and addressed some of the concurrent adverse childhood experiences.[36]

Psychiatrist and psychoanalyst Dr Roberto D'Angelo has written about his psychotherapeutic work with trans people and the psychological dilemmas they face.[37] He expresses concern about how a biomedical framing of GD misses the importance of the interpersonal and social context in which a child develops. The historical and contextual relevance of that person's experience of gender-related distress is then simplified into the degree to which the family and culture are supportive (or not) of the child's expressed feelings about gender identity. The child's gender identity is conceptualised as existing *a priori*, as though it is an essential quality of the child that is beyond the reach of social and environmental influences. Family dynamics, traumatic experiences, social issues, cultural exposure to how masculinity and femininity are constructed and regulated, all become irrelevant in this framework. This gets transformed into an ideological stance that can hinder more fluid and open understandings, and may obstruct the potential for other, less medically invasive, avenues to psychological change.

He notes how many 'queer' theorists argue that neoliberal capitalism generates feelings of inadequacy in individuals that locks them into a lifetime of endless production and consumption.[38] When we encourage children to narrow their focus on discovering a 'true gender self', are we not also colluding in avoiding talking about why they may feel so alienated, despairing or disempowered? Are we not just offering another consumable by promising liberation through gender change? By distracting ourselves with the project of reconfiguring our appearance and body as a cure for how we feel, do we not accidentally reinforce existing cultural stereotypes of gender norms? Rather than a radical challenge to gender norms, is it simply an iteration of consumer capitalism that promotes an endless array of possibilities for self-reinvention?

By remaining afraid of having conversations that discuss how and why a person concluded they wanted to change sex, do we collude with how the culture expects them to be as a boy or a girl? Are gender-dysphoric children responding to the way rigid gender constructions still saturate our culture at multiple levels, via advertising, education, popular culture, social media, pornography, and so on? Indeed, does an unproblematic acceptance that they should change sex not further reinforce those social norms?

In the MHIC project where all feeling-states are to be viewed with suspicion on the one hand and an exploitable entity on the other, the onset of the biological and psychological changes of puberty are a precious resource. The prepubertal freedom of being starts to vanish under pressure of sexualised societal expectations, preoccupation with appearances, difficult bodily changes (from periods to wet dreams), and a greater capacity for abstract and existential thinking. An awareness of expectations and judgementalism makes adolescence a potentially psychologically hazardous territory. There can be a sadness over the loss of prepubertal freedom and deeper questions to ponder, including what it means to become a man or woman in the society you live in. Sexual feelings awaken amid a pornified and marketised relational field, and despite progress same-sex attraction can occur against a backdrop of homophobia and playground jibes about being 'gay'. Hegemonic models of masculinity and femininity can be hard to kick back against in the hyper-competitive environments of the institutions that young people attend.

Could the demand for 'gender affirmation' also be seen as a form of objectification, something many feminists have fought against? Is creating an idea of identity as something fixed – at least partly through bodily appearance – rather than fluid and changeable with context, life events and relationships, not itself a form of oppression? How different are puberty blockers, cross-sex hormones and gender reassignment surgery to cosmetic treatments? Don't we critique cosmetic surgery as a product of commodifying bodies to exploit people's (particularly women's) concern with appearances? What price are young people paying for this culture which leads them to make war on the perfectly healthy body they inhabit? I don't profess to know the definitive answer to these questions, but I do think it's important to raise them.

Neurodiversity, gender and identity

We should understand and treat trans people with the same acceptance, dignity and compassion that everyone should expect. Something couldn't have felt good or right or comfortable for much of their lives to subsequently take the big step of changing their sex. To continue to take hormones, to undertake major surgery and risk judgement and judgementalism is an enormous and psychologically challenging set of procedures to take on. On top of that many trans people experience violence and hostility. In demonising trans people, some even see their presence as a threat to society. None of that is acceptable. Some of the most insightful and psychologically aware conversations I have had have been with young people in my clinic who express a wish to transition.

People should be free to live as they wish, as long as they do not harm others in the process. They should not be discriminated against in housing, employment, health care, education, and all other areas of citizenship. We must remember, as with any identity category, these are real people trying to live meaningful lives, not just symbolic presences in the body politic. We also shouldn't be afraid to discuss the health, political and cultural issues associated with the growth of trans identities.

GD begins its existence as a rare condition mainly seen in boys who have had a wish to become female since childhood. Numbers considered to have GD rapidly expand over the last decade and the predominant group becomes young women who did not have the idea that they were in the wrongly sexed body until adolescence. By then it has entered political life with accusations of 'woke' culture undermining society on one side and labelling people as transphobes or even genocidal fascists on the other. Talking about the subject matter and, most importantly for me as a child psychiatrist, what this all means for young people in distress, becomes difficult.

There are political parallels in terms of a left-wing perspective that have some echoes of the debate with Damien Milton that I discussed at the beginning of this chapter. While we both see autism as a social construct, Damien accepts the idea that such a construct alludes to some sort of natural world essential difference; whereas for me empiricism needs to establish that 'neuro' basis first, and therefore the very idea that autism refers to some essential characteristic differences that can be abstracted into a thing is the social construct. This, I think, is more foundational and the implications further reaching.

It mirrors strands of left-wing thinking where subjective reality can be disconnected from material reality. It takes us into the world of how we feel, what we think others think of us, and the micropolitics of relationships. At its more extreme end, some postmodern perspectives encourage an idea that language projects and creates the world of meaning that we inhabit. An alternative viewpoint contends that our world is made of social relationships that have a material basis (the classes of society for example), which project inward to create the language and world of meaning we inhabit.

An area of quite visceral conflict seems to have emerged around trans people between a more traditional feminism and recent iterations. Their fight takes place on this dimension of how meaning and reality are constructed. Traditional feminists insist that there are material differences between the sexes, from their chromosomes to genitals, from body functions to carrying a baby, and these are important in understanding the nature of the relationships that have emerged between the sexes. When biological sex is no longer recognised as the starting point, the concern is not just for safe spaces for women, but the cause of women's rights more generally. There is disquiet as to why young women are increasingly attracted to becoming men and how this could reflect sexism in society. After all, it's still a man's world.

For the supporters of the idea that biological sex is itself a construct, we see similar arguments to Damien's about autism – that dispositional tendencies are just as 'real' and the starting point for an identity community. You are a woman if you feel that you're a woman, whether you have XX or XY chromosomes. Reality is projected from the inside and carried into the world and made real there. The task becomes a different cultural one, that of accepting these personal diverse self-constructions and fighting for their rights.

A similar conflict has cropped up in the gay community. Some express a concern that the construction of a trans identity has emerged from ongoing homophobia, which may not be as visible but is nonetheless there. Unable to accept that their sexual orientation is towards someone of the same sex, the person then concludes they must actually be the opposite sex. The solution of transitioning seems easier to deal with emotionally than accepting they are homosexual. On the opposite side there are those in the gay community who draw parallels between the years of hostility and prejudice they endured (and still endure in many countries), including homosexuality being a psychiatric diagnosis in the US right up until 1973. They see a camaraderie in the trans rights movement, particularly with the attacks they get from the far right and certain religious groups, who may still not accept homosexuality.

The political problem for me is the same one I've discussed with neurodiversity. By disembodying the idea of ADHD or autism from any need for correspondence in material reality something peculiar happens. Material reality comes from an individualistic inside. They are made socially real by essentially bypassing any need for biological reality, and then arriving at an idea that there is nevertheless something made real in the material world (the mind and bodies of those taking on these identities) by imagining it to be so. Through social looping and contagion these constructs (ADHD, autism, neurodiversity, trans) come to be viewed as real, and become a naturalised category. This makes them ideal for commodification and profit mining. What happens to the people thus exploited is irrelevant to the markets that trade on them.

In her book *End of Love*, Eva Illouz, professor of sociology at the Hebrew University of Jerusalem, talks about how even relationships are marketised and commodified.[39] Psychological self-management is nothing but the management of a pervasive uncertainty in interpersonal relationships. Consumer capitalism has led people to think of themselves and others as goods and commodities that inevitably become less profitable over time and must be replaced by new ones.

Sexual desire has become incorporated into the fashion-cosmetics complex, mass media and, not least, pornography, and has turned desire into a visual performance. Exploited for profit, the display of eroticised bodies, particularly women's bodies, has become commonplace in advertising and the workplace, and sexual desire has become an essential unit of the economy. This consumerism penetrates subjectivities and, as a result, the private sphere has been distorted by an ideology of what Illouz calls 'radical personal freedom'. Relationships become at risk of being viewed through an individualised lens of 'what's in it for me'. Identities mixed with individual desire is a potent concoction leading to inescapable disappointments and dissatisfactions. Perfect for profiteering.

This is the breeding ground of 'identarianism' in both the mental health and political fields and the natural destiny of MHIC. In the next chapter, I continue this journey into the political backdrop shaping, influencing and now being influenced by mental health ideology. In the book thus far, I have problematised the way we imagine and construct the 'what is wrong with me' dilemma and in this chapter how that leads to an essentialised idea of 'I am different'. By implication there is a normal from which it is imagined the disordered or different have deviated. The next two chapters ponder the question of where our ideas of 'normal' come from and what might be their implication.

13. Living in a compare-and-compete culture

'Capitalism is the astounding belief that the most wickedest of men will do the most wickedest of things for the greatest good of everyone.'

John Maynard Keynes

In April 1995 I had my first experience of talking to the press. I was a senior trainee in child and adolescent psychiatry at the internationally renowned eating disorder service at Great Ormond Street Children's Hospital, which was holding its second international conference on eating disorders.[1] Professor Bryan Lask, a highly organised and busy man, who always held a large leather-bound notebook into which he regularly scribbled notes, had decided that we should announce the preliminary findings of a research project I was involved in. The study examined regional cerebral blood flow, using radioisotope scans, in fifteen females aged between eight and sixteen who had been given a diagnosis of anorexia nervosa (AN). It was found that thirteen of the fifteen had 'hypoperfusion' (reduced blood flow) on one side of a part of the brain called the temporal lobe.[2] The 1990s was labelled the 'decade of brain', and brain scans of various types were the in-thing in psychiatric research.

A press release about this study was arranged for the first day of the conference, highlighting that our team had discovered evidence suggesting AN may be caused by a brain-based abnormality. Several TV and radio stations said they wanted to cover the story in their morning news bulletins. When I arrived Professor Lask asked me if I could do the press interviews as he was busy opening and chairing the conference. That morning I was ferried by taxi to a radio studio and a couple of TV stations for brief interviews that explained our findings. In the following days and weeks, our eating disorder department at Great Ormond Street Hospital received numerous phone calls from patients and their carers asking about the research and what they could do about having an 'abnormal' brain. The most memorable was from a young woman who said 'I heard that I have a hole in my brain'. As I have been arguing, what model you publicise (in this case AN being caused by a brain abnormality) has consequences.

In the months prior to, and after, this conference I was getting to grips with various aspects of neuroanatomy, neurophysiology, brain scanning and the issues that emerged – from the technical challenges to the potential meanings of different findings. I began to understand that there were some problems with the claim that we had evidence for a potential biological abnormality. A dilemma known as the 'trait versus state' issue is working out whether brain-functioning differences are a consequence of starvation and/or a reflection of a way of thinking that characterises anorexia (state), or the consequence of a pre-existing and ongoing abnormality (trait)? But even more challenging is understanding the significance of differences in blood flow for a complex whole system like the brain, when nothing is abnormal about the structures themselves. The hope at the time was that this research would lead to a 'biological marker' for AN, which, as with most psychiatric presentations, hasn't of course materialised. But the shift from understanding AN in more psychosocial terms was under way.

There is something a little different about AN compared with the other examples from the mental health literature that I have been discussing in this book. Notice that, unlike most psychiatric diagnostic categories, anorexia nervosa is not followed by the word 'disorder'. Perhaps that's because it appears to have a proximal cause – not eating or restricted eating to a physically dangerous degree because of a fear of fatness/desire for thinness. The other difference is that there is an empirical anchor through which to measure recovery – weight.

However, there are also many similarities to the issues with diagnosis I have been discussing. The idea that AN is caused by body-image distortion has resulted in (what seems to me) pointless arguments in clinical practice about whether to label someone whose eating is restricted to a dangerous degree as having an 'eating disorder' (there's that word again) or what is now being clinically referred to as 'disordered eating' (therefore not an eating disorder). For example, if a young woman who has previously been diagnosed with autism now decides to restrict her eating, even if they do say they don't like feeling fat, then as long as she claims she's avoiding some foods because they don't like their texture (for example), some practitioners will argue that what they have is 'disordered eating' as a result of autism, and not therefore AN.

Stopping, restricting or otherwise controlling (or not) how much you eat is a behaviour. The reason for that behaviour is something to be discovered with each person who shows it. The motivation of fear of fatness is a common one, but mainly found in females in Western societies. The academic literature three decades ago acknowledged AN as a 'culture-bound' syndrome likely related to idealisation of slim body shapes for women in the West.[3]

The predominance of female sufferers led to many feminist writers seeing these young women's anguish as relating to problems and challenges that Western women face in their everyday life. AN thus used to be understood as having important political, cultural and social dimensions.[4]

As MHIC built up its structures and reach, AN from the mid-1990s onwards was increasingly viewed in diagnostic terms, and gradually cut off from its sociocultural context in academia and research. A study examining all issues of the pre-eminent eating disorders journal the *International Journal of Eating Disorders*, from when it was first published in 1981 through to September of 2021, yielded only three articles with 'feminism' or 'feminist' in the title, and only nine between 2011 and 2021 that had those terms anywhere in the article.[5] AN had become understood in individualised terms as a condition related to internal psychological and psychiatric attributes.

AN was also exported to the non-Western world, as not only had Western body ideals been exported alongside Western culture, but so was the concept of AN itself. Ethan Watters's discussion of rising rates of anorexia in Hong Kong in the 1990s explained how AN wormed its way into the minds of a population. Following the death of a young girl struggling with self-starvation, and who passed away on a public street while waiting for the bus, Western professionals were widely interviewed in the press. Once Western views of anorexia were publicised, AN presentations among women began to rise rapidly. It seems that the idea of anorexia nervosa itself – prepackaged in its *DSM* diagnosis form and explained by a host of Western experts – was the likely reason that it caught on so quickly in Hong Kong.[6]

This story of the development of AN from a rare but serious condition that has psychosocial roots into one that becomes individualised and exported, should be a familiar one by now for readers of this book. Having worked with so many young women with eating problems and their families for many years, there is, for me, something about AN that encapsulates the theme of this chapter. Compare (myself to others or an imagined idea of what I should be like) and compete (the obsession with weight loss takes on a dangerous desire to keep doing it better and further).

As we came out of Covid lockdowns a hidden epidemic that had spread across the land revealed itself in clinics and hospitals. There was an outbreak of young people starving themselves, exercising for hours on end, losing weight and becoming dangerously ill. Paediatric wards were inundated with such patients who were refusing to eat, necessitating force-feeding through nasogastric tubes to save their lives. Mental health units for young people found themselves grappling with an influx of – nearly all female – youths who were nutritionally compromised. Eating disorder community services were overwhelmed by referral numbers. According to a UK study, over the two years from March 2020, eating disorders were 42 per cent higher than would be expected for females aged thirteen to sixteen, and 32 per cent higher for those aged seventeen to nineteen.[7]

What was going on? A recurrent theme emerged from what these youngsters told us. In the loneliness of lockdowns, where school was online and friendships on WhatsApp, a sense of purpose, structure and focus diminished and the days became an amorphous sameness. In this social emptiness, trained by a culture of competition, some young people found a new 'hobby'. With TV and online keep fit instructors telling us how to stay healthy, warning about the dangers of weight gain while in confinement, a preoccupation with body weight was turbocharged. A new goal emerged. A personal battle to lose weight and keep fit became a competitive obsession. With the appeal of a number (kilograms or pounds) that could be used to judge success, keep fit regimes, healthy eating and dieting, and distress at any sign that weight was not going down, sometimes spiralled out of control. The impulse to double down and go further became stronger after returning to post-lockdown schools and facing their peers.

It's hard to escape the arena of competition, and the pressure to perform. What we refer to as 'anorexia nervosa' is more than the desire for thinness, promoted as an ideal for women in Western culture. It is also the internalisation of the values of competition and performance. It provides a sense of control and mastery through being the best and most determined to achieve a singular goal that has been given social value (thinness).

In this chapter I go wider and deeper into the social and cultural milieu that has developed in Western capitalism to explore what sort of model of human is nurtured by its economic and political foundations. AN is but one example of what Western capitalism can promote.

The principles of neoliberal capitalism

What are the values that emerge out of a capitalist political and economic ideology?

Neoliberalism is essentially capitalism with minimal restraints that evolved in response to the major economic crises of the 1970s. It revolves around a restructuring of class forces and social priorities in favour of competitiveness and private profits. No other capitalism is on offer today. It valorises aggressive free market economics based around competition as the best way to organise and develop pretty much every aspect of society. It's generally associated with policies of economic liberalisation that promote privatisation, deregulation, globalisation, austerity, and increasing the role of the private sector across all sections of the economy.[8]

The term neoliberalism was first used at a meeting in Paris in 1938, where two men, Ludwig von Mises and Friedrich Hayek, argued that social democracy and a greater role for the government in running society (for example, through having a welfare state) causes a collectivism that eventually results in a loss of individual freedoms. In his 1944 book *The Road to Serfdom*, Hayek argued that government planning crushed the creative potential of the individual and would inevitably lead to totalitarian control such as that seen in fascism or communism.[9]

Whether by design or ignorance, this neoliberal ideology dismisses the enormous role states have played in passing laws, whether in relation to property rights or trade agreements that favour whoever the ruling class is, and so the importance of controlling the organs of state is also central to capitalist economies. Hayek and his followers ignored how the development of fascism was supported by the capitalist ruling classes in Germany, Italy, Spain and other countries during the 1930s as a counterforce to suppress the rise and popularity of communism among the working classes.[10] German fascism was built on the back of spreading the myth of a Jewish-Bolshevik conspiracy theory and communists were in the vanguard of those who fought against fascism.[11]

Hayek's ideas received enthusiastic support from millionaires, corporations and their supported foundations (such as the Institute for Economic Affairs founded in 1955 and still supported by many multinationals today), which saw in this philosophy an ideology that would strengthen their economic interests. By the 1970s some governments started to incorporate their ideas into policy.

Despite the illusion of freedom, the first full trial of neoliberalism took place, under the guidance of US advisers, in the brutal military dictatorship of Augusto Pinochet.[12] Pinochet assumed power in Chile in a US-supported and -financed military coup that overthrew the democratically elected socialist government of Salvador Allende in 1973. Under Pinochet's military dictatorship, tens of thousands were executed, and many hundreds of thousands more arrested and tortured.

By the mid-1970s, developed countries were experiencing crippling economic crises. This created an opportunity for elements of neoliberalism, especially its prescriptions for monetary policy, to be adopted by Jimmy Carter's administration in the US and James Callaghan's government in Britain. After Margaret Thatcher (in the UK) and Ronald Reagan (in the US) took power, the rest of the neoliberal package soon followed: tax cuts for the rich, the crushing of trade unions, deregulation, privatisation, and outsourcing and competition in public services.

International financial and economic institutions such as the International Monetary Fund (IMF), the World Bank and the World Trade Organization soon prescribed similar policies. When the IMF or World Bank lent money to a developing economy it now came with neoliberal strings attached, forcing their governments to adopt marketisation- and globalisation-friendly policies as conditions of loans, while compelling them to implement austerity measures to cut government spending. Much of the global economy was now being structured by capitalist neoliberal ideology.[13]

Egyptian economist Samir Amin long ago pointed out the neocolonial nature of this type of economics of development in his 1974 book *Accumulation on a World Scale*.[14] According to Amin, capitalism evolved into a single integrated global system, composed of 'developed countries', which constitute the *centre*, and 'underdeveloped countries', which are the *peripheries* of the system. Development and underdevelopment are inherent features of globalised capitalism. Underdeveloped countries should not be considered as lagging behind because of the specific social, cultural or even geographic characteristics, but as the result of the forced permanent structural adjustment of these countries to the needs of accumulation (of wealth and power) that benefits the system's centre countries. He believed that the self-liberating efforts of the nations and peoples of the peripheries would eventually lead to an awakening of the Western (centre) working classes.[15]

Peripheral country economies became providers of raw materials and cheap labour, and the centre economies made the high-value items from them to reap the major share of profits. The centre countries accumulated capital (income) and became exporters of capital (loans) to the rest of the world (whether directly through their banks or through the institutions they set up like the IMF and World Bank). The peripheral countries then provide even more profit to the centre economies by having to pay interest on these loans, while they go further into debt, requiring more loans in a never-ending cycle of profit extraction. The elite in the centre economies are enabled to buy ever-expanding assets (a resource with economic value such as property or stocks and shares), furthering inequality within and between countries. The US finds a place at the top of this tree of exploitation and the dollar becomes, by far, the dominant currency in international trade and finance, and therefore the preferred reserve currency for the central banks of pretty much every country on earth.[16]

To undermine the growing call for a radical redistribution of wealth and the potential of class power to block the upward flow of wealth, right-wing politics that supported the shift to neoliberalism took aim at collectivism and the idea of state support. Emblematically captured by Margret Thatcher pronouncing that there is no such thing as society, a decisive shift to a more individualistic model of human relations was taking place.[17] Unions, now depleted of social power, became industrial relations arbiters, and most lost their militancy. Left-wing politics lost its class consciousness as traditional First World 'Socialist' and 'Labour' parties cosied up to business and took up identity and access (to the elite class) causes. The lack of black or women CEOs was no longer related to long-standing class structures that militate disproportionately against certain groups, but the result of racism and sexism. The solution was to fight on identity issues rather than change the nature of economic structures.

People needed to work longer hours or pick up extra jobs. Personal debt increased and young people could no longer expect a wealthier life than their parents. Capitalism's fundamental drive to subordinate as much as possible to its logic reaches its zenith under neoliberalism. Work, social relations, social institutions, nature, emotions, identity are all exposed to the unrelenting discipline of competitiveness and resulting hierarchies.

A strange corollary happens to the central valorised value of freedom. As these negative shifts in well-being occur, populations need to be subjugated through more careful scrutiny and control. There are dangerous tendencies that cannot be allowed to gain a voice. As neoliberalism advances so does militarism abroad and more draconian controls at home. The 'war on terror' allowed greater scope for population-wide spying. We get the rise of conspiracy theories on the one hand (and the ease with which you can label any critical analysis as a conspiracy theory) and cancel culture (both left and right) on the other. With Covid-19 we saw (whether justified or not) how easily fear could be used to invoke population-wide shutdowns and policing. Narrative control by cultural means, such as invoking culture wars, or direct state policing, was, and is, becoming increasingly common. Fear and division have always been useful tools.

The person in capitalism

The importance of competition, efficiency and performance had thus spread widely, including into state and welfare institutions. How would this affect our model of human functioning, relationships and society? How do we construct our beliefs about what it means to be human? How does the model that becomes dominant inform our ideas about how best to organise our societies?

Social constructionists view much of the knowledge we might take for granted as 'common sense' or simply accept as true, as being constructed. This means much of what passes for widely accepted concepts, beliefs, norms and values are formed through continuous interactions among society's members, instead of through objective observation of physical reality. There are many influences at play in how we then develop our cultural beliefs and practices about what we consider to be 'normal' or expected.

The 1966 book *The Social Construction of Reality* by sociologists Peter Berger and Thomas Luckmann is considered a seminal work that gathered historical strands of social constructionist theory. Including thinkers such as Karl Marx, Emile Durkheim and George

Mead, they put forward a cohesive argument that social 'knowledge' arises out of human relationships, with the role of language and power (such as political and economic power) being key to understanding how social constructs emerge and become popularised.[18]

Karl Marx was perhaps the original social constructionist, making clear how difficult it is to imagine a world that operates in a way that is different to the world of social relations a person inhabits. He criticised the dominant themes in philosophical and cultural debates in nineteenth-century Europe that were attempting to distil an abstract idea of 'human nature'. Instead, he proposed that human nature and consciousness are shaped by the social and material circumstances people exist in. In effect he was arguing that what passes for our beliefs about what human nature is cannot escape the logics embedded in the dominant forms of economic and therefore social organisation that we exist in.[19]

Italian Marxist philosopher, journalist and politician Antonio Gramsci, who was imprisoned in 1926 by the fascist regime of Benito Mussolini, wrote more than thirty notebooks during his time in prison. These prison notes would later become highly influential across academia and social activism. In writing about how states can 'manufacture consent', he analysed how ideas and beliefs were shaped, and 'hegemony' (being the strongest and most powerful and therefore able to control others) was reproduced in cultural life through the media, universities, religious and political institutions. These then create legitimacy for the ruling classes.

Hegemony is a key term and concept that Gramsci used to refer to the dominant norms and ideas in any given society or social grouping. Hegemony gives those in power access to the main sources of influence that convince 'the masses' that the way the society is run is the way it should be.[20] *Manufacturing Consent* would later become the title of an influential 1988 book by American social critics Edward Herman and Noam Chomsky, who argued that the mass communication media of the US and the West more broadly are effective and powerful ideological institutions that carry out a system-supportive propaganda function.[21]

All this means that the ways in which we imagine what it means to be human, and how a society should operate, emerge out of economic and political power structures and reflect the best interests of those with class privilege. What then are the implications for how we expect our psychological functioning to be in a neoliberal-dominated society?

Central to the capitalist conception of human nature is a Darwinian-like competition for resources where the 'fittest' wins. Citizens in a capitalist society are said to engage in a competitive field where the most talented will be the most successful (a meritocracy). Their success will be measured through their accumulation of wealth. Differing wealth strata can then be conceptualised as the outcome of an extended version of the hit business-styled reality TV show *The Apprentice*, where the least talented is kicked off early and the worthiest (according to Donald Trump or Alan Sugar, or whichever international version you watch) is selected to join the elites and have their business idea financed.

In this model, a hyper-individualism is promoted, where people are encouraged to implicitly view themselves as if they were a 'mini business' with a 'brand' that needs to stand out in some unique way and where they must triumph over others around them in the social jungle. It is a vision of human nature that's primarily orientated to serve selfish needs and where democratic choices are best exercised through consumerist edicts of purchasing preferences. A creeping alienation from each other develops as our instinct to socially connect is reshaped as a vehicle to gain advantage. A degree of distrust and paranoia pervades relationships as we silently compare our social status to those around us, wondering where we stand and how others perceive us. This can also lead to viewing relationships (with friends, family or romantic) through the lens of 'what's in it for me' or 'is this relationship good for me'. The practice of non-commitment in our relationship-building mimics the rise of the gig economy, precarious work and the breakdown of worker solidarity.[22]

Competition is a key economic driver and so this then also becomes a prominent social and cultural value. Many are then subject to the ongoing fear of falling behind and becoming defined (and/or self-defined) as being a member of a class of 'losers'. To live in a social scenario where you perceive that you are in the loser class and where this is individualised is obviously painful. Capitalism, however, has commodities to sell to help you deal with this.

Defining people as 'vulnerable' or 'ill' allows marketisation and exploitation of this mental pain, insecurity and/or disappointment. Childhood, parenting, mood, stress – and professional approaches to intervening in these – all become subjects of commodification (the act of turning something into an item that can be bought and sold). Human suffering, which follows from the pressures inequality puts on people's material and psychological well-being, is turned into opportunities to create individualised explanations and treatments. The growth of this commodification contributes to both an increase in certain mental problems and the continual expansion of the repertoire of behaviours and emotional states considered to be 'abnormal' (and therefore in need of correcting and treating with this or that product) or a sign of some valorised difference. 'Scientism' is used to sell brands with an aura of being scientific, so that the actual science is buried underneath the power of the profit motive.

More collectivist values such as duty, compassion and solidarity are brought forth only if they give you some sort of advantage in the people market. As we become image (brand) conscious, we are enticed into an ongoing search for self-improvement. In today's world you must learn how to 'sell yourself'. Not only the macro-economy but everyday relationships become regulated by a version of market logic, where a sense that you are failing, or could fail at any moment, is hard to escape.

Richard Wilkinson and Kate Pickett's 2010 book, *The Spirit Level*, examined empirically and theoretically the effects of inequality on societies across the world. Although, in my opinion, they didn't properly account for the impact of regional cultural differences and historical drivers, and I have some reservations about their interpretation of the data (for example, through the unquestioning use of psychiatric diagnoses), they nonetheless provide a strong case that it is not just poverty per se, but *levels of inequality* in any given society that have the biggest impact on health and well-being outcomes. Inequality – the gap between richest and poorest – has profound impacts on people. The prevalence of mental disorders, stress, unhappiness, substance misuse and a variety of physical health outcomes all worsen with rising levels of inequality.[23]

The drivers of self-doubt and insecurity about being judged are exacerbated by inequality. A belief in meritocracy means that any failure is deemed a personal failure. According to Wilkinson and Pickett, greater inequality heightens social threat and status anxiety, evoking feelings of shame, which feed into our instincts for withdrawal, submission and subordination. When the social pyramid gets higher and steeper, status insecurity increases.

The social and cultural demarcations of class, from what we eat and how we talk to what culture we consume, are also rigorously upheld in more unequal societies, making all sorts of discriminations much easier.[24] These social divides exacerbate the individualisation of social phenomena. Change doesn't occur through organised class-based action, but through individuals acting in a 'responsible' way. Saving the world from the proliferation of pollutant plastics is through individuals being more conscious about their use of plastics, rather than through governmental policy. Then we can point the finger at those feckless idiots who are ruining the environment for the rest of us, while turning a blind eye to putting controls on the fashion industry – one of the planet's biggest polluters. Class-based divide and rule emerges from behind the individualisation smokescreen as we fall in line with stereotypes of what these irresponsible 'chavs' that ruin things for everyone else look like.[25]

In neoliberalism, market forces are free to govern all aspects of societal functioning, including institutions previously owned, regulated or managed by the state. From transport to schools, the dominant ideology is that competition will improve standards. The value of competition will then percolate down from the staff to the customers of those institutions. This pressure to perform thus invades all strata of contemporary life. From corporate management to academic practices, from image to games, performance has become central. Knowledge is produced through measuring a system's (and by extension an individual's) performance – be it organisational, cultural or technological. Institutions and individuals are subject to ongoing surveillance and monitoring of their accomplishments using surrogate measures of efficiency (from exam results and school league tables to work appraisals and stock market share values). Knowledge and power are thus created through the production of competitive performance-related information.[26]

The effect of absorbing this ideology is to privatise individuals to the degree where obligations to others and harmony with the wider community can become obstacles rather than objectives. In this 'look after number one' value system, other individuals are there to be competed against as they too chase after their personal desires. Figuring out who is the top dog in what, and once achieved how to stay there, is more defining of personhood than how we support each other.

Children are cultured into the virtues of competition and consumerism, through competitive performing across a variety of arenas and by living within societal institutions (such as schools) that are forced, through policy, to embody these values. The emotional correlates of failure such as misery, fear and demoralisation are naturalised, individualised and so depoliticised.[27] When you get feelings of insecurity, anxiety and stress, and 'epidemics' of self-harm, eating disorders, depression, loneliness and social phobia, these are simply the disorders of individuals with 'dysfunctions'. They are medical conditions that arise from internal failings and that require health professionals to correct. They are most certainly not the outcome of the 'winner' and 'loser' social structure.

The impact of competitive performance starts young. An analysis of the academic performance of the entire state school population of England in 2013 replicates a common finding, which is that the fortunes of the youngest in the class compared to the eldest are different over the course of a lifetime. August-born children (the youngest in the class) get consistently lower results in school exams, are more likely to leave education early, get a diagnosis of ADHD, report feeling unhappy, and have a lower chance of getting into a high-performing university.[28] Performative competition, it seems, starts young and its impact continues for years.

Even the successful can't escape the edict to perform well. The entrepreneurial individual is often regarded as someone who can take risks. But if you don't succeed, or if you succeed and then fail, or if you succeed but can't seem to find a sense of contentment, or if you never feel like you've done enough succeeding – well, it may be because you have a disorder (like ADHD) which has resulted in these disappointments. It's certainly not because this is a system designed to disavow contentment. Capitalism needs a degree of chaos and performance anxiety.

Maintaining the concept of 'freedom' in neoliberal societies means that control is often through mechanisms that encourage populations to internalise, self-monitor and self-sensor.[29] When a young person is not reaching the expected high-level efficiency or shows what are considered deviations from the expected predestiny inscribed for successful neoliberal subjects (such as being able to have fun at the same time as achieving academic success), introspection on personal failures and a search for an individualised solution is deepened.

Commodification distances people from a more considered and involved understanding of the problems being experienced. It also disconnects people from the possibility that they already possess the knowledge to know how to deal with their subjective states. Instead, you're encouraged to buy expert/technically developed commodities, such as particular diagnoses, medications and psychotherapies, which you're led to believe will enhance your quality of life with little adverse effects. The time and relational support needed to learn how to bear and work through emotional pain is at risk of disappearing in such consumerist excess.

Once this system is set in motion, we can predict several things will happen. Commodities tend to give only temporary experiences of satisfaction, as markets must keep selling to keep the monetary flow going and so must keep convincing consumers that there is a better product available. They must also be taught that if they stop consuming the brand (e.g. renounce a diagnosis or stop a medicine) their life will deteriorate. Once an area of life has been subject to market commodification, it will grow in volume as the pressure to make a profit continues.

Of course, none of this is absolute and I am describing tendencies that will get promoted rather than recipes that we all blindly follow. The human spirit is tremendously resilient. We have not succumbed as a species to the isolationist demands of the Hayekian free market vision. No culture can be boiled down to single stories. While neoliberalism promotes a particular version of the human subject, many others coexist. Solidarity, compassion, altruism and even love for our fellow humans keep breaking out. Our instinct to care for each other is intact. My many years of meeting and working with families have reassured me that caring for each other is a fundamentally human trait that cannot be snuffed out.

Before discussing the colonial nature of the push to globalise MHIC, I would like to finish this chapter by highlighting how Western governments are experiencing a wave of political crises that is likely amplifying the dynamics I have been outlining. The US empire is in decline, as are its allies. This sense of decline, of being broken, that we can no longer trust the idea that life will get better, permeates our culture and sets us up for MHIC to sweep in and radiate its messages to all corners and sections of society.

All is not well

In the summer of 1989, an article titled 'The End of History' by American political scientist Francis Fukuyama was published and became an instant hit.[30] Fukuyama argued that with the imminent collapse of the Soviet Union, the last ideological alternative to Western capitalist democracy and liberalism had been eliminated. The world would now converge on a single political and economic model. This would herald 'the end of history'; that is, the endpoint of mankind's ideological evolution and the universalisation of Western liberal democracy as the final form of human government. There would be global marketisation and a new era of international relations would result in the world finally achieving homeostasis.

It didn't take long for history to start again. Capitalist democracy and free trade would not only be rather fragile, but the postcommunist imperialist triumphalism would instead sow the seeds of its potential demise. Markets need a state to protect the interests of the elite. Western states are now riven with political instability, polarisation of public opinions, unpopular leaders and the spread of the feeling that society is broken.

The avarice for consumerism has been fruitful for selling an image of plenty and choice and for preying on our hedonistic desires (which we all have). Behind it a trail of destruction is created, and as it becomes harder to ignore, this love of capitalist excess is wearing thin. The leader of the 'free world', the US, loves to lecture others (and invade, overthrow or otherwise sanction them) about freedom and democracy. But what is life like for most people who live there, let alone those who live in the countries US imperialism has intervened in?

Since the late 1970s, wages for the bottom 70 per cent of earners have been essentially stagnant, and between 2009 and 2013, real wages fell for the entire bottom 90 per cent of the wage distribution. Even wages for the bottom 70 per cent of four-year college graduates have been flat since 2000.[31] In April 2022, with stagnant wages and inflation at a forty-year high, over 60 per cent of US consumers lived pay cheque to pay cheque, a 9 per cent increase from April 2021.[32] Many of these people will be on the brink of joining the 600,000 homeless people wandering around in a country with more than 17 million empty homes.[33] An estimated 34 million people, including one in eight children, experience hunger, with 53 million using foodbanks in 2021,[34] while almost 40 per cent of the entire US food supply is thrown away into landfills every year.[35]

More than 46 million people in the US live with water insecurity — either no running water or water that may be unsafe to drink.[36] The US has been experiencing a historic decline in life expectancy, from 78.8 years in 2019 to 76.1 years in 2021; so much so that today the average Cuban, despite six decades of illegal blockades and hybrid warfare against them, lives around three years longer than the average American.[37]

American people live in one of the most economically unequal societies in human history. Over 20 per cent of income flows to the top 1 per cent, whose share of the country's wealth is approaching 40 per cent. The top 0.1 per cent holds roughly the same share of US wealth as the bottom 90 per cent.[38] While most working-class Americans face difficulties in meeting their everyday needs, billionaire wealth surged in 2022 with rapidly rising food and energy profits. Elon Musk, one of the world's richest men, paid a true tax rate of about 3 per cent between 2014 and 2018. Aber Christine, a flour vendor in Uganda, makes $80 a month and pays a tax rate of 40 per cent.[39]

Far from being the 'beacon of democracy', the US, along with its allies across the Western world, has a democracy created for and by the rich – an oligarch class that keeps the economy siphoning money upwards.* This is what they do across the globalised world, where trade agreements and transnational corporatism keep the 'rule-based' order working in their favour. Economic elites and organised groups representing business interests have substantial independent impacts on US government policy, while average citizens and mass-based interest groups have little or no influence.[40]

According to a 2021 poll, over 60 per cent of Americans were dissatisfied with the two-party system and were ready for third-party alternatives,[41] and by 2023 only 16 per cent approved of what Congress was doing.[42] Opinion polls in July 2022 found that Americans' confidence in news media was just 16 per cent for newspapers and 11 per cent for TV. In the US, six media companies are in charge of 90 per cent of mass media consumption and distribution.[43] US media outlets have been characterised as having a symbiotic relationship with the government, Wall Street and powerful corporations.[44] Similar trends can be found in most Western allies of the US. For example, trust in the main political parties in the UK fell to 12 per cent in 2023, down from 20 per cent in 2022.[45]

More than half of US tax spending goes to sustaining the world's most expensive military (spending more than the next ten countries combined).[46] The military–industrial complex is in overdrive.

---

*There is a habit of referring to oligarchs as the super-rich in countries we don't like, but not to extend a similar label to such a stratum in our own countries; on the contrary, individuals like Jeff Bezos, Elon Musk and Bill Gates are often seen in more heroic terms as great innovators.

Headed by the giants of Lockheed Martin, Boeing, Raytheon and Northrop Grumman, we are getting accustomed to endless war – just not on our lands (yet). After the Cold War and the anti-colonial hot wars, the war machine became, for a while, an unstoppable force leaving millions of dead. Afghanistan, Iraq, Libya, Syria, Yemen, Somalia, the old Yugoslavia and the countless others where CIA operatives tried (sometimes successfully, sometimes not) to engineer regime change.

The US has over 750 foreign military bases spread across eighty nations. After the US is the UK with 145 bases. Russia has about three dozen foreign bases, and China just five. The US military budget accounts for about 40 per cent of the total global military spend. The US has three times as many bases outside its country as all other countries combined.[47] But all this wealth and power has not resulted in sustained victories, so that even the medieval cult of the Taliban defeated them after twenty years in Afghanistan, leaving the country, one of the poorest in the world, in an arguably worse state than when it was first invaded in 2001.

The US has also been using its economic muscle through imposing sanctions (and freezing dollar-based assets, so that the countries they belong to cannot access them) against an expanding number of countries. Many emerging economies are seeking, and finding, ways to conduct trade in non-dollar currencies, a process known as de-dollarisation.[48] New non-dollar trading contracts are being implemented, the most noteworthy perhaps being that for the first time in forty-eight years, oil-rich Saudi Arabia is now open to trading in currencies besides the US dollar.[49] The BRICS (Brazil, Russia, India, China, South Africa) economic group announced in August 2023 that Argentina, Egypt, Ethiopia, Iran, Saudi Arabia and the United Arab Emirates have all been invited to become members of the alliance (Argentina has since declined to join). More than forty countries have shown interest in joining BRICS, including twenty-two countries which have formally requested to join.[50]

The hegemony of the US both militarily and economically, while still considerable, is weakening.[51] Signs of the declining power are multiple. From economic stagnation for the masses, to the fading ability to dictate to other countries what they can and can't do. The US and its Western allies remain powerful and seem hell-bent on setting ablaze any part of the world that doesn't bow down to their will. Whether in Ukraine, West Asia or Western Africa, American and Western imperialism would rather sow chaos than allow any rival power to emerge peacefully.

There are an increasing number of books and articles predicting a terminal decline in US hegemony.[52] In his latest book, John Gray predicts that Western liberalism is in its death throes with the growth of what he calls 'hyper-liberalism', a form of hyper-individualism in which we have unlimited autonomy to create whatever identity we like. Although I disagree with Gray's view of human nature (as being prone to a Hobbesian selfishness and violence), his conclusion that the Western empire is in deep trouble seems to me correct. The hyper-liberal ideology operates as a distraction from a failing capitalism. Identity politics then demonises those who economically suffer the most, from Hillary Clinton's contemptuous 'basket of deplorables' reference to the labelling of Brexit voters as racist. Those voting out of anger at a system that excludes them are derided as stupid, brutish or conned. Anxiously clinging to the fringes of middle-class life, those who may have only a passing acquaintance with the larger society engage in virtue-signalling self-righteousness. As a result, a crisis of legitimation is now sweeping across most Western 'democracies', with deep divisions meaning that most leaders are seen as illegitimate by a substantial portion of their population.[53]

This is the political, economic and therefore cultural backdrop to our everyday lives. Rather than being angry at the warmongering capitalist class, MHIC, alongside identity politics, channels those feelings back into internal conflicts, to be managed, treated or commodified by gaining rights for this or that minority group. Structural inequalities and imperialist power are saved, at least for now, from potential class solidarity.

While the neoliberal empire is in decline, MHIC is on the rise and conditions to conquer the rest of the world were developing. MHIC had already incorporated the colonial mentality of Western imperialism, which is what I discuss next.

14. Colonial psychiatry

'When we revolt it's not for a particular culture. We revolt simply because, for many reasons, we can no longer breathe.'

Frantz Fanon

Vieda Skultans, a professor of social anthropology at the University of Bristol, left Latvia in 1945 as a refugee aged six months. In 1990, she returned for the first time and in 1992 began her many years of fieldwork there. She sat in on psychiatric consultations and tape-recorded over three hundred of these. She interviewed psychotherapists, psychiatrists and neurologists, as well as many of the patients who attended their clinics. She arranged focus groups and attended several conferences organised by pharmaceutical companies that attracted hundreds of psychiatrists from the region.

Skultans had a unique opportunity to investigate what happens when a society coached in collectivism undergoes the sort of rapid change that happened in the ex-Soviet states in the 1990s, after a capitalist economy was introduced almost overnight. How did this radical change in the economic base affect not just levels of distress but the very concepts used in understanding what distress is? In her seminal paper, Skultans describes how Latvia was invaded by the ideology of MHIC, with the previously virtually unknown diagnosis of depression becoming commonplace and the previously common concept of '*nervi*' more or less disappearing.[1]

After the downfall of the USSR, the new governments in the Baltic states were keen to sever ties with their Soviet past. Like many ex-Soviet states, Latvia embarked on a rapid programme of de-collectivisation, marketising the economy, and restructuring existing state institutions such as the health service. Living conditions deteriorated for much of the population and many faced an increased sense of unpredictability and precariousness.

At the same time, the influx of Westernised media and advertising held out the promise of infinite possibilities for those with skills and aspirations. Self-control and self-reliance had been features of Latvian culture for a long time, but with the restraint provided by a collectivist ideology gone, they were reinforced and magnified by the capitalist ethic. One consequence was that individuals suffering from physical and psychological disabilities became ashamed of their problems and reluctant to share them with others.

Despite distrust of the state under Soviet rule, individuals were integrated in many ways with the '*kolektivs*' (the collective group) and now felt on their own and isolated. A paradoxical feature of a social philosophy that places an emphasis on freedom of choice is that people end up with less autonomy in the management of health and illness. Health care in Soviet Latvia was organised around the polyclinics staffed by groups of specialists, including neurologists and psychiatrists. The system accorded the individual a considerable amount of autonomy in choosing treatment. Government policy after independence was premised on the view that Latvians were over-doctored and that there was a wasteful duplication of resources. The number of specialists was reduced and at the same time a rapid growth in the number of private psychotherapists occurred.

Conferences organised by pharmaceutical companies proliferated and psychiatrists and family doctors were 'educated' about (what to them were) new diagnostic categories used in the West such as depression. The language of depression represented a radical departure from older languages that were central both to Soviet psychiatry and to lay conceptualisations of distress.

Traditional values advocated stoicism and contentment with one's lot. During Soviet times the language of *nervi* had become commonplace. *Nervi* referred to being in a tense state, but also to showing or requiring a kind of courage and contempt of danger. To suffer from or live with *nervi* was seen as an inevitable consequence of living under Soviet rule. The discourse of *nervi* placed patients and their ailments within this broader social context of a shared past history and living circumstances.

To ask about a person's *nervi* was to invite a life story. People spoke of what their *nervi* had been through and experienced or survived. Talk of *nervi* pointed outwards, offering a way of understanding the world and its subjective importance, and inwards towards disclosing a person's nature and values. In Latvian discourse about *nervi* there was a sense of dialectic tension between a state of sociality and one of opposition and withdrawal, between a self at ease with its environment and one that stands apart.

The concepts that came with Westernisation introduced to Latvian society a range of hitherto unrecognised syndromes and illnesses, foremost among them was 'masked depression'.

Depression as a concept represented the internalisation of a heightened sense of accountability and responsibility for one's life circumstances, even though opportunities for changing those circumstances were only available to a few of the more privileged of the Latvian population. Westernisation was seen as desirable and connected to the project of modernisation, freedom and abundance. Thus, Western psychiatry was imagined to be more scientific with a greater capacity to explain the causes of human distress.

Unlike in the West, patients did not describe their suffering with internalising language (such as low mood, guilt, negative thinking). This meant that discovering depression could not occur using the classic 'symptoms' found in diagnostic manuals. This was because, so the argument goes, depression was being 'masked' by cultural practices. It was still the depression that was described and placed in the diagnostic manuals developed in the West – it just presented differently. Where have we heard the concept of 'masking' before? It's a useful trick that enables you to shoehorn whatever you wish into your predetermined conceptual framework.

As the concept of depression sank into the minds of psychiatrists and psychotherapists, the nature of consultations no longer invited a person to talk about the social and historical context of their struggles. Distress was no longer part of a shared struggle, but one that pointed to something medically wrong within the person, which required treatment with drugs or therapy. Consultations now had a primarily educative function, teaching distressed patients the meaning of depression and convincing them to accept the 'correct' treatment. Rates of depression rose, and, thanks to MHIC, a rich and meaningful psychosocial history was buried.

Depression goes global

In 1996 an influential book on global disease burden, published by the World Health Organization (WHO), predicted that by 2020 depression would be the second-leading cause of disease burden globally.[2] Linking depression to suicides, the acceleration of the global export of MHIC to countries like Latvia that had differing local idioms for understanding and expressing states of distress, was embedded into global institutional policy.

Since then, there have been multiple programmes funded to spread Western mental health ideology. Introduced in 2008, the WHO mental health Gap Action Programme (mhGAP) aims at scaling up services for 'mental, neurological and substance use disorders in countries, especially those in the low- and middle-income categories'.[3] The priority conditions addressed by mhGAP are: 'depression, psychoses, suicidal ideation, epilepsy, dementia, disorders due to use of alcohol and psychoactive substances, mental and behavioural disorders in children and other conditions including medically unexplained somatic complaints and emotional, physical or behavioural problems after exposure to an extreme stressor'.[4] Notice how psychiatric 'disorders' sit alongside known neurological ones such as epilepsy. This allows depression and suicidal ideation (for example) to be thought of as being in the same realm of brain conditions.

MhGAP's prescriptive tools leave little room for local understandings of distress and practices that might disrupt or diverge from the assumed universality of the conditions it seeks to recognise. Constructed around psychiatric diagnostic conceptualisations of distress, it has all the hallmarks of cultural and political colonisation.[5]

A March 2023 WHO guidance to policymakers around the world

described 'depressive disorder' as a common mental disorder that affects an estimated 5 per cent of adults worldwide, is more common in women than men, is a leading cause of suicide, that there is effective treatment for this condition, but that more than three-quarters of those living in low- and middle-income countries receive no treatment.[6]

This way of discussing depressive disorder already assumes that it's a universal disease that can respond to the same interventions no matter where in the world it's found. The depressive disorder the WHO is talking about derives from the definitions found in the diagnostic manuals created by Western psychiatry. What then happens is similar to what happened in Latvia. The concept of depression is treated as if it has a universal applicability, as if it's capable of defining 'case-ness'. It's then exported around the world and when it encounters local cultures where the 'symptoms' listed in diagnostic manuals cannot be found, then the idea of 'masked' depression enables the construct to survive intact in virtually any location.

Here it is assumed that it's still this illness of depression, but that cultural traditions have resulted in different ways of expressing this supposed underlying condition. Masking allows the symptoms listed to become irrelevant and to create forms of magical intuition where the 'expert' no longer needs symptoms or anything other than deep awareness to spot the 'depression' that's hiding behind (for example) a multitude of bodily pains. There are many other consequences of collapsing and disappearing local idioms. It depoliticises social and economic sources of distress and suicide, as well as taking away the deeper cultural significance and meanings attached to mental suffering, which in many traditions is a source of growth, a path to accepting the limits of human capacity, and a mechanism for strengthening social bonds.

This globalisation-led 'depression as a concept' helped its transformation from being an extremely rare diagnosis in much of the world to one that is thought to be one of the most common.

Some presentations create interesting challenges in knowing how to enact the colonial process of converting and collapsing local knowledge into Western universals. A common presentation among some South East Asian men is locally referred to as *'dhat'*, which manifests as a feared 'semen loss', interpreted as causing a subsequent draining of energy and weakness.[7] *Dhat* in psychiatric diagnostic terms is often interpreted as a localised presentation of a depressive disorder.

In a paper illustrating the process that takes place when we substitute a local belief for an imposed Westernised one, Professor Sushrut Jadhav, a psychiatrist of South Asian origin who works in inner-city London, imagined what it would be like to reverse the process. What might happen, he wondered, if we assumed that *dhat* was the universal and the symptoms we imagine as 'depression' was really 'masked *dhat*'. He analysed case histories of forty-seven white Britons who had a diagnosis of a depressive disorder and found that what they *really* had was a semen-retention syndrome that's a variation of *dhat*. Consequently, he concluded, the undue focus previously on mood idioms by both white British patients and their health professionals leads to a mistaken diagnosis of depression rather than recognising they have 'masked *dhat*'.[8] This might seem amusing and nonsensical to populations trained in MHIC ideology, but doesn't it illustrate what happens when we use Western-developed (and as I have been arguing consumerist) products and impose them unproblematically on diverse populations around the world?

Suffering in a Buddhist context could result in mistaking enlightenment for a depressive condition.[9] In Buddhism, as with many Eastern religions, suffering plays an important role in deepening an understanding of the nature of human consciousness. Far from being a sign of something wrong in you, it can be a vehicle for generating valued spirituality. In any case, no society really knows how to distinguish between mental suffering that's a sign of illness from experiences that are not. Sorrow and grief are often linked with inner depth and dignity, not pathology.[10] Given these alternative perspectives of experiencing the world, some anthropologists have argued that the high rate of depression in the US is itself a product of a culture that prioritises the pursuit of happiness and consumption as a basic aim of human existence.[11]

Post-natal depression is considered a major public health issue across the developed world but is not universally discussed or even recognised elsewhere.[12] Anthropologists have found that certain social rituals seem to protect women from low mood and distress after giving birth in parts of Africa, Asia and the Pacific. In those societies protective measures include social seclusion from the wider community in the postpartum period, mandated rest, assistance in tasks, and recognition (through rituals and gifts) of the new social status of the mother.[13]

Japan has (apparently) not only shown markedly lower rates of what has been assumed to be depression than its Western counterparts, but unlike depression in other developed countries, slightly more men than women appear to suffer from it. Is it still the same 'depression'? What does this difference tell us about social and cultural interpretations of low mood? Anthropologist Margaret Lock suggested this was because many Japanese women did not recognise 'depression' as such. The women in Lock's study, even those in trying socio-economic circumstances, kept telling her that their suffering was insignificant, that they were even fortunate, when compared to their own mothers, who had survived the Second World War and its aftermath.[14]

In China a few decades ago a common diagnosis made by psychiatrists was 'neurasthenia'. Neurasthenia refers to a complaint of increased fatigue, bodily weakness and exhaustion after minimal effort. This had some crossover with a more traditional condition of *'fan nao'*, which is characterised by fatigue, and subjective feelings of being worried and distressed with conflicting thoughts and unfulfilled desires. It may manifest as overt irritability. Fatigue as an expression can be seen as a culturally constructed entity symbolising the consequences of 'busyness' and productivity, while the lack of it might betoken indolence. The complaint of fatigue, therefore, has layers of social meanings embedded within it. Since neurasthenia was treated more as a physical than psychological diagnosis in China, it would connote less personal responsibility in its causation than the diagnosis that was soon to replace it – that of depression.[15]

In the last couple of decades there has been a dramatic transformation of neurasthenia in China. The American system of classification (the *DSM*) gained increasing influence as China became more integrated into the global economic system. Neurasthenia as a psychiatric category became contested, was progressively marginalised, and instead reconstituted as the 'disease' of depression.[16]

Suicide has become a major issue in many countries. In India, farmers have been committing suicide in record numbers. More than 5,500 agricultural labourers committed suicide in 2022, an increase of 9 per cent from 2020, and 29 per cent from 2019. Farmers in India have to routinely face crop failures, rising input costs and low market prices that then trap them in a spiralling cycle of debt.[17] Agricultural policies of liberalisation and globalisation during the 1990s prioritised open markets and had a disproportionate and adverse effect on small farms, as the state withdrew subsidies with minimum support.[18] Narratives from these farmers' families suggest that a combination of financial and moral debt when accrued within a web of family and caste-related relationships result in patterns of personal and familial humiliation, producing a profound sense of hopelessness.[19]

These political and cultural factors can be rendered invisible by suggesting that the primary problem leading to suicide is depression. In this framework, it's the lack of attention to their mental health needs that is causing these suicides. This school of thought recommends early psychiatric intervention as the primary preventive measure.[20] Most papers published in mental health journals on Indian farmer suicides urge a reduction to the access of the means of suicide and an increase in access to psychiatry, psychology and medication. This relocates the central issue away from the political sphere, where social justice and policy reform are needed, to within the individual, where treatment is needed.[21]

These cultural differences and nuances go missing in the WHO mental health Gap Action Programme I mentioned earlier. This hasn't stopped it being promoted by one of the top medical journals, the *Lancet*. In 2007 the *Lancet* produced a series on global mental health,[22] and in 2018 the *Lancet Commission* argued that the global mental health agenda should be expanded from a focus on reducing the treatment gap to improving the mental health of whole populations by addressing gaps in prevention and quality of care.[23]

A film, released in 2023, on the *Lancet* 200 website provides an update on the global mental health movement it's promoting.[24] The film, meant to celebrate achievements and encourage further expansion of the movement, never once questions what we mean by mental health. Nearly all those who appear in the film are based in London and the injunction to scale up services is based on improving access to treatments largely developed in Western mental health systems. The one non-Western-developed idea in the film is a 'friendship bench', first developed in Zimbabwe. One of the counsellors who staff this service explains that they 'train counsellors to talk to people' and that 'people come to talk about their social and relationship issues'. So, this mental health technology is providing a bench for people to come and talk about their problems, which turn out to be mainly relational and social. Do you need training to do that? Do you have to become a qualified 'counsellor' to talk to people about their social (often financial and living conditions) and relationship problems?

In his 2010 book *Crazy Like Us*, Ethan Watters documents how this global mental health movement has encouraged interventions that have discounted and then worked to change local beliefs. Mental illnesses popularised in America and the West have spread across the globe. In post-tsunami Sri Lanka, Watters describes how Western trauma counsellors who, in their rush to help, inadvertently trampled on local expressions of grief, suffering and healing. As I mentioned in the last chapter, in Hong Kong, he retraces the last steps of the teenager whose death sparked an epidemic of the American version of anorexia nervosa, after Western 'experts' covered the local media with talk about eating disorders and how to recognise them. Watters also reveals how a multimillion-dollar campaign by drug companies worked to change the Japanese experience of unhappiness by consciously marketing the disease of depression. Discussing the better outcomes found for psychosis in non-industrialised countries, Watters contrasts those achieved by a woman in Zanzibar, whose family took a relaxed, non-judgemental and spiritual view towards her psychotic experiences, with those of someone from another local family who was accessing Western-style psychiatric services and medication.[25]

MHIC has been a remarkably successful export.

Colonial mindsets

It's hard to understate how deeply colonial, and frankly racist, mental health ideology has been. European colonialism devastated societies and economies, particularly those across the African continent. It required justifying principles such as the need to civilise the purportedly backward peoples, who were painted as so psychologically primitive that being slaves to a master was good for them. The task of civilising was referred to as the 'white man's burden', a term popularised by Rudyard Kipling's 1899 poem of the same title. The philosophy underpinning this alleged burden consisted of the three 'C's of colonialism: 'Civilisation, Christianity and Commerce'.

Christianity unsettled traditional African religious beliefs as well as the entire economic and political stability of the continent. Congo, one of the worst affected countries, had rules inflicted on its population like banning the practice of non-European religions. Missionaries were sent to teach the native people about the true God they should worship. They were introduced across the countries of the Empire with little to no information on local circumstances. Their objective was to 'save souls'.[26]

The belief in a civilising mission can still be found alive and well in the colonial missionaries of MHIC. Non-Western populations need scientific enlightenment to relieve them of the superstitions that led them to believe in primitive notions like *dhat* and *nervi*. They need educating to recognise depression and all the other glorious revelations that can be delivered through the book of *DSM*. Their poor souls have been tarnished with the stigma that their superstitions bring, and we can free them by helping them see that depression is just another illness that can be recognised and cured. Psychoanity will send its missionaries to save you and you will show thanks when the drug companies hand round their pots for your contributions.

Prior to the global MHIC putsch, so steeped was Western psychology and psychiatry in the idea of human cultural and moral hierarchies, that colonised 'natives' were assumed to be psychologically 'primitive'. Unlike the civilised Europeans, they had not developed 'psychological mindedness'. Well into the second half of the last century, psychiatrists were discussing the causes of the lack of depression among non-Westerners and suggesting it was due to their psychological immaturity, lack of insight and a lack of Christian guilt. Some echoed Jean-Jacques Rousseau's theme of 'noble savages', claiming that natives were not prone to depression because of their lack of personal and social responsibility.[27]

Psychiatrist Suman Fernando, who migrated from Sri Lanka to the UK in the early 1960s, has written extensively on the ubiquitous nature of racism in the history of mental health ideology and its stubborn resistance to attempts to expunge it. In his book *Institutional Racism in Psychiatry and Clinical Psychology*, he argues that the theories and technologies of psychiatry and psychology have helped to shore up racist ideologies and contributed to the 'othering' of certain social groups. During the centuries of European colonial expansionism, skin-colour racism, colonialism and imperialism worked to reinforce one another. Non-white natives of the colonies were seen as immature and childlike, and therefore incapable of ruling themselves.[28]

Alienists (as early psychiatrists were called) were involved in conjuring up diagnostic categories that authorised enslavement. *Drapetomania* – a form of madness that compelled slaves to run away – is perhaps the best-known example, while *dysaesthesia aethiopis* was a term used for a deficiency in the psychic capacity to cope with civilised life.

The founding fathers of psychology contributed theories that served to hold racism in place. In the UK, Sir Francis Galton began the eugenics movement with his 1883 book, *Inquiries into Human Faculty and Its Development*. In their quest for a better society, eugenicists believed it was possible to perfect people through selective breeding leading to racial improvement (often referred to as 'racial hygiene'). The philosophy of eugenics spread across the Eurocentric world so that most industrialised countries had organisations devoted to promoting it by the end of World War I. By World War II eugenics reached its ultimate destination in Nazi gas chambers.[29]

Stanley Hall, founder of American psychology and the first president of the American Psychological Association, was a firm proponent of racial eugenics. Like others of his time, he invoked evolutionary principles to posit a hereditary racial hierarchy. In the face of the large-scale migration of impoverished people to the US in the early twentieth century, psychologist Henry Goddard, another committed eugenicist, set up an intelligence testing station at Ellis Island, a main port of entry to the US. His goal was to weed out those with hereditary 'feeble-mindedness'. According to the results that Goddard obtained, 70–80 per cent of Jews, Italians and Hungarians were 'morons' or 'imbeciles'. At the same time, an eminent Stanford psychologist, Lewis Terman, argued for race-based differences in intelligence. In the latter part of the twentieth century, a string of psychologists – such as Hans Eysenck, Arthur Jensen, Richard Herrnstein and Phillipe Ruston – also put forward what they claimed (incorrectly) was evidence that demonstrated race-based differences in intelligence.

All this invocation of racial, cultural and even moral hierarchies had (and continues to have) profound effects on the personhood of the coloniser and the colonised. After writing about the experience of being black in racist post-Second World War France in his 1952 book *Black Skins White Masks*,[30] Frantz Fanon, a French West Indian psychiatrist, psychoanalyst and philosopher who became involved in the anti-colonial struggles in Algeria, describes, in his 1961 book *The Wretched of the Earth*, what it's like psychologically to be colonised.[31] He claimed the colonised must 'ask themselves the question constantly: "who am I?"' The colonial logic divides settlers from natives and necessitates the dehumanisation of the latter to facilitate their exploitation. This impacts the psychological reality of both the coloniser and colonised.

A European 'self' develops in its relation and encounter with the 'other' (non-European). To deal with the sense of psychological inadequacy, the native tries to be as white as possible, by adopting the Western values, religions and practices. Fanon calls this phenomenon donning white masks over black skins, resulting in an almost psychotic duality. Further, the sense of inadequacy and insecurity in the colonised psyche results in violence, which can be seen as a form of self-assertion, an attempt to combat this sense of inadequacy. As a result, the natives are then further compartmentalised by being demonised for their perceived inherently violent nature. They are declared insensible to ethics; they represent not only the absence of values, but also the negation of values. In this sense they are required to represent the embodiment of evil for the coloniser.

In his 1978 book *Orientalism*, American Palestinian author Edward Said establishes the term 'Orientalism' as a critical concept to describe the West's commonly contemptuous depiction and portrayal of the East. Said shows how Orientalist writings and ideologies actively shape the world they describe, and how they perpetuate views of Middle Eastern and Far Eastern people as inferior, subservient and in need of saving. As a result, these racist and sometimes romanticised stereotypes create a world view that justifies Western colonialism and imperialism.[32]

Gayatri Spivak developed and applied Foucault's term of 'epistemic violence' to describe the destruction of non-Western ways of perceiving the world and the resultant dominance of Western traditions for conceptualising humanity. She used the term 'subaltern' to designate colonial populations who are socially, politically and geographically excluded from the hierarchy of power and from the metropolitan homeland of an empire. The term subaltern was originally coined by Antonio Gramsci to identify the cultural exclusion that displaces specific people and social groups from socio-economic institutions of society, in order to deny their agency and voice. Spivak was particularly concerned with what she saw as the epistemic violence that relates to women from the colonised subaltern, who are pushed to the social margins with their non-Western ways of perceiving, understanding and knowing the world.[33]

Residue from these racialised and ethnocentric ideals continued to be found in later twentieth-century psychological and psychiatric discussions that depicted Westerners as introspective and intellectually articulate 'psychologisers' and non-Westerners as un-reflexive and more instinctual 'somatisers'.[34] Non-Westerners are cast as incapable of recognising psychological distress, which instead would be expressed as bodily symptoms. Women and the working classes were also often seen as 'somatisers' well into the late twentieth century.[35]

Hierarchy of minds is deeply woven into the ideologies that gave birth to MHIC.

Incorporating and defenestrating racism

The brutal death of George Floyd profoundly impacted people across the US and then across most of the Western world. There were widespread feelings of anger, sadness and revulsion at the latest in a long line of deaths of black Americans in a society where an extraordinary number of young black men become incarcerated in the prison industrial complex or at the receiving end of police brutality. Protests spread from city to city, and in that energy, calls for a radical change of policy and an acknowledgement of structural disadvantage became louder and impossible to ignore.

I have already discussed in Chapter 12 how the resulting Black Lives Matter movement was hijacked by corporate marketing. There is a similar story to tell about institutional psychiatry.

In the week after George Floyd's killing on 25 May 2020, a discussion grew on the UK-based Critical Psychiatry Network email list that I am a part of. We decided it was an opportune time to write to the newly elected president of the Royal College of Psychiatrists.

We penned an open letter to Dr Adrian James, stating that psychiatry had a difficult and at times shameful history, including collusion with eugenic mass murder in Nazi Germany and labelling civil rights protesters and political dissidents as mentally ill. We noted that we continue to disproportionately incarcerate black patients and coerce them into treatment. The letter discussed the profession's history of not only ignoring the effects of discrimination on patients, but of painting other cultures as psychologically primitive. We urged the new president to establish a full independent commission to assess all training curricula and practice guidelines that the college produces, so as to examine these with respect to race and culture. The letter got a decent amount of publicity and I and others had interviews with both televised and written media.[36]

Following an exchange of letters, our suggestion of an independent commission was (perhaps predictably) turned down by Dr James.

However, the royal college created a new race and equality taskforce process and conducted an in-house investigation into racism and discrimination in mental health services. I took part in some of the invited sessions. To me, it felt like identity politics writ large. Psychiatrists talked about their own experience of racism holding back promotions, and attitudes from white patients to black and brown psychiatrists. These are important issues, but the patient-focused discussion was about early access to treatment, efforts to destigmatise mental illness in certain communities who may be reluctant to attend, and the importance of educating them about mental health and illness.

Questions of race and culture were being boiled down to visibility. The inherent bias in our diagnostic practice was never discussed. Worse, the idea that minority communities needed education because of their tendency to stigmatise, illustrated that the prevailing colonial hierarchical model was still institutionally embedded. The power of narratives, guild interests mixing with personal ones, and the ignoring of anything that went further (literally) than skin-deep was not adequately, or even minimally, discussed.

The college's Equality Action Plan was published in January 2021.[37] The plan seemed like a retreat into corporate managerialism. A list of abstract and process-based recommendations about having more data and better education made up the bulk of the suggested solutions. There was nothing about the nature of the concepts, the history and the cultural specificity of the system we use for diagnosis and treatment. The obligatory public relations exercise had been satisfactorily completed without any fundamental change being demanded.

Dr James finished his three-year term as president of the Royal College of Psychiatrists in June 2023. The new president, Dr Shubulade Smith, was one of the two presidential leads for race and equality appointed by James. In an interview about her hopes for her presidency, Smith stated that she wants to work with the college's international partners to influence global mental health and has innovative ideas about how to do this, saying, 'Wouldn't it be great if the World Bank made mental health provision a condition of loans?'[38]

MHIC is in safe hands.

15. Rehabilitating emotions

'The ultimate, hidden truth of the world is that it is something that we make and could just as easily make differently.'

David Graeber

I had been seeing Charlotte on and off for the last two years. She was now seventeen. Before my involvement, she had been seen by our service and received several different therapeutic interventions since she was thirteen years old. All sorts of strategies had been tried. I'd seen her on her own, with her mother, with her father (the parents were separated), even once with her boyfriend. We'd looked at her thoughts, discussed her traumas, we'd even tried medication (which she discontinued, after initially feeling it was great and then after a couple of months coming to the opposite conclusion). I'd spent a lot of time noticing her strengths and natural resilience. I'd discussed her with colleagues and brought their feedback to her. Over those two years she'd have better periods and then at some point would crash, take to her bed, and withdraw for days, sometimes weeks. Periodically she would have other experiences and behaviours such as intrusive thoughts and images of her or others dying horrible deaths, periods where her food intake was poor, and sometimes health anxieties such as thinking she had a brain tumour.

Now she was in another down period. I was wondering what to say, when she blurted out with an angry passion, 'How can I get rid of this thing in my head?'

Me: 'What thing? What do you mean?'

Charlotte: 'This depression, this whatever it is that I can't get rid of.'

Me: 'Can you say more?'

Charlotte: 'There's obviously something wrong with me, a

chemical imbalance or some sort of brain problem. Like a mental illness or something. Whatever it is I can't shake it off.'

It struck me that I had never really had a conversation with Charlotte, or indeed most of my patients, about what sort of theory or model they had about the nature of their problems. How stupid of me. This was many years ago, but most young people already had access to Google and of course were using it to try and make sense of the dilemmas they were experiencing.

Me: 'What do you mean? There's nothing wrong with you. You're just reacting the way human beings are meant to react. There's no chemical imbalance or brain problem. When you have your better periods, you've shown you have an excellent, capable, imaginative, empathic brain. It works perfectly well.'

Charlotte goes quiet, looks at the floor for a minute or so, her long auburn hair draped around her shoulders, partly going down her back and partly either side of her bowed head. She looks up somewhat quizzical. 'But surely there's something wrong in my brain, something not right. Like . . . I feel it.'

Me: 'The feelings are real, powerful, and distressing. I've seen how badly they affect you. What if it's believing that there's something wrong in your brain or in your mind that's making it hard for you to be able to recover? What if the problem is that you believe the problem is in you?'

For the rest of that session and the following couple of sessions we talked more about the power of the belief that there is something wrong in her brain/mind. We talked about the conversations she's had with friends, what she's heard on the media, and what she's found on Google. The idea that there was nothing wrong *in her* seemed strange, so woven into her sense of self and identity had it become. She was both attached and simultaneously disparaging of whatever this was that she felt was a part of her. It seemed like she was in a perpetual battle trying to suppress, ignore, control and desperate to get rid of this part of her. It wouldn't go away. It must be impossible to get rid of.

Sometimes that felt OK, maybe even desirable – she had a reason why she couldn't manage to do what she wanted to. It wasn't her fault. Other times she was so frustrated or despondent or numb or overwhelmed when she thought about this 'thing', this 'mental health', this 'depression', this 'disorder', this 'dysregulation' that was always there. Even when she was feeling happier, having good days, it was lurking in the shadowland of her mind. She could never just enjoy herself, or feel any sense of peace or contentment, because it was there. Always there, somewhere. Sooner or later that shadow would swallow her up again. She was 'treatment-resistant'. Every time she hoped she was finally in recovery, back it would come. She stopped hoping. But still did. Which was the part that still hoped? Was it her unconscious that stopped hoping and her conscious part that still hoped or was it the other way round? Maybe it's this treatment or the next one or the one after that will finally slay the demon. But who is she without this?

The penny started to drop. The belief that there was something wrong in her had become the primary driver of her feeling so bad. It was how she felt about her feelings that made the original feelings seem so awful and that perpetuated the mutual belief (which I shared) that getting better meant feeling better, as opposed to changing how you feel about your feelings. This accords (albeit very loosely) with the psychoanalytic concept of internal objects and how we relate to our internal objects. Depression/mental illness/symptoms had become an internalised object (a part of her), which she found threatening/dangerous, but also strangely alluring at times. The cultural stories we hear about depression/mental illness/symptoms strengthen the boundaries, presence and concreteness of that internal object. A collection of feelings gets tied into the object and the power of this object upon us grows.

Charlotte's attachment to the belief in this inner mysterious entity that had kidnapped her began to melt. The next bad patch she had lasted three days. She resisted the idea of 'oh no here we go again'. She found that after three days in bed she was ready to get up and get on with things. Something had changed. Depression/mental illness were no longer chains wrapped around her body wherever she went, whatever she did. Soon after, for the first time, Charlotte told me she was ready for discharge.*

In the years since meeting Charlotte, I've understood that the problem a large and growing proportion of patients have is the belief that they have a 'mental health' problem. This is very different to saying that they don't have a problem, or that they are attention-seeking, or that they are being 'snowflakes', or that their distress isn't real. Very different. The suffering is real, tangible, visceral, disabling, and can be extremely dangerous, resulting sometimes in serious self-harm and suicide.

'I want to know what's wrong with me . . . I want to understand why I feel like this . . . I want to know what my diagnosis is.'

I am asked versions of this regularly.

Me: 'So, if you got a diagnosis what difference do you imagine it would make to you?'

'I would understand the reason for feeling like this . . . I would know what's wrong with me . . . It would explain why I feel this way . . . I could look up the diagnosis online . . . You would know what the right treatment is.'

Me: 'So, if you understood what was wrong with you and there was a right treatment, what difference do you imagine this might make?'

'I wouldn't feel so low . . . I would stop being anxious . . . I wouldn't have these intrusive thoughts . . . I would stop having these mood swings . . . I wouldn't get so angry all the time.'

And so, we get to an idea that there is something you have to get rid of rather than learn to live with/alongside. That's understandable. When it's constructed as 'symptoms', then that's something you want to eliminate. Treatment then becomes structured around getting rid of a mental experience.

MHIC has influenced our culture to such a degree that we are

---

*Charlotte, like all the case examples in this book, is a fictional patient, but she embodies real presentations and dilemmas taken from clinical practice. The patient who first revealed the power of this meaning-making framework of believing that they have an illness/disorder happened many years ago.

suspicious of a range of emotional experiences, and by implication believe that improving our mental health involves getting rid of a variety of feelings that are now labelled as not just undesirable, but alien, destructive and dangerous. Undesirable feelings are illnesses, diseases, disorders, powerful cancer-like entities that can spread, infect and take over our minds. They are modern versions of possession states that erupt from our genes into misfiring brain chemicals. Beware of that feeling – it's not a feeling, or an experience, it's a 'symptom'. Early intervention is the key. If you let that symptom grow it will take control, become difficult to excise and the modern priests of MHIC will have a hard time performing their scientific exorcisms. These are long-term illnesses anyway, and like diabetes you will need our insulins for the rest of your life. Emotions are dangerous. They must be controlled.

Brooke Siem is a writer, speaker and award-winning chef. I first met her when we were both speaking at a conference organised by the Richard Fee Foundation at Virginia Beach in January 2023. What struck me about her was what I think of as the extra-ordinary courage of the ordinary. Brooke was first prescribed antidepressants as a fifteen-year-old for 'depression' and 'anxiety'. After more than a decade cycling through a variety of antidepressants, she wondered who she might be without them. Brooke made the decision to come off her psychiatric drug prescriptions. She experienced the agony of withdrawal symptoms that no medical professional had warned her about. It took her a year or so to wean herself off them, but eventually she did, and recovered from what she was told would be a lifelong illness. Her moving 2022 book *May Cause Side Effects* recounts this journey.[1] Her recovery happened six years before I first met her.

Talking to Brooke reminded me of Charlotte and the many others I have met who have been convinced or taught to believe they had a dreadful illness from which they may never recover. Looking back, Brooke feels that her own capacity to get through a painful experience (in her case the death of her father when she was fifteen) was undermined by the fear that suffering was not survivable. This was not necessarily Brooke's fear, but that of others around her and the health professionals she was taken to see. And so began a journey of relapses, medication changes, suicidal feelings, hopelessness, and a sense of a never-ending struggle. It takes someone extraordinary like Brooke to recognise that there may be something wrong with the narrative she was being sold. Maybe the problem wasn't depression. Maybe the problem was the belief that she had a 'depression' that needed treatment.

Brooke, I think, demonstrates the courage that I believe we all have but that many of us don't realise we have, particularly in a culture that is so suspicious of suffering. Brooke is extraordinary and started to recognise that ordinary courage. She didn't have anyone who encouraged her to reappraise her life story – she had to go on a journey of her own making. She wishes others around her, and the professionals she met, could have enabled what she now calls 'radical acceptance' – a capacity to live alongside pain and suffering and the knowledge that it won't stay forever. In fact, the fear that our pain will never change is enabled by labelling it as a sign of something wrong in you. A battle to get rid of or suppress ordinary and/or understandable suffering in fact perpetuates it. Brooke's story reminds us that it's never too late. Recovery may be more possible than many of us realise.[2]

Sociologists have understood the adverse consequences of internalised labels, whether sexist, classist or racist, for a long time. Anybody who thinks that psychiatric labels are empowering may not be familiar with this literature or perhaps they have dismissed its relevance to mental health. A 2023 study of young people identifying (or not) with a psychiatric label used longitudinal data that followed 427 youths over two years. Identifying with a psychiatric label was associated with decreasing self-esteem, while discarding a psychiatric label was associated with an increase in self-esteem.[3]

The good, the bad and the ugly of emotional control

I hope I have convinced you that the mental health industry is an economic force tied to capitalist consumption logic, with scant scientific basis. The commercialisation and monetisation of emotional distress and behavioural difference has had the profound effect of alienating us from the diversity of states of mind and behavioural orientations that human beings possess. This is not a liberation. We would not be so starry-eyed about diversity if it was (as it should be) in the realm of the ordinary. We would not need the increasing categories of human typologies being created and mansplained all over the place.

Humans have a vast capacity for emotional experiences. When we declare war on certain emotional states, not only do we deprive people from deepening their reservoir and gaining meaning from the variety of responses they experience, but we obfuscate the fluid motion that is an inescapable feature of being alive. Emotions are dynamic and change over time in response to events and different contexts (both relationally and occupationally). Like other dynamic systems such as the weather, the one constant is motion and change. By freezing them into labelled entities mistakenly called 'diagnosis', we turn the flowing turbulence of our emotional streams, lakes and rivers into a thick slurry as we attempt to dam or drain our emotional waterways.

The war against emotions means that as a culture we are curtailing emotional depth, the capacity to live through unpleasant feelings, and therefore our relational patience. The terrain of the ordinary keeps shrinking with sink holes appearing hither and thither from the minefield laid out by profiteers and their accomplices. We become scared to speak our mind for fear of inadvertent offence and our tolerance of difference/disagreement/upset in relationships diminishes.

Services that emerge from this culture are resorting to labelling the response to almost anything difficult in life as potential signs of a disorder. It's as though there's no imagination or possibility of 'bearing with' an intense – or indeed any – emotion considered undesirable. Not everybody needs a service to deal with difficult emotions. When services *are* involved, they shouldn't feel the need to label. They can be involved in encouraging an engagement with life in the broadest sense. Too often services seem to overlook the importance of helping people get on with their lives.

When we can't tolerate the frustration associated with our own lack of omnipotence, with our own relative smallness in the grand scheme of things, we (both patient and practitioner) imagine that we can bypass emotional pain or unpleasantness. We are likely to create increasingly aggressive approaches to numbing suffering. We are likely to lurch from one mind-altering epiphany to another, imagining the mundaneness of the everyday can be permanently eclipsed. We teach ever more desperate remedies. In the process, we create more and more chronic mental health conditions and a system whose preoccupation is an alchemist's obsession with making gold out of the dreariness of a decaying society. Still, it sells.

As a fourteen-year-old patient beginning to realise what her last two years of believing she had a mental disorder told me: 'My generation know too much. At school we have lessons where they teach us about different disorders and mental health symptoms. I avoid those lessons now.'

And as a parent commenting on the dilemmas she sees her children and their friends experiencing: 'There's too much talk at school and online about identity, sexuality, body image, and even about how self-harm is a coping mechanism. No wonder kids are confused.'

Emotions play a vital role in developing, strengthening and then maintaining interpersonal bonds. When we romanticise a Hollywoodised version of love detached from the patient and ongoing working through of difference, when we imagine that the forms of acceptable emotion are narrow, and we combine this with an individualist entitlement that commodification encourages, it's not surprising that relationships become at risk of the one-way traffic of 'what am I getting out of this?'. The task of bearing the agony of fallouts, deferring personal desire, and moving beyond the injunction to have fun, all become harder.[4]

MHIC affects our physical health too. We have long recognised that physical ailments, life expectancy and childhood well-being are all related to social class and what are broadly referred to as the social determinants of health. Inequality is bad for you in a myriad of ways. The wellness industry sweeps the resulting human desperation into new pockets, knowing demand will be potentially limitless.

What can the medical profession do about this? Prescribe more antidepressants? Send people to therapy?

Or help to rehabilitate emotions.

Australian child psychiatrist Jon Jureidini wrote in a paper that received a hostile response from establishment psychiatrists in his country: 'We seem to dislike it when young people are angry, ashamed, frightened, sad, or disappointed. There is strong encouragement to consider such distress as being a precursor of disease, so that parents, doctors, and teachers are prone to label and intervene rather than sit with ordinary, healthy, but distressing feelings.' Instead, he recommends, 'We would do better to trust children's capacity to survive and benefit from strong uncomfortable feelings; be more respectful of the time and space that is required to do so; and tolerate and manage the anxiety we experience through not intervening.'[5]

In those few sentences Jon summarises one of the main ambitions of this book.

What if a major driver of mental health problems is the belief that we have a problem?

What if the 'solution' is sometimes as easy as getting rid of the idea that we have a problem needing a solution?

What if it's simply a matter of rehabilitating a respect and appreciation for the ordinariness and necessity of the full range of emotional experiences we can have? We have personal histories and social contexts; these shape us by interacting with our biology. We are then exposed to narratives that structure the meanings we give our experiences. It is the narratives structuring our meanings that can have profound effects on how we subsequently feel.

Beyond the scientism of the mental health industrial complex

In a post-MHIC world, services would start with the assumption that the people they see are doing the best they can in the circumstances they find themselves in. They would assume the person's struggles are in the realm of the ordinary and/or understandable – they are responding in the myriad ways humans respond to adversity or existential pain. It would put relational awareness at the centre. Listening and bearing witness to suffering has always played an important role in healing. There would be another assumption that everyone has natural resilience, usually discovered through facing adversity and surviving. There would be a deep respect for the capacity of each human being. There would be a political commitment to a more just and equal society.

In my clinical work with young people, I am increasingly being called to help them understand the trap they fall into when they come to believe that they have a mental disorder. I try to help them recognise their natural resilience, which they stop noticing when possessed by the conviction that there is something wrong/damaged/broken/dysfunctional in them.

Much of what we refer to as mental disorder/illness stems not from emotions themselves, but from the labels and meanings we give to our emotional experiences. I call these 'meta-emotions' (the way we feel about how we feel). MHIC has proved itself to be destructive and malevolent in its mystification of emotions by the way it encourages us to construct our meta-emotions. In a medicalised/technicalised model, becoming preoccupied with the 'why' question (why do I feel this way?) contributes to creating long-term patients. An initially difficult but survival problem can multiply, thicken and crystallise. Our sympathy, empathy and desire to help may accidentally burden the patient with baggage they never needed. Diagnosis is given to answer the why question. If things don't improve more treatment and/or more diagnoses emerge. A process I describe as 'the problem becomes the problem' emerges.

I often use insomnia as an analogy to explain this process. Because many people have had some experience of insomnia, they can usually relate to it. I used to get insomnia frequently and would struggle with it. Then one day my wife said, 'You do like to make a fuss about your sleep.' It was just a throwaway comment. It must have played on my mind because I recall a few days later having something of an emotional epiphany (I don't know how else to describe it). I understood, at a level beyond language and intellect, that my struggle with insomnia was because I was struggling with insomnia. I understood how after a while insomnia causes insomnia, and to interrupt that process, I had to stop taking it so seriously and refrain from trying to find a solution to it. Let me explain.

Insomnia first happened because I was stressed and upset and had things on my mind, so I sometimes had trouble falling asleep or would wake up in the middle of the night and my mind would spring into action about whatever was preoccupying me, and I couldn't then get back to sleep (by the way, waking up at night and not being able to get back to sleep is often considered a key symptom of a 'depressive disorder'). After a while, it was the fact that I couldn't get to sleep, or back to sleep when I woke up, that kept me awake. I would worry that I was going to have another sleepless night. I might do some clock-watching, thinking another hour had passed and I still hadn't got to sleep, but I had to get up for work in a few hours. Even though I'm sceptical when it comes to mainstream media, now of course I was noticing reports and articles about how we all need our sleep and how lack of sleep causes all sorts of health and other problems.

So I started to look for ways to solve this, because insomnia was now achieving the status of a problem that was interfering with my daily life. I read articles about dealing with insomnia, changed bits of my lifestyle, downloaded apps, changed my bedtime routine, and so on. Some produced an improvement (which may have been just coincidental), but after a while the insomnia just came back. My relationship to insomnia, in other words my feelings about insomnia, were now veering towards the hopeless. I felt I had a problem that I couldn't shift, and it was occupying an increasing amount of mental space.

My wife's comment and my subsequent epiphany ruptured the hypnotic attachment I had developed to insomnia. Insomnia doesn't deserve the status of a problem needing a solution. People are resilient. Ask any parent of a baby or young child. We can still operate effectively on very little sleep. Insomnia is irritating, but nothing more than an ordinary experience. I had placed insomnia into the category of 'a problem', then of 'a problem affecting other aspects of my life' and 'a problem needing a solution'. I had concluded that for my life to improve I had to eliminate the problem or at least control it better. It was no longer an ordinary and/or understandable experience – it was now a symptom to be treated. *The problem becomes the problem.* The original reasons I couldn't sleep had passed long ago. I was being kept awake because I was worried about whether I would sleep or not. The insomnia was causing my subsequent insomnia.

My wife's comment provoked something. Why was I making such a fuss about my sleep? What made it a problem? Why did I need to keep seeing it as a problem? There was that pesky persecuting internal object I spoke about earlier. It didn't need to be like this. I didn't need to view insomnia as a problem that needed to be solved. I could change my relationship, my feelings, my meta-emotions towards insomnia. Insomnia was just an understandable reaction to a situation. It was in the realm of the ordinary. I didn't need a strategy for it. The more I looked for a solution, the more I strengthened the belief that insomnia was a problem. The more these solutions didn't sustain, the further I was falling into my problem-focussed trance, with hope sapping away about the possibility that life could ever be better and I could get back to an idealised pre-insomnia life.

And it turned out to be as simple as that. Once I stopped viewing insomnia as anything other than ordinary and/or understandable, as not a problem, as just something that I must accept comes and goes, then insomnia stopped causing insomnia. Now I have nights when I don't sleep well, for whatever reason, but other nights are fine. I don't clock-watch any more. If I don't sleep, I don't sleep. I don't whoop for joy after getting a good night's sleep or become despondent after a bad night. Intermittent insomnia is just a part of my life, as I suspect it is for most people from time to time.

Many problems that become what we consider and categorise as mental health problems start as understandable and/or ordinary reactions, often to various adversities. We are then influenced by the cultural stories about how we are meant to be. The spread of 'mental health awareness' has sensitised the population to becoming suspicious of a whole variety of ordinary and/or understandable emotional reactions and to see in them potential disease, disorder, dysregulation and dysfunction.

Once we tread down the path of 'there is something wrong with my emotions and/or behaviour', we risk entering into the *Alice in Wonderland* rabbit hole where the problem becomes the problem. Being anxious becomes anxiety-provoking, being depressed is depressing. We enter the hall of mirrors where our problem is detached from the ordinary and stares back at us mocking our attempts to ignore it. We develop an antagonistic relationship to aspects of our life, particularly our emotional life, seeing it as possessing qualities of disease, accentuating our suffering, and sucking out meaning from the experience beyond that of a potential medical or psychological 'abnormality' that needs solving and/or removing. Suffering becomes the meaningless torture of disease.

Now you enter into the marketplace of McDonaldised MHIC, where the array of brands (diagnoses) and associated goods (medication, therapies, self-help, wellness products) are offered. Once co-opted into brand consumption, antagonism towards your emotional life is further strengthened. You are now entering into the dangerous territory of the alienated. You are set up into fighting and trying to control, suppress and eliminate aspects of your emotional life. Your relationship to and feeling about your problem occupies more mental space if the solutions offered don't work or only provide temporary respite. The internal object becomes more persecuting.

Now you are ready for the final stage – entry into the world of the chronic patient, waiting for the right expert, brand, medication or therapy to quell the disorder that keeps rising again and again. The original issues are long since gone. The problem has become the problem.

This understanding has made me much more aware of how services can and do make a person's mental health worse and in the process destroy their natural resilience and curtail their sense-making skills. Mental health services, it seems, are often bad for your mental health.

Not always

There are many examples of successful projects which draw on shared experiences, strengths and resources. They all seem to promote the importance of relationships and context, and give little value to diagnostic-based treatment pathways.

Some of these projects have a long history. In 1961, an Italian psychiatrist called Franco Basaglia started refusing to bind patients to their beds in the lunatic asylum of Gorizia. He resisted the established methods of the time and began what is probably the single biggest revolution in modern mental health care. Basaglia had been appalled by what he observed as the conventional regime of institutional 'care' in Italy at the time: locked doors – only partly successful in muffling the weeping and screams of the patients – and institutional responses to human suffering that included physical restraint, straitjackets, ice packs, bed ties, isolation rooms, electric shocks and insulin-coma therapies. He felt the purpose of these 'therapies' was primarily institutional – to 'quieten' the patient.

From his initiative at Gorizia, a wide theoretical and practical debate spread all over Italy. The establishment railed against him and his allies, but the movement he started managed to convince politicians to change the country's laws. In 1978 a national reform bill was passed that approved the gradual but radical closure and dismantling of state mental hospitals in the whole country, with the aim of moving all mental health care into the community.[6]

Law 180 is known as the 'Basaglia Law' and was approved by the parliament of Italy on 13 May 1978. Full implementation of the psychiatric reform law was accomplished in 1998, which marked the end of the state psychiatric hospital system in Italy. The movement Basaglia inspired is often referred to as 'Democratic Psychiatry' and has influenced, at least to some degree, mental health laws in many countries, with community-based psychiatric care becoming more of a priority than institutional care.

However, Law 180 remains unique in mental health law around the world, as Italy is the only country where traditional state-run psychiatric hospitals no longer operate. Instead, there are psychiatric wards in general hospitals with a limited number of beds. Italy has the lowest number of psychiatric beds in Europe relative to the population. It has very stringent criteria for compulsory treatment, which doesn't include risk as a criterion, only urgent treatment, and only for a maximum of fourteen days.

Alarmist predictions about how a system like this wouldn't work, and would not only lead to diminished health for those with mental illnesses, but would also increase the risks for the public, proved to be wide of the mark. While the system has had its problems and challenges, it has unleashed the creativity of mental health practitioners, and many projects have since developed in Italy that have taken mental health work out of the clinic and into being a social activity that involves connecting with patients' families and the wider community.

Some years ago, a colleague of mine went to visit one of these projects – the Users and Relatives as Experts (UFE) – in Trento, Italy.[7] She stayed at a B&B that was managed and staffed by current and ex-service users. She was taken to see some of the businesses they ran and sat in on some of the sessions at one of the local community mental health centres. What most amazed her was the lack of locked doors anywhere. This felt alien for someone who came from a UK mental health systems background. She recalls talking to service users over breakfast and feeling welcome, calm and safe. There was none of the 'them and us' you find in the mental health services she was used to.

In 2021 the World Health Organization published a comprehensive package of guidance on community mental health services that promoted 'person-centred and rights-based approaches'. The series had twenty-eight examples from all over the globe that had transformed mental health systems and services to align with international human rights standards, including the UN Convention on the Rights of Persons with Disabilities. The guide showcased a selection of comprehensive regional and national mental health service networks that incorporate an understanding of social determinants of health and actively collaborate with other sectors, such as housing, education and employment.[8]

The example that ticked all the boxes of what a mental health service should look like came from Trieste, a city with a population of about a quarter of a million, in the north-east of Italy. Trieste became the centre of the Democratic Psychiatry experiment, which has continued long after Basaglia's untimely death at the age of fifty-six in 1980, with human rights becoming a central concern of mental health services as inpatient institutions were replaced by a network of community services.

In a 2019 short film on the BBC entitled 'Trieste's mental health revolution', it was described as the best place in the world to become mentally unwell.[9]

Within the Trieste community mental health system, a 'whole person, whole system, whole community' approach to mental health care has been developed. It places a major emphasis on working with the wider community to develop a fully integrated system of support with open doors and no restraint. People are supported as much as possible in their own homes and localities so that they can maintain links with their communities. Mental health services collaborate with other health and welfare services, the juridical system, cultural institutions, regional and city authorities, and other community organisations, to enhance the social capital of service users and the whole city. The development of broad partnerships with peers, staff, trainees, volunteers, family members and social networks promotes a 'whole life' approach.

The ethos of the mental health centres revolves around concepts of 'doing with', and 'being with'. The intake assessment is problem-based, rather than diagnosis-based, and first-person narratives are used to understand people's life story and circumstances. Formalities are kept to a minimum. There is a comprehensive set of rehabilitation and residential support services working in partnership with a wide range of non-profit organisations, such as social cooperatives, volunteers and social promotion associations, including those of peers and carers.

The changes in Trieste have been substantial since the reforms initiated in the 1970s. From 1971 to 2018 the number of psychiatric beds was reduced from 1,160 to 219, while the number of people treated per year by the mental health service has quadrupled. The suicide rate has also fallen from 25 per 100,000 population in the period 1971–94, to 13 per 100,000 by 2015. The number of people subjected to involuntary treatment each year dropped from 150 in 1971 to 18 in 2019. The number of people in forensic hospitals fell from 15 in 1977 to zero from 2016 onwards.[10]

These are impressive achievements, and though Trieste may be a standout example, across Italy similar improvements have happened. A comparison of the annual rate of involuntary hospitalisation between 2008 and 2017 for twenty-two countries across Europe, Australia and New Zealand found a twentyfold variation. Italy had by far the lowest rate, with 14.5 involuntary hospitalisations per 100,000. The median rate was 106.4 and the highest rate (Austria) was 282 per 100,000.[11] Italy has seen a substantial decline in the number of inpatient psychiatric beds over the past forty-plus years.[12]

Another well-developed and enduring example, known as 'Open Dialogue', comes from Western Lapland in Finland. Open Dialogue is a model of mental health care which involves a family and social network approach, where treatment is carried out via whole system/network meetings, which always include the patient. It is a philosophical/theoretical approach to people experiencing a mental health crisis and their families/networks, as well as a system of care.

In the 1980s, psychiatric services in Western Lapland were in a poor state, in fact they had one of the highest incidences of 'schizophrenia' in Europe. The mental health team there, drawing on a Scandinavian model of narrative therapy and incorporating ideas from family and systems theory, embarked on a project to change the way their service operated. They trained together, discussed their ideas, and democratised the process of treatment, so that hierarchies were flattened, and the agency of patients and their families was respected.

All the team members – psychiatrists, psychologists, nursing staff and therapists – adopted the philosophy of seeing people's experiences through the prism of human rather than technical challenges. Diagnosis was not used, medication used sparingly and mostly short-term, and the meaningful social network was engaged from early in the patient's care. Most of the meetings enabled an open exploration of the possible meanings that arose from the stories patients and those around them told, to create a collaborative effort to make sense of what had happened and what might help.

After twenty years of running their regional mental health service using these principles, they documented the best outcomes for psychosis in the Western world. For example, a five-year follow-up study found that 82 per cent did not have any residual psychotic symptoms, 86 per cent had returned to their studies or a full-time job, and only 14 per cent were on disability allowance.[13] Nineteen-year follow-up data suggests these improvements are maintained.[14] Remember, these are outcomes for some of the severest mental health presentations.

What is particularly striking about the Open Dialogue approach is that it is not an alternative to standard psychiatric services or an add-on (such as having an Open Dialogue clinic), it is *the* psychiatric service in Western Lapland.

Working with families and social networks, as much as possible in their own homes, Open Dialogue teams help those involved in a crisis to be together and to engage in dialogue. It has been their experience that if the family/team can bear the extreme emotion, and tolerate the uncertainty, then in time shared meanings that are useful for all can emerge. There is no attempt at didactic teaching this or that strategy, and therefore a much lower risk of disempowering the patient and their families.

The Power Threat Meaning Framework, published in 2018, is a remarkable piece of work from the UK. It was developed, over the course of five years, by a group of UK-based senior psychologists and service-user campaigners to serve as an alternative to models based on psychiatric diagnosis. Rather than an example of a service, the *Framework* is a theoretical manuscript that summarises and integrates a great deal of evidence about the role of various kinds of power in people's lives, the kinds of threat that misuse of power poses to us, and the ways we have learned to respond to those threats. It provides an umbrella of principles to help organise services through acknowledging the role of adversity and the meanings people attach to their experiences, without forgetting the strengths and capacities people have.[15]

Running to more than 400 pages, with a detailed critical analysis of existing research, the *Framework* aims to offer a non-medicalised perspective on why some people struggle with overwhelming emotions and experiences, such as despair, fear, hopelessness, self-harm, low mood, hearing voices, eating difficulties, and so on. It argues that distress of all kinds is part of understandable human responses in the contexts of our relationships, social circumstances, and wider structures, norms and expectations of the societies we live in. It provides a way of helping people to create more hopeful stories about their lives and the difficulties they have faced or are still facing, instead of seeing themselves as blameworthy, weak, deficient or 'mentally ill'. It highlights and clarifies the links between wider social factors such as poverty, discrimination and inequality, along with traumatic experiences such as abuse and violence, and the resulting emotional distress or troubled behaviour that can sometimes then emerge.

It also shows why those of us who do not have an obvious history of trauma or adversity can still struggle to find a sense of self-worth, meaning and identity. As such it is a philosophy that radically departs from medicalised and consumer-friendly approaches, creating meanings that are not reduced to 'symptoms' or 'disorders'. Instead, it looks at how we make sense of these experiences and how messages from the wider culture can increase our feelings of shame, self-blame, isolation, fear and guilt.

Like most worthwhile projects that challenge mainstream hegemony, the *Power Threat Meaning Framework* has received criticism from establishment institutions and academics, as it has not yet been shown in research to improve outcomes. This may reflect a misunderstanding of what the *PTMF*'s goals are. It's not an intervention or model of therapy, but rather a theoretical summary of evidence and the production of principles that could help orientate services away from diagnostic models. It will be interesting to see in coming years whether incorporating *PTMF* principles influences the care given and the outcomes achieved.

Post-mental health industrial complex

There are many other examples I could have discussed, including feedback-informed treatment models, medication-free psychiatric wards in Norway, school-based teacher-support projects that de-medicalise distress, and 'Soteria' houses that exist in several countries to provide a community space for people experiencing mental distress or crisis. The examples I have outlined illustrate that what we imagine mental health to be will influence how we then organise services. When we free ourselves and our societies from imagining that there are diseases inside our minds or brains, we free our imaginations to engage with human dilemmas rather than medical hallucinations.

Humanising our paradigms of care should open us all to the ordinary and understandable nature of diverse behaviours and experiences, including distressing and unwanted ones. We live in a strange world where we are told that our politics are about increasing our acceptance of the diversity of populations, but in our individualised and atomised units we are simultaneously self-policing these diversities by pigeonholing people into typologies, many of which I feel are anti-diverse.

As we ease off the value base of compare and compete, we allow our emotional experiences greater depth and diversity and our behavioural manifestations less need for careful inspection for signs of 'abnormality'. We will then be able to reduce the panopticon of self-surveillance and be less inclined to freak out at the intensity of our emotional lives. We will allow our children to grow up differently while enjoying their unique world views and letting them make discoveries at their own pace and in their own time.

The reformed mental health service will act as a preventative and protective shield against the violence inflicted by the psycho(therapeutic) state. In fact, it may no longer be called 'mental health'. The word 'mental' has too many connotations and contains a slippery construct that evades capture.

We would recognise that we are not dealing with broken brains. We would acknowledge how humans can be resilient and understand that practitioners in this area, including doctors, will primarily use therapeutic philosophies rather than technical knowledge to help their patients.

We would be political, advocating for policies that create environments that are more nurturing for us all in a society that helps provide people with meaning, a sense of community and a sense of civic duty. Reduced levels of inequality through a more socialist-orientated economy would be a good starting point, but by itself would not be sufficient. Recapturing the narrative so that the hegemony of the mental health/mental illness model can be loosened, is an ongoing struggle.

Alternatives are there. The evidence is there. Technocratic diagnostic philosophies do not work in mental health. They make things worse. They trap patients into becoming long-term consumers. It's time to scrap them.

Epilogue
The changing narrative

'A journey of a thousand miles begins with a single step.'

Confucius

New mental health epidemics have seen a ballooning of diagnoses like autism and ADHD. At the same time the Western world has been experiencing social and economic decay. The post-war dream of looking forward to a better life than your parents has faded. Job insecurity, high rents, poor housing, homelessness, crumbling infrastructure, crippling debts, food banks and mental health epidemics are normalised.

In the general gloom, an octopus-like siren was extending its tentacles far and wide, creeping into the minds of the masses as they lay awake at night searching for the meaning of their isolation, self-loathing, sense of failure and sleepless fatigue. Like a virus it spread. First in little pockets here and there, it soon engulfed a family, then its neighbourhood, then the city. It crept along the information highways now reaching out into towns, villages and hamlets. Clinging to droplets of data, transmitting its language through the airwaves, sowing doubt, cracking open minds, a new pandemic was emerging. We felt defenceless.

Through the hypnotic drumbeat of a million shamans, a mind-bending illusion was being fomented, making us see shadows where none existed. Apparitions began possessing us and we knew not how to expel them. The siren made real by imagination, became real in our bodies, we could feel it. In our twenty-first-century common sense, we lament how previous generations did not understand the evident truth that 'mental illness' exists as concretely as broken bones or diabetes.

From before the start of the new millennium, the concept of mental illness had been encroaching further and further into the territory of the ordinary. Yet it was nearly impossible to find any article, report or even academic paper that made clear what was meant by terms such as mental 'disorder', 'problem', 'illness' or even 'mental health'. An assumption took root. The assumption turned an abstract concept into concrete, embodied reality. It turned a map into the territory, a picture into something you could walk into, a hallucination into a persistent presence, a cultural delusion into a new faith. Mental health and mental ill health had arrived in Western folklore, now bypassing any pretence at scientific curiosity and the necessity of empirical falsifiability.

Yet stories of hope kept lingering around in our personal narratives, our family ones and even geopolitical ones. They were easily overlooked in the rush to purchase the latest mental life hack. But they were there and once seen cannot be unseen. I do not think we are about to annihilate humanity, that a new wave of despotism will destroy our societies, or that mental health ideology is forever lost in a sea of individualised commodification.

I have outlined how the current dominant mental health systems are failing, but also the history that shows exceptions, experiments and ideas are always developing. New forms will continue to emerge here and there and eventually become more widespread. There will be conflict, unpleasantness and discord. Revolutionary changes can happen peacefully but will always result in some who lose power and are (understandably) therefore reluctant to let go. Thus, there will likely be some degree of nastiness. When the new cadre eventually becomes the institutional masters, new problems will emerge, and a new generation of critics will hopefully stand up and make their voices heard.

In his book *Capitalist Realism*, Mark Fisher explains how anything that can be marketised for profit will be, including all manner of anti-capitalist rhetoric and icons.[1] Climate change, diversity, identity politics, BLM, MeToo, democracy, all these can become Trojan Horses that infiltrate political movements for change, denude their potential, and deliver them into the hands of ruling-class control. Mental health has always had revolutionary potential.[2] Distress is often the consequence of oppressive social conditions imposed upon us. MHIC is the Trojan Horse that brought capitalism with its individualising and marketizing tendencies into the mental health world, appearing to defenestrate any progressive political force it might contain.

I call for a radical shift, a revolution no less, in which there will be no more use of psychiatric diagnoses, a dramatic decrease in the use of psychiatric medication, and the promotion to the public of a narrative that will help rehabilitate emotions back into the sphere of the ordinary and/or understandable. Is this possible while capitalism exists in its current form? Can there be a meaningful change when emotions are so easily available for financialisation? I say yes. Critical movements have been growing and ultimately the tearing down of the current paradigm is, I predict, inevitable, whether it takes five or fifty years.

A good friend of mine, a psychiatrist now practising in New Zealand, has a T-shirt he likes with *De cerca nadie es normal* (Up close no one is normal) written on it. Perhaps that's the best conclusion a search for normal can come to. It's the other side of the coin that says we're all variations of normal. The creation of human typologies and the substitution of symptoms for experiences is a sign of the intolerance of diversity, not its recognition.

In *Madness and Civilization: A History of Insanity in the Age of Reason*, French philosopher and historian Michel Foucault examined the rise of asylums in Europe, the starting point for what later develops into the mainstream mental health ideologies of today. He proposed that the creation of the asylum was not an act of generous humanity but an effort to impose a damagingly rationalised system of order on those who came to be categorised as 'insane'. Before the birth of the asylum, he argued, the mad were in fact better off. They were visible and unconfined by their surroundings. Their voices could be heard and could be said to be in dialogue with the voices of reason. The asylum was designed, Foucault believed, to induce conformity. Far from liberating the insane from the fetters of the past, to Foucault the asylum signalled the birth of a powerful 'moral imprisonment' of the lunatic.[3]

Mental health ideology would later step out of the confines of the asylum, spread its wings, and cast its shadow across all sections of the population from the cradle to the grave, and across all territories from the global North to the global South. Population control would remain part of its function but delivered by turning people into their own policemen and women. Mental health products would become desirable consumables supporting the individualisation of distress and difference, allowing them to slip seamlessly, and almost invisibly, into a merger with identity politics. It would reach its zenith as the US-led empire was declining. In the gloom and confusion that rippled out into a sea of pessimism and despair, broken society would be transformed into broken minds.

But.

In underground movements and trickle-up information wars, new ideas and possibilities have kept emerging. The fire-setting maniacs could not always prevail. The dominance of the dollar is under threat. Neocolonial economics is being shaken. New mental health ideology is finding its voice.

The old world is dying, and the new world struggles to be born.
It will be born.

Acknowledgements

Without the love and support of my family none of this, or my other writings, would have been possible. My wife, Kitty, has probably taught me more than anyone else. My children, Michelle, Lewis and Zoe, have all had their struggles and triumphs. Watching, connecting and being with them has helped me understand the resilient nature of the human spirit. We have discussed much of this book's content, and I owe many insights to them. My parents and my brothers, Keith and Hazim, and their families have helped broaden my perspectives. Other members of my extended family, alive and lost, have always been a presence and an influence.

My friends, who are mostly doctors in other branches of medicine, for the many enlightening discussions we've had about health care and society more broadly – thanks, Steve, Kenny, Duncan, Paul, Johnny, Dale, Ash, Neeraj, Colin and many others.

I've learned more from my communications and conversations with many thoughtful and creative people in the field than from reading books about theory and practice. Thanks to my mentors in clinical work, in research, in management, in academia, and in particular to everyone in the Critical Psychiatry Network, International Institute for Psychiatric Drug Withdrawal, Council for Evidence-based Psychiatry and A Disorder for Everyone.

A big thanks to colleagues in the child and adolescent mental health teams in Lincoln. You are wonderful people, and I am blessed in being able to work alongside you.

A special thanks to Michal Shavit, publisher at Penguin Random House, who took a chance with accepting this book proposal, gave me great advice, encouraged and allowed me the freedom to write what I wish. Many thanks for the thoughtful feedback and wisdom from Michal, Douglas Pepper, David Milner, Seán Hayes and Katherine Fry in their editorial suggestions that enhanced the breadth, depth and readability of this manuscript. A special thanks also to

Zoe, Kitty, Keith, Rosa, Paul, Dale, Johnny and Dave for their thoughtful feedback and suggestions on earlier drafts of some sections.

Finally, to the people who have taught me the most – all the patients and their families whom I have had the privilege to accompany for part of their journeys through the rocky landscapes of distress.

Notes

1. Changing times

1 MTA Cooperative Group, 'Multimodal Treatment Study of Children with ADHD', *Arch Gen Psychiatry*, December 1999, 56(12): 1073–86.
2 P.S. Jensen et al., '3-year follow-up of the NIMH MTA study', *J Am Acad Child Adolesc Psychiatry*, August 2007, 46(8): 989–1002.
3 National Institute for Health and Clinical Excellence, *Attention Deficit Hyperactivity Disorder: Diagnosis and management of ADHD in children, young people and adults*, National Clinical Practice Guideline Number 72, 2008.
4 J. Moncrieff, S. Timimi, 'The social and cultural construction of psychiatric knowledge: an analysis of NICE guidelines on depression and ADHD', *Anthropol Med*, April 2013, 20(1): 59–71.

2. What is mental health?

1 https://www.who.int/news-room/fact-sheets/detail/mental-health-strengthening-our-response
2 Genesis 2:7.

3. Psychiatric diagnoses are facts of culture not nature

1 See for example, Ahmed Samei Huda, *The Medical Model in Mental Health: An Explanation and Evaluation*, Oxford University Press, 2019.
2 E.I. Fried, R.M. Nesse, 'Depression is not a consistent syndrome: An investigation of unique symptom patterns in the STAR*D study', *J Affect Disord*, 1 February 2015, 172: 96–102.
3 Peter Gøtzsche, *Deadly Medicines and Organised Crime*, Radcliffe Publishing, 2013.

4 See for example, Ben Goldacre, *Bad Pharma: how drug companies mislead doctors and harm patients*, Fourth Estate, 2012.
5 Suman Fernando, *Mental Health, Race and Culture: Third Edition*, Red Globe Press, 2010.
6 R.D. Strous, A.A. Opler, L.A. Opler, 'Reflections on "Emil Kraepelin: Icon and Reality"', *Am J Psychiatry*, 1 March 2016, 173(3): 300–1.
7 I.I. Gottesman, A. Bertelsen, 'Legacy of German psychiatric genetics: hindsight is always 20/20', *Am J Med Genet*, 26 July 1996, 67(4): 317–22.
8 https://link.springer.com/chapter/10.1007/978-3-031-01987-6_5
9 Suman Fernando, *Cultural Diversity, Mental Health and Psychiatry: The Struggle Against Racism*, Routledge, 2003.
10 Ronald Bayer, *Homosexuality and American Psychiatry: The Politics of Diagnosis*, Princeton University Press, 1987.
11 J. Leff et al., 'The International Pilot Study of Schizophrenia: five-year follow-up findings', *Psychol Med*, February 1992, 22(1): 131–45. A. Jablensky et al., 'Schizophrenia: manifestations, incidence and course in different cultures. A World Health Organization ten-country study', *Psychol Med Monogr Suppl*, 1992, 20: 1–97.
12 Robert Whitaker, *Mad in America*, Basic Books, 2002.
13 Robert Whitaker, *Anatomy of an Epidemic*, Crown, 2010.
14 Robert Whitaker, Lisa Cosgrove, *Psychiatry Under the Influence: Institutional Corruption, Social Injury, and Prescriptions for Reform*, Springer, 2015.
15 F. Leichsenring et al., 'The efficacy of psychotherapies and pharmacotherapies for mental disorders in adults: an umbrella review and meta-analytic evaluation of recent meta-analyses', *World Psychiatry*, February 2022, 21(1): 133–45.
16 For example: James Davies, *Sedated: How Modern Capitalism Created our Mental Health Crisis*, Atlantic Books, 2021; Charles E. Dean, *The Skeptical Professional's Guide to Psychiatry: On the Risks and Benefits of Antipsychotics, Antidepressants, Psychiatric Diagnoses, and Neuromania*, Routledge, 2020; Thomas Insel, *Healing: Our Path from Mental Illness to Mental Health*, Penguin Press, 2022; Andrew Scull, *Desperate Remedies: Psychiatry's Turbulent Quest to Cure Mental Illness*, Harvard University Press, 2022; Hugh Middleton, *Toxic Interactions and the Social Geography of Psychosis*, Routledge, 2023.

17 https://www.nytimes.com/2021/04/01/health/mental-health-treatments.html
18 https://time.com/6308096/therapy-mental-health-worse-us/
19 L.V. Kessing et al., 'Lifetime Incidence of Treated Mental Health Disorders and Psychotropic Drug Prescriptions and Associated Socioeconomic Functioning', *JAMA Psychiatry*, 1 October 2023, 80(10): 1000–8.
20 Peter Gøtzsche, *Deadly Psychiatry and Organised Denial*, Art People, 2015.
21 M.M. Nour, Y. Liu, R.J. Dolan, 'Functional neuroimaging in psychiatry and the case for failing better', *Neuron*, 17 August 2022, 110(16): 2524–44.
22 N. Drury, 'Mental health is an abominable mess: Mind and nature is a necessary unity', *N Zealand J Psychol*, January 2014, 43(1): 5–17.
23 See my book *Insane Medicine* and Robert Whitaker's *Anatomy of an Epidemic*.
24 G. Schomerus et al., 'Changes in mental illness stigma over 30 years – Improvement, persistence, or deterioration?', *Eur Psychiatry*, 4 November 2022, 65(1): e78. J. Read et al., 'Prejudice and schizophrenia: a review of the "mental illness is an illness like any other" approach', *Acta Psychiatr Scand*, November 2006, 114(5): 303–18.
25 S. Saha, D. Chant, J. McGrath, 'A systematic review of mortality in schizophrenia: is the differential mortality gap worsening over time?', *Arch Gen Psychiat*, October 2007, 64(10): 1123–31.
26 J.F. Hayes et al., 'Mortality gap for people with bipolar disorder and schizophrenia: UK-based cohort study 2000–2014', *Br J Psychiat*, September 2017, 211(3): 175–81.
27 R. Whitaker, 'Viewpoint: do antipsychotics protect against early death? A critical view', *Psychol Med*, December 2020, 50(16): 2643–52.
28 N. Bansal et al., 'Antidepressant use and risk of adverse outcomes: population-based cohort study', *BJPsych Open*, 13 September 2022, 8(5): e164.
29 E.M. van Weel-Baumgarten et al., 'Treatment of depression related to recurrence: 10-year follow-up in general practice', *J Clin Pharm Ther*, February 2000, 25(1): 61–6.
30 P. Cuijpers et al., 'The outcomes of mental health care for depression over time: A meta-regression analysis of response rates in usual care', *J Affect Disord*, 1 August 2024, 358: 89–96.

31 M.A. Posternak et al., 'The naturalistic course of unipolar major depression in the absence of somatic therapy', *J Nerv Ment Dis*, 2006, 194: 324–9.
32 D. Goldberg et al., 'The effects of detection and treatment on the outcome of major depression in primary care: a naturalistic study in 15 cities', *Br J Gen Pract*, December 1998, 48(437): 1840–4.
33 S.B. Patten, 'The impact of antidepressant treatment on population health: synthesis of data from two national data sources in Canada', *Popul Health Metr*, 1 November 2004, 2(1): 9.
34 S. Rix et al., 'Impact of a national campaign on GP education: an evaluation of the Defeat Depression Campaign', *Br J Gen Pract*, February 1999, 49(439): 99–102.
35 R.D Goldney et al., 'Changes in the prevalence of major depression in an Australian community sample between 1998 and 2008', *Aust N Z J Psychiatry*, October 2010, 44(10): 901–10. A.F. Jorm, N.J. Reavley, 'Changes in psychological distress in Australian adults between 1995 and 2011', *Aust N Z J Psychiatry*, April 2012, 46(4): 352–6.
36 S. Viola, J. Moncrieff, 'Claims for sickness and disability benefits owing to mental disorders in the UK: trends from 1995 to 2014', *BJPsych Open*, 13 January 2016, 2(1): 18–24.
37 https://www.madinamerica.com/2023/04/answering-awais-aftab
38 A.J. Rush et al., 'Acute and longer-term outcomes in depressed outpatients requiring one or several treatment steps: a STAR*D report', *Am J Psychiatry*, November 2006, 163(11): 1905–17.
39 I. Kirsch et al., 'Do outcomes of clinical trials resemble those of "real world" patients? A reanalysis of the STAR*D antidepressant data set', *Psychol of Consciousness: Theory Res Practice*, 2018, 5(4): 339–45.
40 H.E. Pigott et al., 'Efficacy and effectiveness of antidepressants: current status of research', *Psychother Psychosom*, 2010, 79(5): 267–79.
41 Whitaker, Cosgrove, *Psychiatry Under the Influence*.
42 H.E. Pigott et al., 'What are the treatment remission, response and extent of improvement rates after up to four trials of antidepressant therapies in real-world depressed patients? A reanalysis of the STAR*D study's patient-level data with fidelity to the original research protocol', *BMJ Open*, 25 July 2023, 13(7): e063095.
43 https://www.psychiatrictimes.com/view/star-d-dethroned

4. Concept expansion

1 https://www.reuters.com/world/us/more-high-school-girls-suffered-poor-mental-health-than-boys-us-data-2023-02-13
2 https://www.theguardian.com/commentisfree/2023/jun/13/mental-health-crisis-young-people-bernie-sanders
3 https://docs.google.com/document/d/1diMvsMeRphUH7E6D1d_J7R6WbDdgnzFHDHPx9HXzR50/edit
4 https://www.hhs.gov/about/news/2022/10/20/us-surgeon-general-releases-new-framework-mental-health-well-being-workplace.html
5 https://www.bma.org.uk/bma-media-centre/shameful-statistics-show-a-mental-health-crisis-that-is-spiralling-out-of-control-as-demand-far-outweighs-capacity-warns-bma
6 https://www.rcpsych.ac.uk/news-and-features/latest-news/detail/2021/04/08/country-in-the-grip-of-a-mental-health-crisis-with-children-worst-affected-new-analysis-finds
7 https://www150.statcan.gc.ca/n1/pub/75-006-x/2023001/article/00011-eng.htm
8 The Mental Health Million Project, *The Mental State of the World in 2022*, Sapien Labs, 2023.
9 https://www.youtube.com/watch?v=KqgEUjQv_oU
10 Gabor Maté, *The Myth of Normal: Trauma, Illness & Healing in a Toxic Culture*, Vermilion, 2022.
11 Peter Berger, Thomas Luckman, *The Social Construction of Reality*, Doubleday/Anchor, 1966.
12 https://www.dailymail.co.uk/news/article-11959615/Parents-slam-primary-school-bans-pupils-playing-tag.html
13 Ian Hacking, *The social construction of what?*, Harvard University Press, 1999.
14 N. Haslam, 'Looping effects and the expanding concept of mental disorder', *J Psychopath*, 2016, 22: 4–9.
15 B. Wright, 'Documentary Reports Mental Health Crisis Amongst Young People', 2019. Retrieved from https://happiful.com/documentary-reports-mental-health-crisis-amongst-young-people

16 J. Deighton et al., 'Prevalence of mental health problems in schools: poverty and other risk factors among 28 000 adolescents in England', *Br J Psychiatry*, September 2019, 215(3): 565–67.

17 S. Murata et al., 'The psychiatric sequelae of the COVID-19 pandemic in adolescents, adults, and health care workers', *Depress Anxiety*, February 2021, 38(2): 233–46.

18 N. Haslam, 'Concept Creep: Psychology's Expanding Concepts of Harm and Pathology', *Psychol Inq*, 2016, 27: 1–17.

19 N. Haslam, J.S.Y. Tse, S. De Deyne, 'Concept Creep and Psychiatrization', *Front Sociol*, 16 December 2021, 6: 806147.

20 P.J. Jones, R.J. McNally, 'Does broadening one's concept of trauma undermine resilience?', *Psychol Trauma*, April 2022, 14(S1): S131–9.

5. The creation of ADHD

1 American Psychiatric Association (APA), *Diagnostic and Statistical Manual of Mental Disorders, Fifth Edition (DSM-5)*, APA, 2013.

2 https://www.theguardian.com/commentisfree/2021/jun/04/tiktok-accidentally-detected-my-adhd-for-23-years-everyone-missed-the-warning-signs

3 https://www.cosmopolitan.com/uk/body/health/a39536361/tiktok-adhd

4 K.N. Anderson et al., 'Attention-Deficit/Hyperactivity Disorder Medication Prescription Claims Among Privately Insured Women Aged 15–44 Years – United States, 2003–2015', *MMWR Morb Mortal Wkly Rep*, 19 January 2018, 67(2): 66–70.

5 https://www.nbcnews.com/health/health-news/adhd-women-symptoms-overlooked-rcna60240

6 https://www.independent.co.uk/news/uk/home-news/adhd-women-gender-differences-b1993364.html

7 https://archive.org/details/b21445060/page/n9/mode/2up

8 Pat Thane, Tanya Evans, *Sinners? Scroungers? Saints? Unmarried Motherhood in Twentieth Century England*, Oxford University Press, 2012.

9 C. Tasca et al., 'Women and hysteria in the history of mental health', *Clin Pract Epidemiol Ment Health*, 2012, 8: 110–19.

10 L. Oliveira et al., 'Jean-Martin Charcot's influence on Sigmund Freud's career', *Neurology*, April 2018, 90(15 Suppl.): P5.309
11 H. Pérez-Rincón, 'Pierre Janet, Sigmund Freud and Charcot's psychological and psychiatric legacy', *Front Neurol Neurosci*, 2011, 29: 115–24.
12 R. Yadav, 'Freud and penis envy – a failure of courage?', 2018, https://www.bps.org.uk/psychologist/freud-and-penis-envy-failure-courage
13 J. Benjamin, 'A desire of one's own: Psychoanalytic feminism and intersubjective space', in T. de Lauretis (ed.), *Feminist Studies/Critical Studies: Language, Discourse, Society*, Palgrave Macmillan, 1986.
14 Lucy Johnstone et al., *The Power Threat Meaning Framework: Towards the identification of patterns in emotional distress, unusual experiences and troubled or troubling behaviour, as an alternative to functional psychiatric diagnosis*, British Psychological Society, 2018.
15 A. McMunn et al., 'Gender Divisions of Paid and Unpaid Work in Contemporary UK Couples', Work Employment Society, 2020, 34(2): 155–73.
16 B. Laslett, J. Brenner, 'Gender and social reproduction: historical perspectives', *Annu Rev Sociol*, 1989, 15: 381–404. I. Bakker, 'Social Reproduction and the Constitution of a Gendered Political Economy', *New Political Econ*, 2007, 12(4): 541–56.
17 Christime Delphy, *Close to Home: A Materialist Analysis of Women's Oppression*, Verso Books, 2016. N. Fraser, 'Contradictions of capital and care', *New Left Review*, July/August 2016, available at https://newleftreview.org/issues/ii100/articles/nancy-fraser-contradictions-of-capital-and-care
18 B.L. Fredrickson, T.-A. Roberts, 'Objectification Theory: Toward Understanding Women's Lived Experiences and Mental Health Risks', *Psychology of Women Quarterly*, 1997, 21(2): 173–206. S. Loughnan et al., 'Objectification leads to depersonalization: The denial of mind and moral concern to objectified others', *Eur J Soc Psychol*, 2010, 40: 709–17. E. Holland et al., 'Sexual objectification in women's daily lives: A smartphone ecological momentary assessment study', *Br J Soc Psychol*, 2017; 56(2): 314–33. J.M. Tyler, R.M. Calogero, K.E. Adams, 'Perpetuation of sexual objectification: The role of resource depletion', *Br J Soc Psychol*, 2017, 56(2): 334–53.
19 Frazer Benya, Shiela Widnall, Paula Johnson (eds), *Sexual Harassment of Women*, National Academies Press, 2018.

20 Daniel Freeman, Jason Freeman, *The Stressed Sex: Uncovering the Truth About Men, Women, and Mental Health*, Oxford University Press, 2013.

21 M. Rutter, A. Caspi, T.E. Moffitt, 'Using sex differences in psychopathology to study causal mechanisms: unifying issues and research strategies', *J Child Psychol Psychiatry*, November 2003, 44(8): 1092–115.

22 S. McManus et al., 'Mental Health and Wellbeing in England: Adult Psychiatric Morbidity Survey 2014', NHS Digital, 2016. NHS Digital, 'Mental Health of Children and Young People in England: Wave 1 follow up to the 2017 Survey', 2020.

23 Royal College of Psychiatrists, *Public Mental Health Implementation*, RCPsych, 2022.

24 https://www.justice.gov/opa/pr/united-states-sues-telehealth-providers-and-executives-unfair-and-deceptive-conduct

25 https://www.bloomberg.com/news/features/2022-03-11/cerebral-app-over-prescribed-adhd-meds-ex-employees-say

26 https://www.additudemag.com/cerebral-adhd-telehealth-diagnosis-medication-report

27 https://medtigo.com/news/digital-mental-health-companies-draw-scrutiny-and-growing-concerns/

28 https://bhbusiness.com/2023/02/27/cerebral-quietly-closes-medication-assisted-treatment-program-lays-off-15-of-staff

29 https://www.dailymail.co.uk/health/article-11957869/Experts-sound-troubling-warning-number-people-given-stimulants-rockets.html

30 https://www.theguardian.com/society/2023/jan/13/adhd-services-swamped-say-experts-as-more-uk-women-seek-diagnosis

31 https://adhduk.co.uk/adult-adhd-screening-survey

32 G.F. Still, 'Some abnormal psychiatric conditions in children', *Lancet*, 1902, I: 1008–12, 1077–82, 1163–8.

33 C. Bradley, 'The behaviour of children receiving Benzedrine', *Am J Psychiat*, 1937, 94: 577–85.

34 Alfred Strauss, Laura Lehtinen, *Psychopathology and Education of the Brain Injured Child*, Grune and Stratton, 1947.

35 Matthew Smith, *Hyperactive: The Controversial History of ADHD*, Reaktion Books, 2012.

36 Sami Timimi, *Naughty Boys: Anti-Social Behaviour, ADHD and the Role of Culture*, Palgrave Macmillan, 2005.

37 American and Psychiatric Association, *Diagnostic Statistical Manual of Mental Disorders, Second Edition (DSM-II)*, APA, 1966.
38 American and Psychiatric Association, *Diagnostic Statistical Manual of Mental Disorders, Third Edition (DSM-III)*, APA, 1980.
39 American Psychiatric Association, *Diagnostic and Statistical Manual of Mental Disorders, Third Edition Revised (DSM-III-R)*, APA, 1987.
40 American Psychiatric Association, *Diagnostic and Statistical Manual of Mental Disorders, Fourth Edition (DSM-IV)*, APA, 1994.
41 American Psychiatric Association, *Diagnostic and Statistical Manual of Mental Disorders, Fifth Edition (DSM-5)*, APA, 2013.
42 Timimi, *Naughty Boys*.
43 John Fischer, Ann Fischer, *The New Englanders of Orchard Town*, John Wiley and Sons, 1966.
44 Sami Timimi, Jonathan Leo (eds), *Rethinking ADHD: From Brain to Culture*, Palgrave Macmillan, 2009.
45 I. Singh, 'A disorder of anger and aggression: children's perspectives on attention deficit/hyperactivity disorder in the UK', *Soc Sci Med*, September 2011, 73(6): 889–96.
46 E.M. Mann et al., 'Cross-cultural differences in rating hyperactive-disruptive behaviors in children', *Am J Psychiatry*, November 1992, 149(11): 1539–42.
47 A. Brewis, K.L. Schmidt, 'Gender variation in the identification of Mexican children's psychiatric symptoms', *Med Anthropol Q*, September 2003, 17(3): 376–93.
48 E. Carpenter-Song, 'Caught in the psychiatric net: meanings and experiences of ADHD, pediatric bipolar disorder and mental health treatment among a diverse group of families in the United States', *Cult Med Psychiatry*, March 2009, 33(1): 61–85.
49 A.W.W.A. Wong, S.D. Landes, 'Expanding Understanding of Racial-Ethnic Differences in ADHD Prevalence Rates among Children to Include Asians and Alaskan Natives/American Indians', *J Atten Disord*, March 2022, 26(5): 747–54.
50 Yaakov Ophir, *ADHD is Not an Illness and Ritalin is Not a Cure*, World Scientific Publishing, 2022.
51 https://www.incb.org/documents/Psychotropics/technical-publications/2022/Psychotropics-2022-ebook-Final.pdf

52 M.L. Danielson et al., 'Prevalence of Parent-Reported ADHD Diagnosis and Associated Treatment Among U.S. Children and Adolescents, 2016', *J Clin Child Adolesc Psychol*, March–April 2018, 47(2): 199–212.

53 S.N. Visser et al., 'Trends in the parent-report of health care provider-diagnosed and medicated attention-deficit/hyperactivity disorder: United States, 2003–2011', *J Am Acad Child Adolesc Psychiatry*, January 2014, 53(1): 34–46.e2.

6. Is ADHD an evidence-based construct?

1 For example, Jay Joseph, *The trouble with twin studies: A reassessment of twin research in the social and behavioural sciences* (Routledge, 2014) and *Schizophrenia and Genetics* (Routledge, 2023).

2 N.M. Williams et al., 'Rare chromosomal deletions and duplications in attention-deficit hyperactivity disorder: a genome-wide analysis', *Lancet*, 23 October 2010, 376(9750): 1401–8.

3 https://www.bbc.co.uk/blogs/thereporters/ferguswalsh/2010/09/the_genetics_of_adhd.html

4 S.V. Faraone, H. Larsson, 'Genetics of attention deficit hyperactivity disorder', *Mol Psychiatry*, April 2019, 24(4): 562–75.

5 J.A. Collister, X. Liu, L. Clifton, 'Calculating Polygenic Risk Scores (PRS) in UK Biobank: A Practical Guide for Epidemiologists', *Front Genet*, 18 February 2022, 13: 818574.

6 R. Plomin, S. von Stumm, 'Polygenic scores: prediction versus explanation', *Mol Psychiatry*, January 2022, 27(1): 49–52.

7 M. Hoogman et al., 'Subcortical brain volume differences in participants with attention deficit hyperactivity disorder in children and adults: a cross-sectional mega-analysis', *Lancet Psychiatry*, April 2017, 4(4): 310–19.

8 https://www.madinamerica.com/2017/04/lancet-psychiatry-needs-to-retract-the-adhd-enigma-study/

9 L. Batstra et al., 'Subcortical brain volume differences in participants with attention deficit hyperactivity disorder in children and adults', *Lancet Psychiatry*, June 2017, 4(6): 439.

10 S. Bejerot, G. Nilsonne, M.B. Humble, 'Subcortical brain volume differences in participants with attention deficit hyperactivity disorder in children and adults', *Lancet Psychiatry*, June 2017, 4(6): 437.

11 L. Eliot et al., 'Dump the "dimorphism": Comprehensive synthesis of human brain studies reveals few male-female differences beyond size', *Neurosci Biobehav Rev*, June 2021, 125: 667–97.

12 J.L. Rapoport et al., 'Dextroamphetamine: cognitive and behavioral effects in normal prepubertal boys', *Science*, 3 February 1978, 199(4328): 560–3. J.L. Rapoport et al., 'Dextroamphetamine. Its cognitive and behavioral effects in normal and hyperactive boys and normal men', *Arch Gen Psychiatry*, August 1980, 37(8): 933–43.

13 N. del Campo et al., 'A positron emission tomography study of nigrostriatal dopaminergic mechanisms underlying attention: implications for ADHD and its treatment', *Brain*, November 2013, 136(Pt 11): 3252–70.

14 V. Parlatini et al., 'A state-of-the-art overview of candidate diagnostic biomarkers for Attention-deficit/hyperactivity disorder (ADHD)', *Expert Rev Mol Diagn*, April 2024, 24(4): 259–71.

15 M. Whitely et al., 'Attention deficit hyperactivity disorder late birthdate effect common in both high and low prescribing international jurisdictions: a systematic review', *J Child Psychol Psychiatry*, April 2019, 60(4): 380–91.

16 Sami Timimi, *Naughty Boys: Anti-Social Behaviour, ADHD and the Role of Culture*, Palgrave Macmillan, 2005.

17 Elizabeth Wurtzel, *More, Now, Again: A Memoir of Addiction*, Virago, 2003.

18 https://www.dailymail.co.uk/health/article-11957869/Experts-sound-troubling-warning-number-people-given-stimulants-rockets.html

19 https://drugfreeadhd.substack.com

20 L. Hennissen et al., ADDUCE consortium, 'Cardiovascular Effects of Stimulant and Non-Stimulant Medication for Children and Adolescents with ADHD: A Systematic Review and Meta-Analysis of Trials of Methylphenidate, Amphetamines and Atomoxetine', *CNS Drugs*, March 2017, 31(3): 199–215.

21 O.J. Storebø et al., 'Methylphenidate for children and adolescents with attention deficit hyperactivity disorder (ADHD)', Cochrane Database Syst Rev, 27 March 2023, 3(3): CD009885.

22 B.S.G. Molina et al., MTA Cooperative Group, 'The MTA at 8 years: prospective follow-up of children treated for combined-type ADHD in a multisite study', *J Am Acad Child Adolesc Psychiatry*, May 2009, 48(5): 484–500.

23 J. Currie, M. Stabile, L.E. Jones, *Do Stimulant Medications Improve Educational and Behavioral Outcomes for Children with ADHD? NBER Working Paper No. 19105*, National Bureau of Economic Research, 2013. Government of Western Australia, Department of Health, *RAINE ADHD Study: Long-term Outcomes Associated with Stimulant Medication in the Treatment of ADHD in Children*, Department of Health, 2010.

24 K. Boesen et al., 'Extended-release methylphenidate for attention deficit hyperactivity disorder (ADHD) in adults', *Cochrane Database Syst Rev*, 24 February 2022, 2(2): CD012857.

25 O.J. Storebø et al., *Cochrane Database Syst Rev*.

26 C. O'Connor, F. McNicholas, 'What Differentiates Children with ADHD Symptoms Who Do and Do Not Receive a Formal Diagnosis? Results from a Prospective Longitudinal Cohort Study', *Child Psychiatry Hum Dev*, February 2020, 51(1): 138–50.

27 L. Kazda et al., 'Association of Attention-Deficit/Hyperactivity Disorder Diagnosis with Adolescent Quality of Life', *JAMA Netw Open*, 3 October 2022, 5(10): e2236364.

28 L. Zhang et al., 'Attention-Deficit/Hyperactivity Disorder Medications and Long-Term Risk of Cardiovascular Diseases', *JAMA Psychiatry*, 2023, doi: 10.1001/jamapsychiatry.2023.4294.

29 K. Curtin et al., 'Increased risk of diseases of the basal ganglia and cerebellum in patients with a history of attention-deficit/hyperactivity disorder', *Neuropsychopharmacology*, December 2018, 43(13): 2548–55.

7. The creation of autism

1 L. Kanner, 'Autistic disturbances of affective contact', *Nervous Child*, 1943, 2: 217–50.

2 V. Lotter, 'Epidemiology of autistic conditions in young children: I. Prevalence', *Soc Psychiat*, 1966, 1: 124–37.

3 H. Asperger, '"Autistic Psychopathy" in Childhood', in U. Frith (ed.), *Autism and Asperger Syndrome*, Cambridge University Press, 1991. Originally published as 'Die "Autistischen Psychopathen" im Kindesalter', *Archiv für Psychiatrie und Nervenkrankenheiten*, 1944, 117: 76–136.
4 Edith Sheffer, *Asperger's Children: The Origins of Autism in Nazi Vienna*, W.W. Norton & Company, 2018.
5 F. Muratori, S. Calderoni, V. Bizzari, 'George Frankl: an undervalued voice in the history of autism', *Eur Child Adolesc Psychiatry*, August 2021, 30(8): 1273–80.
6 Steve Silberman, *Neurotribes: the legacy of autism and the future of neurodiversity*, Avery, 2015.
7 L. Eisenberg, L. Kanner, 'Childhood schizophrenia: symposium, 1955, VI. Early infantile autism, 1943–55', *Am J Orthopsychiatry*, July 1956, 26(3): 556–66.
8 L. Wing, 'Asperger's syndrome: a clinical account', *Psychol Med*, February 1981, 11(1): 115–29.
9 M. Rutter, 'Diagnosis and definition of childhood autism', *J Autism Child Schizophr*, June 1978, 8(2): 139–61.
10 Judith Singer, 'Odd People In: The Birth of Community Amongst People on the Autistic Spectrum: A personal exploration of a New Social Movement based on Neurological Diversity', an Honours Thesis presented to the Faculty of Humanities and Social Science, University of Technology, Sydney, 1998.
11 For example, https://www.science.org/content/article/disorder-or-difference-autism-researchers-face-over-field-s-terminology
12 https://www.cdc.gov/mmwr/volumes/72/ss/ss7202a1.htm?s_cid=ss7202a1_w
13 G. Russell et al., 'Time trends in autism diagnosis over 20 years: a UK population-based cohort study', *J Child Psychol Psychiatry*, June 2022, 63(6): 674–82.
14 https://sparkleclass.com/2022/03/08/famous-autistic-women
15 https://www.mirror.co.uk/3am/celebrity-news/celebs-who-bravely-opened-up-25475735
16 https://www.clinical-partners.co.uk

17 C. Allison, B. Auyeung, S. Baron-Cohen, 'Toward brief "Red Flags" for autism screening: The Short Autism Spectrum Quotient and the Short Quantitative Checklist for Autism in toddlers in 1,000 cases and 3,000 controls [corrected]', *J Am Acad Child Adolesc Psychiatry*, February 2012, 51(2): 202–12.e7.
18 https://www.nice.org.uk/guidance/CG142
19 https://www.additudemag.com/autism-in-women-adhd-signs-symptoms-treatment/
20 https://www.autism.org.uk/advice-and-guidance/professional-practice/autistic-masking
21 Sami Timimi, Brian McCabe, Neil Gardner, *The Myth of Autism: Medicalising Boys' and Men's Social and Emotional Competence*, Palgrave Macmillan, 2010. Katherine Runswick-Cole, Rebecca Mallet, Sami Timimi (eds), *Re-thinking Autism: Diagnosis, Identity, and Equality*, Jessica-Kingsley, 2016. Sami Timimi, *Insane Medicine: How the Mental Health Industry Creates Damaging Treatment Traps and How you can Escape Them*, Independently published, 2021.
22 See Michel Foucault, *Discipline and Punish: The Birth of the Prison*, Vintage Books, 1977.
23 Jean Baudrillard, *Simulacra and Simulation* (translation, S.F. Glaser), University of Michigan Press, 1994 (originally published 1981).
24 Jodi Dean, *Comrade: An Essay in Political Belonging*, Verso, 2019.
25 Roy Richard Grinker, *Unstrange Minds*, Basic Books, 2007.
26 Y.S. Kim et al., 'Prevalence of autism spectrum disorders in a total population sample', *Am J Psychiatry*, September 2011, 168(9): 904–12.
27 https://apps.who.int/iris/bitstream/handle/10665/103312/?sequence=1
28 J. Zeidan et al., 'Global prevalence of autism: A systematic review update', *Autism Res*, May 2022, 15(5): 778–90.

8. Is autism an evidence-based construct?

1 https://blogs.exeter.ac.uk/exploringdiagnosis/
2 S. Timimi et al., 'Deconstructing Diagnosis: Four Commentaries on a Diagnostic Tool to Assess Individuals for Autism Spectrum Disorders', *Autonomy (Birm)*, 12 June 2019, 1(6): AR26.

3 American Psychiatric Association, *Diagnostic and Statistical Manual of Mental Disorders, Fifth Edition (DSM-5)*, APA, 2013.
4 https://www.autism.org.uk/advice-and-guidance/what-is-autism
5 https://www.acamh.org/cpd-on-demand/myth-busting-autism/
6 L. Rylaarsdam, A. Guemez-Gamboa, 'Genetic Causes and Modifiers of Autism Spectrum Disorder', *Front Cell Neurosci*, 20 August 2019, 13: 385.
7 V. Hughes, 'Epidemiology: Complex disorder', *Nature*, 1 November 2012, 491(7422): S2–3.
8 R. Al-Jawahiri, E. Milne, 'Resources available for autism research in the big data era: a systematic review', *PeerJ*, 12 January 2017, 5: e2880.
9 L. Rylaarsdam, A. Guemez-Gamboa. 'Genetic Causes and Modifiers of Autism Spectrum Disorder', *Front Cell Neurosci*, 20 August 2019: 13:385.
10 D.S. Manoli, M.W. State, 'Autism Spectrum Disorder Genetics and the Search for Pathological Mechanisms', *Am J Psychiatry*, 1 January 2021, 178(1): 30–8.
11 E.A. Maguire et al., 'Navigation-related structural change in the hippocampi of taxi drivers', *Proc Natl Acad Sci U S A*, 11 April 2000, 97(8): 4398–403.
12 Sami Timimi, Brain McCabe, Neil Gardner, *The Myth of Autism: Medicalising Boys' and Men's Social and Emotional Competence*, Palgrave Macmillan, 2010.
13 E. Anagnostou, M.J. Taylor, 'Review of neuroimaging in autism spectrum disorders: what have we learned and where we go from here', *Mol Autism*, 18 April 2011, 2(1): 4. I. Dziobek et al., 'The "amygdala theory of autism" revisited: linking structure to behavior', *Neuropsychologia*, 2006, 44(10): 1891–9.
14 L. Waterhouse, E. London, C. Gillberg, 'ASD Validity', *Rev J Autism Dev Disord*, 2016, 3: 302–29.
15 http://fcon_1000.projects.nitrc.org/indi/abide/abide_II.html
16 G. Auzias, S. Takerkart, C. Deruelle, 'On the Influence of Confounding Factors in Multisite Brain Morphometry Studies of Developmental Pathologies: Application to Autism Spectrum Disorder', *IEEE J Biomed Health Inform*, May 2016, 20(3): 810–17.
17 M.L. Elliott et al., 'What Is the Test-Retest Reliability of Common Task-Functional MRI Measures? New Empirical Evidence and a Meta-Analysis', *Psychol Sci*, July 2020, 31(7): 792–806.

18 P. Howlin, I. Magiati, 'Autism spectrum disorder: outcomes in adulthood', *Curr Opin Psychiatry*, March 2017, 30(2): 69–76.
19 D. Mason et al., 'A Meta-analysis of Outcome Studies of Autistic Adults: Quantifying Effect Size, Quality, and Meta-regression', *J Autism Dev Disord*, September 2021, 51(9): 3165–79.

9. Start them young

1 S Timimi, 'Starting young: Children cultured into becoming psychopharmaceutical consumers – the example of childhood depression', in James Davies (ed.), *The Sedated Society: confronting our psychiatric prescribing epidemic*, Palgrave Macmillan, 2016.
2 S. Timimi, 'The McDonaldization of childhood: children's mental health in neo-liberal market cultures', *Transcult Psychiatry*, November 2010, 47(5): 686–706.
3 Z. Timimi, S. Timimi, 'Psychiatrisation of School Children: Secondary School Teachers' Beliefs and Practices on Mental Health and Illness', in Michael Harbusch (ed.), *Troubled Persons Industries*, Palgrave Macmillan, 2022. S. Timimi, Z. Timimi, 'The dangers of mental health promotion in schools', *J Philos Educ*, 2022, 56:12–21.
4 https://happiful.com/documentary-reports-mental-health-crisis-amongst-young-people
5 J. Deighton et al., 'Prevalence of mental health problems in schools: poverty and other risk factors among 28,000 adolescents in England', *Br J Psychiatry*, September 2019, 215(3): 565–7.
6 A. Caspi et al., 'Longitudinal Assessment of Mental Health Disorders and Comorbidities Across 4 Decades Among Participants in the Dunedin Birth Cohort Study', *JAMA Netw Open*, 1 April 2020, 3(4): e203221.
7 T.J. Bommersbach et al., 'National Trends in Mental Health-Related Emergency Department Visits Among Youth, 2011–2020', *JAMA*, 2023, 329(17): 1469–77.
8 L. Foulkes, J.L. Andrews, 'Are mental health awareness efforts contributing to the rise in reported mental health problems? A call to test the prevalence inflation hypothesis', *New Ideas Psychol*, 2023, 69: 1-6.

9 J.D. Haltigan, T.M. Pringsheim, G. Rajkumar, 'Social media as an incubator of personality and behavioral psychopathology: Symptom and disorder authenticity or psychosomatic social contagion?', *Compr Psychiatry*, February 2023, 121: 152362.
10 I cover the scholarly discussions on the history of Western childhoods in my 2005 book, *Naughty Boys: Anti-Social Behaviour, ADHD and the Role of Culture* (Palgrave Macmillan).
11 Henry Jenkins (ed.), *Children's Culture Reader*, New York University Press, 1988.
12 M. Wolfenstein, 'Fun morality: An analysis of recent child-training literature', in Margaret Mead, Martha Wolfenstein (eds), *Childhood in Contemporary Cultures*, University of Chicago Press, 1955.
13 B. Maitra, 'Culture and the mental health of children: The cutting edge of expertise', in Sami Timimi, Begum Maitra (eds), *Critical Voices in Child and Adolescent Mental Health*, Free Association Books, 2006.
14 James Davies, *The Importance of Suffering: The Value and Meaning of Emotional Discontent*, Routledge, 2011.
15 J. Brownlie, 'Not "going there": limits to the professionalisation of our emotional lives', *Sociol Health Illn*, January 2011, 33(1): 130–44. Kathryn Ecclestone, Dennis Hayes, *The Dangerous Rise of Therapeutic Education*, Routledge, 2008. Frank Furedi, *Therapy Culture*, Routledge, 2004.
16 V. Gillies, 'Social and emotional pedagogies: critiquing the new orthodoxy of emotion in classroom and behaviour management', *Br J Sociol Educ*, 2011, 32: 185–202.
17 K. Brunila, P. Siivonen, 'Preoccupied with the self: towards self-responsible, enterprising, flexible and self-centred subjectivity in education', *Discourse Stud Cultural Pol Education*, 2016, 37: 56–69.
18 P. Stallard et al., 'Classroom based cognitive behavioural therapy in reducing symptoms of depression in high risk adolescents: pragmatic cluster randomised controlled trial', *BMJ*, 5 October 2012, 345: e6058.
19 J.L. Andrews et al., 'Evaluating the effectiveness of a universal eHealth school-based prevention programme for depression and anxiety, and the moderating role of friendship network characteristics', *Psychol Med*, August 2023, 53(11): 5042–5051.
20 J. Montero-Marin et al., 'School-based mindfulness training in early adolescence: what works, for whom and how in the MYRIAD trial?',

Evid Based Ment Health, 12 July 2022, 25(3): 117–24. W. Kuyken el al., 'Effectiveness and cost-effectiveness of universal school-based mindfulness training compared with normal school provision in reducing risk of mental health problems and promoting well-being in adolescence: the MYRIAD cluster randomised controlled trial', *Evid Based Ment Health*, 12 July 2022, 25(3): 99–109.

21 D. Dunning et al., 'The impact of mindfulness training in early adolescence on affective executive control, and on later mental health during the COVID-19 pandemic: a randomised controlled trial', *Evid Based Ment Health*, 12 July 2022, 25(3): 110–16. D. Dunning et al., 'Do mindfulness-based programmes improve the cognitive skills, behaviour and mental health of children and adolescents? An updated meta-analysis of randomised controlled trials', *Evid Based Ment Health*, 12 July 2022, 25(3): 135–42.

22 L.J. Harvey et al., 'Investigating the efficacy of a Dialectical behaviour therapy-based universal intervention on adolescent social and emotional well-being outcomes', *Behav Res Ther*, October 2023, 169: 104408.

23 J.L. Andrews et al., 'Evaluating the effectiveness of a universal eHealth school-based prevention programme for depression and anxiety, and the moderating role of friendship network characteristics', *Psychol Med*, August 2023, 53(11): 5042–51.

24 P. Cuijpers, 'Universal prevention of depression at schools: dead end or challenging crossroad?', *Evid Based Ment Health*, 12 July 2022, ebmental-2022-300469.

10. Conveyor-belt therapy

1 R. Budd, I. Hughes, 'The Dodo Bird Verdict – controversial, inevitable and important: a commentary on 30 years of meta-analyses', *Clin Psychol Psychother*, November–December 2009, 16(6): 510–22. Mick Cooper, *Essential Research Findings in Counselling and Psychotherapy: The Facts are Friendly*, Sage, 2008. Barry Duncan, Scott Miller, Bruce Wampold, Mark Hubble (eds), *The Heart and Soul of Change: Delivering What Works in Therapy: Second Edition*, American Psychological Association, 2010. S. Miller, B. Wampold, K. Varhely, 'Direct comparisons of treatment

modalities for youth disorders: a meta-analysis', *Psychother Res*, January 2008, 18(1): 5–14. J. Sparks, B. Duncan, S. Miller, 'Common factors in psychotherapy: Common means to uncommon outcomes', in Jay Lebow (ed.), *21st century psychotherapies*, Wiley, 2008. Bruce Wampold, Zac Imel, *The Great Psychotherapy Debate: Second Edition*, Routledge, 2015.

2 Barry Duncan, Scott Miller, Jaqueline Sparks, *The Heroic Client: A Revolutionary Way to Improve Effectiveness Through Client-Directed, Outcome-Informed Therapy*, Jossey-Bass, 2004.

3 S. Timimi et al., 'Outcome Orientated Child and Adolescent Mental Health Services (OO-CAMHS): a whole service model', *Clin Child Psychol Psychiatry*, April 2013, 18(2): 169–84.

4 Sami Timimi, Dianne Tetley, Wayne Burgoine, *Outcome Orientated Child and Adolescent Mental Health Services (OO-CAMHS): A Service Transformation Toolkit*, Author House, 2012.

5 J. Edbrooke-Childs, A. Calderon, M. Wolpert, P. Fonagy, *Children and Young People's Improving Access to Psychological Therapies: Rapid Internal Audit, National Report*, Evidence-Based Practice Unit, Anna Freud Centre, 2015.

6 Open Science Collaboration, 'Estimating the reproducibility of psychological science', *Science*, 28 August 2015, 349(6251): aac4716.

7 R.E. Nisbett, T. Masuda, 'Culture and point of view', *Intellectica*, 2007, 46–47: 153–72.

8 M. Finegan, N. Firth, J. Delgadillo, 'Adverse impact of neighbourhood socioeconomic deprivation on psychological treatment outcomes: the role of area-level income and crime', *Psychother Res*, April 2020, 30(4): 546–54. J. Delgadillo et al., 'On poverty, politics and psychology: the socioeconomic gradient of mental healthcare utilisation and outcomes', *Br J Psychiatry*, November 2016, 209(5): 429–30. S. McPherson, M.P. Hengartner, 'Long-term outcomes of trials in the National Institute for Health and Care Excellence depression guideline', *BJPsych Open*, 9 September 2019, 5(5): e81.

9 Budd, Hughes, 'The Dodo Bird Verdict'. N. Drury, 'Mental health is an abominable mess: Mind and nature is a necessary unity', *New Zealand J Psychol*, 2014, 43:5–17. T.J. Johnsen, O. Friborg, 'The effects of cognitive behavioral therapy as an anti-depressive treatment is falling: A meta-analysis', *Psychol Bull*, July 2015, 141(4): 747–68. O. Friborg, T.J.

Johnsen, 'The effect of cognitive-behavioral therapy as an antidepressive treatment is falling: Reply to Ljòtsson et al. (2017) and Cristea et al. (2017)', *Psychol Bull*, March 2017, 143(3): 341–5. J.R. Weisz et al., 'What five decades of research tells us about the effects of youth psychological therapy: A multilevel meta-analysis and implications for science and practice', *Am Psychol*, February–March 2017, 72(2): 79–117.

10 Farhad Dalal, *CBT: The Cognitive Behavioural Tsunami: Managerialism, Politics and the Corruptions of Science*, Routledge, 2019. N.S. Jacobson et al., 'A component analysis of cognitive-behavioral treatment for depression', *J Consult Clin Psychol*, April 1996, 64(2): 295–304. R.J. Longmore, M. Worrell, 'Do we need to challenge thoughts in cognitive behavior therapy?', *Clin Psychol Rev*, March 2007, 27(2): 173–87. G.I. Spielmans, L.F. Pasek, J.P. McFall, 'What are the active ingredients in cognitive and behavioral psychotherapy for anxious and depressed children? A meta-analytic review', *Clin Psychol Rev*, June 2007, 27(5): 642–54.

11 F. Leichsenring et al., 'The efficacy of psychotherapies and pharmacotherapies for mental disorders in adults: an umbrella review and meta-analytic evaluation of recent meta-analyses', *World Psychiatry*, February 2022, 21(1): 133–45.

12 Drury, 'Mental health is an abominable mess'.

13 L. Bickman et al., 'The Fort Bragg continuum of care for children and adolescents: mental health outcomes over 5 years', *J Consult Clin Psychol*, August 2000, 68(4): 710–6. F. Jörg et al., 'Puzzling findings in studying the outcome of "real world" adolescent mental health services: the TRAILS study', *PLoS One*, 2012, 7(9): e44704. B. Weiss et al., 'The effectiveness of traditional child psychotherapy', *J Consult Clin Psychol*, February 1999, 67(1): 82–94. B. Weiss, T. Catron, V. Harris, 'A 2-year follow-up of the effectiveness of traditional child psychotherapy', *J Consult Clin Psychol*, December 2000, 68(6): 1094–101.

14 https://www.nuffieldtrust.org.uk/resource/improving-access-to-psychological-therapies-iapt-programme

15 D. Summerfield, D. Veale, 'Proposals for massive expansion of psychological therapies would be counterproductive across society', *Br J Psychiatry*, May 2008, 192(5): 326–30.

16 N. Hawkes, 'Talking therapies: can the centre hold?', *BMJ*, 9 March 2011, 342: d1459.

17 Rosemary Rizq (ed.), *The Industrialisation of Care: Counselling and Psychotherapy in a Neoliberal Age*, PCCS Books, 2019.
18 M.J. Scott, 'Improving Access to Psychological Therapies (IAPT) – The Need for Radical Reform', *J Health Psychol*, August 2018, 23(9): 1136–47. S. Timimi, 'The diagnosis is correct, but National Institute of Health and Care Excellence guidelines are part of the problem not the solution', *J Health Psychol*, August 2018, 23(9): 1148–52.
19 R. Spence et al., *Focus On: Antidepressant Prescribing: Trends in the Prescribing of Antidepressants in Primary Care*, Health Foundation and Nuffield Trust, 2014.
20 https://pharmaceutical-journal.com/article/news/antidepressant-prescribing-increases-by-35-in-six-years
21 S. Timimi, 'Children and Young People's Improving Access to Psychological Therapies: inspiring innovation or more of the same?', *BJPsych Bull*, April 2015, 39(2): 57–60.
22 P. Fonagy, D.M. Clark, 'Update on the Improving Access to Psychological Therapies programme in England: Commentary on . . . Children and Young People's Improving Access to Psychological Therapies', *BJPsych Bull*, October 2015, 39(5): 248–51. S. Timimi, 'Update on the Improving Access to Psychological Therapies programme in England: author's reply', *BJPsych Bull*, October 2015, 39(5): 252–3.
23 Ronald Purser, *McMindfulness: How Mindfulness Became the New Capitalist Spirituality*, Watkins Media, 2019.
24 Dalal, *CBT: The Cognitive Behavioural Tsunami*.

11. The mental health industrial complex (MHIC)

1 https://www.health.harvard.edu/mind-and-mood/serotonin-the-natural-mood-booster
2 Joanna Moncrieff, *The Myth of the Chemical Cure: A Critique of Psychiatric Drug Treatment*, Palgrave Macmillan, 2007.
3 C.M. France, P.H. Lysaker, R.P. Robinson, 'The "chemical imbalance" explanation for depression: Origins, lay endorsement, and clinical implications', *Professional Psychology: Research and Practice*, 2007, 38(4): 411–20. P.D. Pilkington, N.J. Reavley, A.F. Jorm, 'The Australian

public's beliefs about the causes of depression: associated factors and changes over 16 years', *J Affect Disord*, 5 September 2013, 150(2): 356–62.

4 B. Ang, M. Horowitz, J. Moncrieff, 'Is the chemical imbalance an "urban legend"? An exploration of the status of the serotonin theory of depression in the academic literature', *SSM – Mental Health*, 2022, 2: 100098.

5 https://www.psychiatry.org/patients-families/depression/what-is-depression

6 J. Moncrieff et al., 'The serotonin theory of depression: a systematic umbrella review of the evidence', *Mol Psychiatry*, 20 July 2022, doi: 10.1038/s41380-022-01661-0.

7 https://www.sciencemediacentre.org/expert-reaction-to-a-review-paper-on-the-serotonin-theory-of-depression

8 https://www.madinamerica.com/2022/07/response-criticism-serotonin-paper

9 J.J. Kemp, J.J. Lickel, B.J. Deacon, 'Effects of a chemical imbalance causal explanation on individuals' perceptions of their depressive symptoms', *Behav Res Ther*, May 2014, 56: 47–52.

10 R.D. Goldney et al., 'Changes in the prevalence of major depression in an Australian community sample between 1998 and 2008', *Aust N Z J Psychiatry*, October 2010, 44(10): 901–10.

11 https://www.madinamerica.com/2023/04/answering-awais-aftab

12 S. Viola, J. Moncrieff, 'Claims for sickness and disability benefits owing to mental disorders in the UK: trends from 1995 to 2014', *BJPsych Open*, 13 January 2016, 2(1): 18–24.

13 J.C. Jakobsen, C. Gluud, I. Kirsch, 'Should antidepressants be used for major depressive disorder?', *BMJ Evid Based Med*, August 2020, 25(4): 130.

14 K. Munkholm, A.S. Paludan-Müller, K. Boesen, 'Considering the methodological limitations in the evidence base of antidepressants for depression: a reanalysis of a network meta-analysis', *BMJ Open*, 2019, 9: e024886.

15 V. Faria et al., 'Do You Believe It? Verbal Suggestions Influence the Clinical and Neural Effects of Escitalopram in Social Anxiety Disorder: A Randomized Trial', *EBioMedicine*, October 2017, 24: 179–88.

16 J.C. Jakobsen et al., 'Selective serotonin reuptake inhibitors versus placebo in patients with major depressive disorder. A systematic review

with meta-analysis and Trial Sequential Analysis', *BMC Psychiatry*, 8 February 2017, 17(1): 58.

17 H. Ma, M. Cai, H. Wang, 'Emotional Blunting in Patients With Major Depressive Disorder: A Brief Non-systematic Review of Current Research', *Front Psychiatry*, 14 December 2021, 12: 792960.

18 J.N. Jureidini et al., 'Efficacy and safety of antidepressants for children and adolescents', *BMJ*, 10 April 2004, 328(7444): 879–83.

19 Sami Timimi (2021), *Insane Medicine: How the Mental Health Industry Creates Damaging Treatment Traps and How you can Escape Them*, Independently published, 2021.

20 P. Doshi et al., 'Restoring invisible and abandoned trials: a call for people to publish the findings', *BMJ*, 2013, 346: f2865.

21 J. Le Noury et al., 'Restoring Study 329: efficacy and harms of paroxetine and imipramine in treatment of major depression in adolescence', *BMJ*, 16 September 2015, 351: h4320.

22 J. March et al., 'Fluoxetine, cognitive-behavioral therapy, and their combination for adolescents with depression: Treatment for Adolescents with Depression Study (TADS) randomized controlled trial', *JAMA*, 18 August 2004, 292(7): 807–20.

23 N. Aboustate, J. Jureidini, 'Barriers to access to clinical trial data: Obstruction of a RIAT reanalysis of the treatment for adolescents with depression study', *Int J Risk Saf Med*, 2022, 33(3): 299–308.

24 P.C. Gøtzsche, D. Healy, 'Restoring the two pivotal fluoxetine trials in children and adolescents with depression', *Int J Risk Saf Med*, 2022, 33(4): 385–408.

25 https://www.youtube.com/watch?v=9oH9ovmmAXk

26 Peter Gøtzsche, *Deadly Medicines and Organised Crime: How Big Pharma Has Corrupted Healthcare*, Routledge, 2013.

27 S. Timimi, 'Review of "Death of a whistleblower and Cochrane's moral collapse" by P. Gøtzsche', *Psychosis*, 2020, 12(1): 99–100.

28 Peter Gøtzsche, *Deadly Psychiatry and Organised Denial*, Art People, 2015.

29 Robert Whitaker, Lisa Cosgrove, *Psychiatry Under the Influence: Institutional Corruption, Social Injury, and Prescriptions for Reform*, Springer, 2015.

30 Ghostwriters are people hired to write a journal or magazine article, speeches, or other texts that are then credited to another person as the

author, who then has a collection of publications attributed to them that they didn't write.
31 American Psychiatric Association, *Diagnostic Statistical Manual of Mental Disorders, Third Edition (DSM-III)*, APA, 1980.
32 James Davies, *Cracked: Why Psychiatry is Doing More Harm Than Good*, Icon Books, 2013. J. Davies, 'How Voting and Consensus Created the Diagnostic and Statistical Manual of Mental Disorders (DSM-III)', *Anthropol Med*, April 2017, 24(1): 32–46.
33 D.L. Rosenhan, 'On being sane in insane places', *Science*, 19 January 1973, 179(4070): 250–8.
34 See Adam Curtis's 2007 documentary *The Trap*, where in Episode 1 there is an interview with David Rosenhan.
35 Stuart Kirk, Herb Kutchins, *The Selling of DSM: The Rhetoric of Science in Psychiatry*, Aldine de Gruyter, 1992.
36 Timimi, *Insane Medicine*.
37 Davies, *Anthropol Med*.
38 https://www.nytimes.com/2023/05/16/magazine/does-therapy-work.html
39 S. Forthal et al., 'Mental Health First Aid: A Systematic Review of Trainee Behavior and Recipient Mental Health Outcomes', *Psychiatr Serv*, 1 April 2022, 73(4): 439–46.
40 James Davies, *Sedated: How Modern Capitalism Created our Mental Health Crisis*, Atlantic Books, 2022.
41 M. Martin-Carrasco et al., 'EPA guidance on mental health and economic crises in Europe', *Eur Arch Psychiatry Clin Neurosci*, March 2016, 266(2): 89–124. S. Mathieu et al., 'The Role of Unemployment, Financial Hardship, and Economic Recession on Suicidal Behaviors and Interventions to Mitigate Their Impact: A Review', *Front Public Health*, 6 July 2022, 10: 907052.
42 M. Whitely, M. Raven, J. Jureidini, 'Antidepressant Prescribing and Suicide/Self-Harm by Young Australians: Regulatory Warnings, Contradictory Advice, and Long-Term Trends', *Front Psychiatry*, 5 June 2020, 11: 478.
43 S.B. Goldberg et al. 'Mobile phone-based interventions for mental health: A systematic meta-review of 14 meta-analyses of randomized controlled trials', *PLOS Digit Health*, 2022, 1(1): e0000002.

12. Neurodiversity, gender and new human typologies

1 For the full version of our debate: https://blogs.exeter.ac.uk/exploringdiagnosis/debates/debate-1
2 Walter Benn Michaels: *The Trouble With Diversity: How We Learned to Love Identity and Ignore Inequality*, Metropolitan Books, 2006; *The Beauty of a Social Problem: Photography, Autonomy, Economy*, University of Chicago Press, 2015.
3 https://wersm.com/do-you-hear-us-now-doritos-joins-the-blm-movement
4 https://www.sec.gov/ix?doc=/Archives/edgar/data/1364742/000095017023004343/blk-20221231.htm
5 https://www.blackrock.com/corporate/responsibility/environmental-sustainability
6 https://careers.blackrock.com/life-at-blackrock-2/diversity-equity-and-inclusion
7 https://theintercept.com/2023/02/09/corporate-lobbying-congress-diversity
8 https://www.socialistalternative.org/2021/08/17/woke-capitalism-is-not-the-ally-of-oppressed-people
9 Hannah Barnes, *Time to Think: The Inside Story of the Collapse of the Tavistock's Gender Service for Children*, Swift Press, 2023.
10 https://can-sg.org/2023/03/08/review-of-book-by-hannah-barnes-time-to-think-the-inside-story-of-the-collapse-of-the-tavistocks-gender-service-for-children
11 https://gendercriticalwoman.blog/wp-content/uploads/2022/06/FOI_20-21117_2005_David_Taylor_Report.pdf
12 https://www.theguardian.com/society/2021/may/02/tavistock-trust-whistleblower-david-bell-transgender-children-gids
13 https://medium.com/@kirstyentwistle/an-open-letter-to-dr-polly-carmichael-from-a-former-gids-clinician-53c541276b8d
14 P. Carmichael et al., 'Short-term outcomes of pubertal suppression in a selected cohort of 12 to 15 year old young people with persistent gender dysphoria in the UK', *PLoS One*, 2 February 2021, 16(2): e0243894.

15 You can read Kiera's account of what happened to her here: https://www.persuasion.community/p/keira-bell-my-story
16 https://cass.independent-review.uk/publications/interim-report
17 https://cass.independent-review.uk/home/publications/final-report/
18 https://gids.nhs.uk/about-us/number-of-referrals
19 L. Griffin et al., 'Sex, gender and gender identity: a re-evaluation of the evidence', *BJPsych Bull*, October 2021, 45(5):291–9.
20 Calculated by a Swedish colleague from https://sdb.socialstyrelsen.se/if_par/val.aspx
21 P. Expósito-Campos et al., 'Evolution and trends in referrals to a specialist gender identity unit in Spain over 10 years (2012–2021)', *J Sex Med*, 27 February 2023, 20(3): 377–87.
22 https://www.reuters.com/investigates/special-report/usa-transyouth-data
23 https://williamsinstitute.law.ucla.edu/wp-content/uploads/Trans-Pop-Update-Jun-2022.pdf
24 https://www.pewresearch.org/short-reads/2022/06/07/about-5-of-young-adults-in-the-u-s-say-their-gender-is-different-from-their-sex-assigned-at-birth
25 R. Kaltiala et al., 'Time trends in referrals to child and adolescent gender identity services: a study in four Nordic countries and in the UK', *Nord J Psychiatry*, January 2020, 74(1): 40–4.
26 K. Kozlowska et al., 'Australian children and adolescents with gender dysphoria: Clinical presentations and challenges experienced by a multidisciplinary team and gender service', *Human Systems*, 2021, 1(1): 70–95.
27 R. Kaltiala-Heino et al., 'Two years of gender identity service for minors: overrepresentation of natal girls with severe problems in adolescent development', *Child Adolesc Psychiatry Ment Health*, 9 April 2015, 9: 9.
28 K. Cooper, 'Phenomenology of gender dysphoria in autism: a multi-perspective qualitative analysis', *J Child Psychol Psychiatry*, February 2023, 64(2): 265–76.
29 https://www.tabletmag.com/sections/science/articles/finland-youth-gender-medicine
30 C. Heneghan, T. Jefferson, 'Gender-affirming hormone in children and adolescents', *BMJ EBM* Spotlight, 25 February 2019, https://blogs.bmj.

com/bmjebmspotlight/2019/02/25/gender-affirming-hormone-in-childrenand-adolescents-evidence-review/

31 'Puberty blockers for young people will only be available as part of clinical research, says NHS England',
BMJ, 2023, 381, doi: https://doi.org/10.1136/bmj.p1344.

32 S.B. Levine, E. Abbruzzese, 'Current Concerns About Gender-Affirming Therapy in Adolescents', *Curr Sex Health Rep*, 2023, 15: 113–23.

33 S.C. Mueller, 'Mental Health Treatment Utilization in Transgender Persons: What We Know and What We Don't Know', *Am J Psychiatry*, 1 August 2020, 177(8): 657–9.

34 J. Elkadi et al., 'Developmental Pathway Choices of Young People Presenting to a Gender Service with Gender Distress: A Prospective Follow-Up Study', *Children (Basel)*, 7 February 2023, 10(2): 314.

35 C.M. Roberts et al., 'Continuation of Gender-affirming Hormones Among Transgender Adolescents and Adults', *J Clin Endocrinol Metab*, 18 August 2022, 107(9): e3937–e3943.

36 J. Elkadi et al., *Children (Basel)*. doi: 10.3390/children10020314.

37 R. D'Angelo: 'The man I am trying to be is not me', *Int J Psychoanal*, October 2020, 101(5): 951–70; 'Psychiatry and the ethical limits of gender affirming care', in Michelle Moore, Heather Brunskell-Evans (eds), *Inventing Transgender Children and Young People*, Cambridge Scholars, 2019.

38 Mari Ruti, *The Ethics of Opting Out: Queer theory's defiant subjects*, Columbia University Press, 2017.

39 Eva Illouz, *The End of Love: A Sociology of Negative Relations*, OUP USA, 2019.

13. Living in a compare-and-compete culture

1 S. Timimi S. ' "Eating Disorders '95" Second London International Conference on Eating Disorders', *Clinical Child Psychology and Psychiatry*, 1996, 1(1): 161–3.

2 I. Gordon et al., 'Childhood-onset anorexia nervosa: towards identifying a biological substrate', *Int J Eat Disord*, September 1997, 22(2): 159–65.

3 R. Prince, E.F. Thebaud, 'Is Anorexia Nervosa a Culture-Bound Syndrome?', *Transcultural Psychiatric Research Review*, 1983, 20(4): 299–302. L. Swartz, 'Anorexia nervosa as a culture-bound syndrome', *Soc Sci Med*, 1985, 20(7): 725–30.
4 Patricia Fallon, Melanie Katzman, Susan Wooley (eds), *Feminist perspectives on eating disorders*, Guilford Press, 1994.
5 A. LaMarre et al., 'An open invitation to productive conversations about feminism and the spectrum of eating disorders (part 1): basic principles of feminist approaches', *J Eat Disord*, 19 April 2022, 10(1): 54.
6 Ethan Watters, *Crazy Like Us: The Globalization of the American Psyche*, Free Press, 2010.
7 https://www.manchester.ac.uk/discover/news/researchers-chart-large-rise-in-eating-disorders-and-self-harm-amongst-teenage-girls/
8 Elizabeth Martinez, Arnoldo García, *What is Neo-Liberalism? A Brief Definition*, New Press, 2000.
9 Fredrick Hayek, *The Road to Serfdom*, Routledge, 2001.
10 Michael Parenti, *Blackshirts & Reds: Rational Fascism and the Overthrow of Communism*, City Light Books, 1997.
11 Michael Kellogg, *The Russian Roots of Nazism: White Émigrés and the Making of National Socialism, 1917–1945*, Cambridge University Press, 2005.
12 Marcus Taylor, *From Pinochet to the 'Third Way': Neoliberalism and Social Transformation in Chile*, Pluto Press, 2006.
13 David Harvey, *A Brief History of Neoliberalism*, Oxford University Press, 2007.
14 Samir Amin, *Accumulation on a World Scale: Critique of the Theory of Underdevelopment*, Monthly Review Press, 1974.
15 Samir Amin, *The Law of Worldwide Value*, Monthly Review Press, 2010.
16 Michael Hudson, *Super Imperialism: The Economic Strategy of American Empire, Third Edition*, Islet, 2021.
17 '. . . they are casting their problems on society and who is society? There is no such thing! There are individual men and women and there are families . . .' Margaret Thatcher, interview for *Woman's Own*, 1987.
18 Peter Berger, Thomas Luckman, *The Social Construction of Reality*, Doubleday/Anchor, 1966.

19 Carlos Garrido (ed.), *Marxism and the Dialectical Worldview*, Midwestern Marx Publishing, 2022.
20 George Hoare, Nathan Sperber, *An Introduction to Antonio Gramsci: His Life, Thought and Legacy*, Bloomsbury Academic, 2015.
21 Edward Herman, Noam Chomsky, *Manufacturing Consent: The Political Economy of the Mass Media*, Pantheon Books, 1988.
22 Z. Timimi, 'What we owe our friends', 2024, https://ethics.org.au/what-we-owe-our-friends
23 Richard Wilkinson, Kate Pickett, *The Spirit Level: Why Equality is Better for Everyone*, Penguin, 2010.
24 Pierre Bourdieu, *Distinctions: A Social Critique of the Judgment of Taste* (translation, R. Nice), Harvard University Press, 1984 (originally published 1979).
25 Owen Jones, *Chavs: The Demonization of the Working Class*, Verso Books, 2011.
26 Jon McKenzie, *Perform or Else: From Discipline to Performance*, Routledge, 2001.
27 C.H. Tienken, 'Neoliberalism, Social Darwinism, and Consumerism Masquerading as School Reform', *Interchange*, May 2013, 43(4): 295–316.
28 Clare Crawford, Lorraine Dearden, Ellen Greaves, *When You Are Born Matters: Evidence for England*, Institute for Fiscal Studies, 2013. M. Whitely et al., 'Attention deficit hyperactivity disorder late birthdate effect common in both high and low prescribing international jurisdictions: a systematic review', *J Child Psychol Psychiatry*, April 2019, 60(4): 380–91.
29 Michel Foucault, *Discipline and Punish: The Birth of the Prison*, Vintage Books, 1977.
30 https://www.wesjones.com/eoh.htm, and F. Fukuyama, *The End of History and the Last Man*, Free Press, 1992.
31 https://www.epi.org/publication/causes-of-wage-stagnation
32 https://www.pymnts.com/consumer-finance/2022/report-36-of-consumers-earning-250k-now-live-paycheck-to-paycheck
33 https://usafacts.org/data/topics/people-society/poverty/public-housing/homeless-population
34 https://www.feedingamerica.org/hunger-in-america
35 https://www.rts.com/resources/guides/food-waste-america

36 https://www.fastcompany.com/90858376/were-going-backwards-in-water-access-how-46-million-americans-still-dont-have-safe-drinking-water
37 J.H. Tanne, 'Life expectancy: US sees steepest decline in a century', *BMJ*, 2022,378, doi.org/10.1136/bmj.o2142.
38 https://inequality.org/great-divide/inequality-in-america-far-beyond-extreme
39 https://www.oxfam.org/en/press-releases/richest-1-bag-nearly-twice-much-wealth-rest-world-put-together-over-past-two-years
40 M. Gilens, B. Page, 'Testing Theories of American Politics: Elites, Interest Groups, and Average Citizens', *Perspectives on Politics*, 2014, 12(3): 564–81.
41 https://news.gallup.com/poll/329639/support-third-political-party-high-point.aspx
42 https://news.gallup.com/poll/1600/congress-public.aspx
43 https://www.fool.com/investing/stock-market/market-sectors/communication/media-stocks/big-6
44 Herman, Chomsky, *Manufacturing Consent*.
45 https://www.ft.com/content/cob3a1d1-b887-4b67-ba0e-b6e745e1df7b
46 https://www.commondreams.org/views/2010/04/13/your-tax-dollars-war-more-53-your-tax-payment-goes-military
47 https://www.thesoldiersproject.org/how-many-us-military-bases-are-there-in-the-world/
48 https://fortune.com/europe/2023/06/25/dollar-reserve-currency-brics-brazil-russia-india-china-south-africa/
49 https://www.visualcapitalist.com/de-dollarization-countries-seeking-alternatives-to-the-u-s-dollar/
50 https://www.politico.eu/article/brics-summit-south-africa-six-new-countries-join-alliance
51 https://www.ft.com/content/c8cf024d-87b7-4e18-8fa2-1b8a3f3fbba1
52 The latest at the time of writing is by historian, anthropologist, sociologist and political scientist Emmanuel Todd in his 2024 book *The Defeat of the West*. E. Todd, *La défaite de l'Occident*. Gallimard, 2024.
53 John Gray, *The New Leviathans: Thoughts After Liberalism*, Allen Lane, 2023.

14. Colonial psychiatry

1 V. Skultans, 'From damaged nerves to masked depression: inevitability and hope in Latvian psychiatric narratives', *Soc Sci Med*, June 2003, 56(12): 2421–31.
2 C.J. Murray, L. Lopez, D. Alan, World Health Organization, World Bank, Harvard School of Public Health, *The Global burden of disease: a comprehensive assessment of mortality and disability from diseases, injuries, and risk factors in 1990 and projected to 2020: summary*, WHO, 1996.
3 World Health Organization, *Mental Health Global Action Programme: mhGAP – Scaling up Care for Mental, Neurological, and Substance Use Disorder*, WHO, 2008.
4 https://www.who.int/activities/scaling-up-mental-health-care
5 C. Mills, E. Hilberg, '"Built for expansion": the "social life" of the WHO's mental health GAP Intervention Guide', *Sociol Health Illn*, October 2019, 41 Suppl 1: 162–75. D. Summerfield, 'Afterword: against "global mental health"', *Transcult Psychiatry*, July 2012, 49(3–4): 519–30.
6 https://www.who.int/news-room/fact-sheets/detail/depression
7 Stefan Ecks, *Eating drugs: psychopharmaceutical pluralism in India*, New York University Press, 2013.
8 S. Jadhav, 'Dhis and Dhāt: Evidence of Semen Retention Syndrome Amongst White Britons', *Anthropol Med*, December 2007, 14(3): 229–39.
9 G. Obeyesekere, 'Depression, Buddhism, and the work of culture in Sri Lanka', in Arthur Kleinman, Byron Good (eds), *Culture and depression: studies in the anthropology and cross-cultural psychiatry of affect and disorder*, University of California Press, 1985.
10 B. Good, B.J. Good, R. Moradi, 'The interpretation of Iranian depressive illness and dysphoric affect', in Arthur Kleinman, Byron Good (eds), *Culture and depression: studies in the anthropology and cross-cultural psychiatry of affect and disorder*, University of California Press, 1985.
11 C. Lutz, 'Depression and the translation of emotional worlds', in Arthur Kleinman, Byron Good (eds), *Culture and depression: studies in the anthropology and cross-cultural psychiatry of affect and disorder*, University of California Press, 1985.

12 A.E. Becker, D.T.S. Lee, 'Indigenous models for attenuation of post-partum depression: case studies from Fiji and Hong Kong', in Alex Cohen, Arthur Kleinman, Benedetto Saraceno (eds), *World mental health casebook*, Kluwer, 2002.

13 G. Stern, L. Kruckman, 'Multi-disciplinary perspectives on post-partum depression: an anthropological critique', *Social Sci Med*, 1983, 17(15): 1027–41.

14 Margaret Lock, *Encounters with aging: mythologies of menopause in Japan and North America*, University of California Press, 1993.

15 S. Lee, 'The Vicissitudes of Neurasthenia in Chinese Societies: Where Will It Go From the ICD-10?', *Transcultural Psychiatric Research Review*, 1994, 31(2): 153–72.

16 S. Lee, A. Kleinman, 'Are Somatoform Disorders Changing With Time? The Case of Neurasthenia in China', *Psychosomatic Medicine*, November 2007, 69(9): 846–9.

17 https://www.dw.com/en/india-why-are-suicides-among-farmers-on-the-increase/a-62991022

18 S.V. Menon, 'Globalisation, State and Disempowerment: Study of Farmers Suicide in Warangal', *Munich Personal RePEc Archive*, 2006, http://mpra.ub.uni-muenchen.de/1633/1/MPRA_paper_1633.pdf

19 N.K. Kannuri, S. Jadhav, 'Cultivating distress: cotton, caste and farmer suicides in India', *Anthropol Med*, December 2021, 28(4): 558–75.

20 R. Srinivasa Murthy, 'Farmers suicide: Need for mental health interventions', *Indian J Soc Psychiatry*, 2012, 28: 26–35.

21 S. Kottai, 'Farmers' Protests, Death by Suicides, and Mental Health Systems in India: Critical Questions', *Ethical Human Psychology and Psychiatry*, 2021, 23(2): 70–88.

22 https://www.thelancet.com/series/global-mental-health

23 https://www.thelancet.com/commissions/global-mental-health

24 https://www.thelancet.com/lancet-200/mental-health

25 Ethan Watters, *Crazy Like Us: The Globalization of the American Psyche*, Free Press, 2010.

26 E. Cleall, 'Missionaries, Masculinities and War: The London Missionary Society in Southern Africa, c.1860–1899', *South African Historical Journal*, 2009, 61(2): 232–53. Roland Oliver, *The Missionary Factor in East Africa*, Longmans, 1952.

27 Roland Littlewood, Simon Dein, *Cultural psychiatry and medical anthropology: an introduction and reader*, Athlone Press, 2000. Arthur Kleinman, Byron Good (eds), *Culture and depression: studies in the anthropology and cross-cultural psychiatry of affect and disorder*, University of California Press, 1985.
28 Suman Fernando, *Institutional Racism in Psychiatry and Clinical Psychology: Race Matters in Mental Health*, Palgrave Macmillan, 2017.
29 Adam Rutherford, *Control: The Dark History and Troubling Present of Eugenics*, W&N, 2020.
30 Frantz Fanon, *Black Skins White Masks* (translation, C.L. Markmann), Pluto Press, 1986 (originally published 1952).
31 Frantz Fanon, *The Wretched of the Earth* (translation, C. Farrington), Penguin Classics, 1961; revised edition 2001.
32 Edward Said, *Orientalism*, Pantheon Books, 1978.
33 G. Spivak, 'Can the Subaltern Speak?', in Carl Nelson, Lawrence Grossberg (eds), *Marxism and the Interpretation of Culture*, Macmillan, 1988.
34 G.M. White, 'The role of cultural explanations in "somatization" and "psychologization"', *Soc Sci Med*, 1982, 16(16): 1519–30.
35 Ecks, *Eating drugs*. Kleinman, Good, Good (eds), *Culture and depression*.
36 'Psychiatrists urge royal college to tackle racism', *BMJ*, 2020, 370: m2657, doi.org/10.1136/bmj.m2657; https://www.theguardian.com/society/2020/jul/01/psychiatrists-urge-new-leader-to-rid-profession-of-institutional-racism
37 https://www.rcpsych.ac.uk/docs/default-source/about-us/equality-diversity-and-inclusivity/equality-action-plan---january-2021.pdf
38 https://www.rcpsych.ac.uk/docs/default-source/members/rcpsych-insight-magazine/rcpsych-insight-23---spring-2023.pdf

15. Rehabilitating emotions

1 Brooke Siem, *May Cause Side Effects: A Memoir*, Central Recovery Press, 2022.
2 https://www.youtube.com/watch?v=wQNYEwGmo5I
3 L. Harari, S.S. Oselin, B.G. Link, 'The Power of Self-Labels: Examining Self-Esteem Consequences for Youth with Mental Health Problems', *J Health Soc Behav*, 2 June 2023, doi: 10.1177/00221465231175936.

4 https://ethics.org.au/what-we-owe-our-friends/
5 J.N. Jureidini, 'Let children cry', *Med J Aust*, 17 November 2014, 201(10): 612–13.
6 John Foot, *The Man Who Closed the Asylums: Franco Basaglia and the Revolution in Mental Health Care*, Verso, 2015.
7 https://www.rivistadipsicologiaclinica.it/ojs/index.php/rpc/article/view/589
8 https://www.who.int/publications/i/item/9789240025844
9 https://www.bbc.co.uk/news/av/stories-49008178
10 https://www.who.int/publications/i/item/9789240025844
11 L. Sheridan Rains et al., 'Variations in patterns of involuntary hospitalisation and in legal frameworks: an international comparative study', *Lancet Psychiatry*, May 2019, 6(5): 403–17.
12 C. Barbui, D. Papola, B. Saraceno, 'Forty years without mental hospitals in Italy', *Int J Ment Health Syst*, 31 July 2018, 12:43.
13 J. Seikkula et al., 'Five-Year Experience of First-Episode Nonaffective Psychosis in Open-Dialogue Approach: Treatment Principles, Follow-Up Outcomes, and Two Case Studies', *Psychotherapy Res*, 2006, 16(2): 214–28.
14 T. Bergstøm et al., 'How Do People Talk Decades Later about Their Crisis that We Call Psychosis? A Qualitative Study of the Personal Meaning-Making Process', *Psychosis*, 2019, 11(2):105–15.
15 L. Johnstone, et al, *The Power Threat Meaning Framework: Towards the identification of patterns in emotional distress, unusual experiences and troubled or troubling behaviour, as an alternative to functional psychiatric diagnosis*, British Psychological Society, 2018.

Epilogue: The changing narrative

1 Mark Fisher, *Capitalist Realism*, Zero Books, 2009.
2 This was the theme of a book I co-edited with Carl Cohen, *Liberatory Psychiatry: Philosophy, Politics and Mental Health*, Cambridge University Press, 2008.
3 Michel Foucault, *Madness and Civilization: A History of Insanity in the Age of Reason*, Pantheon, 1965.

Index

Accumulation on a World Scale (Amin), 240
Adams, Nicola, 87
addiction, 56, 76, 115–16, 117–18, 273
ADDitude, 88, 133
adoption studies, 105–6
adverse experiences
    belittlement, 42, 63, 144
    bullying, 40–43, 63, 75, 99, 226
    cognitive parenting, 73–4
    corporal punishment, 23–5, 42, 73
    domestic violence, 221
    gender dysphoria and, 221, 225
    isolation, 37–9
    parental mental illness, 171–2, 225
    parental separation, 42, 65, 66–7, 99, 171–2, 226
    sexual abuse, 221
Afghanistan, 252
Afro-Caribbean people, 12, 54, 80
Alexion, 217
Allen, Lily, 87
Allende, Salvador, 239
American Psychiatric Association, 195, 201, 264
Amin, Samir, 240
amphetamines, 15, 94, 112, 116
Anatomy of an Epidemic (Whitaker), 56
Andrews, Jack, 162–3
anorexia nervosa (AN), 234–8, 262
antidepressants, 23, 56, 59, 60–61, 158, 179, 184, 192–9, 273
antipsychotics, 62, 118, 194
anxiety, 5, 11, 56, 72, 87, 124, 136, 169, 182

Apprentice, The, 244
Arabic, 32–3, 35
Argentina, 252
Aristotle, 142
Asperger, Hans, 126–8, 146, 149
astrology, 20
attachment disorders, 80, 149
attention deficit hyperactivity disorder (ADHD), 5, 11–16, 50, 65, 80–101, 102–23
    autism, relationship to, 108, 118
    awareness campaigns, 170, 210
    behaviour therapy, 13
    brain-imaging studies, 109–11
    chemical imbalance hypothesis, 16, 82, 88, 104, 111–12, 116–17
    cultural dynamics, 96–9
    genetic research, 104–9
    identity, 21, 214
    marketisation of, 72, 77, 87–90, 95–9, 163, 210
    medication, 13–16, 88, 94, 115–21, 158
    men and, 83, 87
    MTA study (1999), 12–16, 119
    NICE Guideline (2008), 15, 119
    null hypothesis, 104–12
    origins of, 90–93
    rates of, 82, 89, 98–9
    social media and, 81–2
    symptoms, 89–90, 113–14, 150
    tests, 89–90
    women and, 82–3, 133
    young-for-class children and, 112–13, 247
atypical autism, 146

auditory hallucinations, 40–43, 62–4
August-born children, 112–13, 247
Australia, 59, 120, 209, 227, 285
authenticity, 69–70
autism, 2, 5, 7–11, 50, 65, 124–41, 142–56, 191–2
    ADHD, relationship to, 108, 118
    awareness campaigns, 170
    brand, 72, 77, 129, 131–9
    cultural dynamics and, 137–8, 144
    definitions of, 146–51
    eating issues and, 236
    gender dysphoria and, 225, 226
    genetic research, 108, 129, 151–2
    identity, 212–13, 215
    infantile autism, 128, 129
    men and, 87
    Nazism and, 54, 125–8
    spectrum, 10–11, 128–30
    symptoms, 10, 132–3, 138, 142–6, 147–50
    tests, 132–3, 142–6
    women and, 84, 133–4, 139, 144, 163
Autism and Developmental Disabilities Monitoring (ADDM), 130
Autism Brain Imaging Data Exchange, 154
Autism Diagnostic Observation Schedule (ADOS), 142–6
awareness campaigns, 25, 59–60, 74, 88, 129, 139, 159, 161, 162–5, 168–70

Barnes, Hannah, 219
Baron-Cohen, Simon, 131
Basaglia, Franco, 282–3, 284
Batmanghelidjh, Camila, 70
Baudrillard, Jean, 135–6
behaviour problems, 7, 11–12, 16, 18, 87, 95, 97, 109
behaviour therapy (BT), 13, 16, 185

Belgium, 98
Bell, David, 220
Bell, Keira, 222–3
Bergen, Norway, 110
Berger, Peter, 242–3
Beyond Blue, 59
big data, 152
Big Society (2010–13), 70
bipolar disorder, 2, 5, 58–9, 66, 72, 78, 84, 191
    genetic research, 108, 109
Black Lives Matter, 216–17, 267, 292
black people, 12, 54, 80
Black Skins White Masks (Fanon), 265
Black Women's Congressional Alliance, 217
BlackRock, 217
Bleuler, Eugen, 125
Blumenthal, Heston, 87
body image, 222, 235, 236–7, 276
Boeing, 252
borderline personality disorder, 84
Boseley, Matilda, 80, 81
Bradley, Charles, 91
brain
    ADHD imaging studies, 109–11
    anorexia imaging studies, 234–5
    autism imaging studies, 152–4
    chemical imbalance hypotheses, 16, 55, 104, 111–12, 116–17, 191–9, 270
    plasticity, 152–3
brands, 71–3
    ADHD as, 72, 77, 87–90, 95–9, 163
    autism as, 72, 77, 129, 131–9
    depression as, 72, 169–70
    psychotherapy, 179–81, 189–90
Brazil, 252
breath, 32–4
Bremner, Rory, 87
Brexit, 253
BRICS, 252

British Medical Association, 68
British Medical Journal, 61
Buddhism, 167, 186–7, 259
bullying, 40–43, 63, 75, 99, 226
burnout, 208

Callaghan, James, 240
Cameron, David, 70
Canada, 68, 98, 163
cancel culture, 215, 242
cannabis, 42, 115
capitalism, 72, 86, 207, 234–53, 254–68, 274
   colonial nature, 240, 253, 254–68
   compare and compete culture, 95, 135, 229, 237–8, 242–9
   identity politics and, 213, 215–16, 228
   neoliberalism, 207, 213, 215, 216, 228, 238–53
Capitalist Realism (Fisher), 292
Care Quality Commission, 224
care system, 102
Carey, Benedict, 56
Carter, Jimmy, 240
caseness, 113–14, 151, 258
Cass, Hilary, 224
catharsis, 186
celebrities, 87, 131, 210
Celexa, 202
Cerebral, 88
Charcot, Jean-Martin, 84
chemical imbalance hypotheses, 16, 82, 88, 104, 111–12, 116–17, 191–9, 270
Child and Adolescent Mental Health Services (CAMHS), 65
childhood disintegrative disorder, 146
Chile, 239
Chiles, Adrian, 87
China, 96–7, 98, 252, 260–61
Chomsky, Noam, 243
Christine, Aber, 251

chronic illness, 19, 29–30, 45, 58, 170, 173, 276, 281
civil rights movement (1954–68), 54
Civilisation, Christianity and Commerce, 263
class, 54, 68, 71, 77, 96, 215–16, 241, 246, 276
Clinton, Hillary, 253
cocaine, 112, 115, 116, 117–18
Cochrane Collaboration, 50, 200, 201
Cochrane Reviews, 119–20
cognitive behavioural therapy (CBT), 20, 169, 180–81, 184–5
cognitive parenting, 73–4
Cold War (1947–91), 92, 252
collectivism, 35, 178, 241, 254–6
Colombia, 55
colonialism, 138, 193, 219, 240, 249, 253, 254–68
Columbia University, 205–6
common factors paradigm, 175–6
communism, 239
competition, 95, 135, 229, 237–8, 242–9
concept creep, 75–7
conduct disorders, 11, 72, 87, 91, 149
confessionals, 186
Congress, US, 217–18
consumerism, *see* marketisation
context, 19, 20, 26, 31–2, 36, 168, 187, 201, 215, 275, 277, 282, 287
   autism and, 133, 139, 143, 144, 145, 146, 150
   gender dysphoria and, 227, 229
copy number variants (CNVs), 106–7
corporal punishment, 23–5, 73
Cosgrove, Lisa, 56, 201, 202
Cosmopolitan, 82
COVID-19 pandemic (2019–20), 3, 16, 68, 237–8, 242
Crazy Like Us (Watters), 262
Critical Psychiatry Network, 267

Cuba, 250
cultural dynamics, 52–5, 96–9, 137, 144, 177–8
   childhood and, 165–8
   eating disorders and, 236
   study population bias and, 177–8
culture wars, 214, 215, 242
Czech, Herwig, 127

D'Angelo, Roberto, 227
Daily Mail, 115
Darwin, Charles, 148
Davies, James, 204, 206–7, 208
Deadly Medicines and Organised Crime (Gøtzsche), 50–51, 200–201
Deadly Psychiatry and Organised Denial (Gøtzsche), 201
Defeat Depression campaign (1992–6), 59
democracy, 249, 251, 292
Democratic Psychiatry, 282–5
Denmark, 57, 98, 225
depression, 2, 5, 18, 23, 26, 37–9, 59–61, 136, 269–72
   awareness campaigns, 59–60, 169–70, 210
   children and, 158, 169–70
   chronic, 170, 173
   diagnosis, 44–8, 50, 56, 59
   globalisation of, 254–62
   marketisation of, 72, 169–70, 210
   medication and, 23, 56, 59, 60–61, 158, 179, 184, 192–9, 273
   polygenic risk scores, 108–9
   post-natal, 259–60
   psychotherapeutic models, 176, 182
   symptoms, 150
   women and, 87
descriptive systems, 30
destigmatisation campaigns, *see* awareness campaigns

development, 19
dhat, 258–9, 263
diabetes, 29–30, 44
diagnosis, 4, 20–21, 43–64, 67, 71, 142–6, 203–7
   concept creep, 75–7, 162
   longitudinal studies, 120–21
   looping effects, 74–5, 162–3, 232
   marketisation of, *see* marketisation
   medication and, 13–16, 55–63
   scientism, 48–52, 245
   sociocultural dynamics, 52–5, 96–9, 137, 144
   treatment pathways, 20, 176–7, 181
Diagnostic Statistical Manual, 54, 93–4, 147, 204–7, 211, 237, 260, 263
dialectical behaviour therapy (DBT), 169
disability benefits, 57, 58, 60, 196–7
disease-centred model, 194
disordered eating, 236
disorders, 25, 27, 46, 52, 55
dissociative identity disorder, 163
diversity, equity, and inclusion (DEI), 217–18
#DiversityAcrosstheAisle, 217
domestic violence, 221
dopamine, 82, 88, 111–12
Doritos, 216–17
drapetomania, 264
drug-centred model, 194
drugs, recreational, 43, 112, 115, 116, 117–18
Duncan, Barry, 176
Durkheim, Emile, 242
dysaesthesia aethiopis, 264

eating issues, 11, 18, 87, 150, 157, 163, 172, 210, 234–8
   anorexia nervosa, 234–8, 262
   autism and, 156, 236

echolalia, 10
economic deprivation, 68, 71, 215–16, 249–53
Edison, Thomas, 148
Egypt, 252
Einstein, Albert, 148
Eisenberg, Leon, 128
elastic band effect, 67, 155
Eli Lilly, 217
emergency department visits, 161–2
emotional experiences, 269–89
    meta-emotions, 269–72, 278, 280
    numbing of, 62n, 197, 276
emotional intelligence, 137, 140
emotional well-being, 168
empathy, 58, 76, 129–30, 137, 140, 148, 149
'End of History, The' (Fukuyama), 249
End of Love (Illouz), 232
Entwistle, Kirsty, 221
epilepsy, 129, 257
epiphanies, 188–9, 276, 278, 279
equal environment assumption (EEA), 105
Estonia, 98
Ethiopia, 252
eugenics, 53, 83, 126, 264, 267
euthanasia, 127
evidence-based medicine (EBM), 50–52, 104, 174
    ADHD and, 102–23
    autism and, 142–56
Eysenck, Hans, 265

false positives, 177
Fanon, Frantz, 254, 265
fascism, 239, 243
feminism, 85–6, 213, 229, 231, 236
Fernando, Suman, 264
Ferox, 217
financial crash (2008), 166
Finland, 98, 113, 225, 226, 285–6
first do no harm, 62
Fischer, Ann and John, 95
Fisher, Mark, 291–2
Floyd, George, 217, 267
fluoxetine, 158, 199, 202
folk psychology, 174–5, 184–7, 188
Food and Drug Administration (FDA), 202
Foucault, Michel, 157, 204, 266, 292–3
Foulkes, Lucy, 162–3
Frankl, George, 126–8
freedom, 248
Freud, Sigmund, 84, 85
friendship bench, 262
Fukuyama, Francis, 249
functional magnetic resonance imaging (fMRI), 154

Galton, Francis, 264
gender dysphoria (GD), 66, 221–33
Gender Identity Development Service (GIDS), 219–24
genetics
    ADHD and, 104–9
    autism and, 108, 129, 151–2
genome-wide association studies (GWAS), 107–9
germ theory, 48, 90
Germany, 98, 110
    Nazi Germany (1933–45), 53–4, 125–8, 165, 264, 267
Gillberg, Christopher, 154
Girl in Red, 191
Goddard, Henry, 265
Goffman, Erving, 204
Gorizia, Italy, 282
Gøtzsche, Peter, 50–51, 57, 199, 200–201

Graeber, David, 269
Gramsci, Antonio, 1, 243, 266
Gray, John, 253
Great Ormond Street Children's Hospital, 234
Grinker, Roy, 137–8
Guardian, 81

Hacking, Ian, 74
Hall, Stanley, 264
Hamburger, Franz, 126
Hardy, Thomas, 7
Harry, Duke of Sussex, 87
Haslam, Nick, 75
Hayek, Friedrich, 239, 249
Healy, David, 199
hearing voices, 40–43, 62–4
Hebrew University of Jerusalem, 232
Herman, Edward, 243
hero fantasies, 176
Herrnstein, Richard, 265
high functioning autism, 146
Hilton, Paris, 87
Hinduism, 33–4
Holocaust (1941–5), 53–4
homeostasis, 117
homosexuality, 54, 222, 224, 229, 231–2
Hong Kong, 236–7, 262
Hoogman, Martine, 110
hyper-liberalism, 253
hypotheses, 49–50, 104
hysteria, 84

Iceland, 98
identified patient, 17–18
identity, 20–21, 35, 212–19
identity politics, 214, 215–19, 233–4, 253, 267–8
  trans rights, 219–33
Illouz, Eva, 232

Improving Access to Psychological Therapies (IAPT), 182–4
India, 55, 138, 252, 258–9, 261
Indian Ocean tsunami (2004), 262
individualism, 35, 37, 70, 77, 95, 134–5, 178, 214
  colonialism and, 254–5
  competition and, 244–9
  hyper-individualism, 253
Indonesia, 96–7
inequality, 54, 77, 209, 215, 216, 241, 245–53, 276
infantile autism, 128, 129
Institute for Economic Affairs, 239
Institutional Racism in Psychiatry (Fernando), 264
internal object, 271, 280, 281
International Journal of Eating Disorders, 236
International Monetary Fund (IMF), 240, 241
intersectionality, 218–19
IQ (intelligence quotient), 110, 111
Iran, 252
Iraq, 35, 242
Ireland, 120
irritability, 5
Islam, 32–3
Italy, 282–5

Jadhav, Sushrut, 259
James, Adrian, 267–8
Japan, 97, 178–9, 260
Jensen, Arthur, 265
Jones, Owen, 87
Joseph, Jay, 105
Judaism, 98
Jureidini, Jon, 197–9, 277

Kaltiala, Riittakerttu, 225, 226
Kanner, Leo, 125–8

Keynes, John Maynard, 234
Kheriaty, Aaron, 40
Kids Company, 70
Kierkegaard, Søren, 22
Kipling, Rudyard, 263
Kohn, Alfie, 124
Korea, Republic of, 98, 138
Kraepelin, Emil, 52–3
Kwarteng, Kwasi, 218

labelling, 20, 136, 162–3, 274, 275, 277, 278, 280
Laing, Ronald, 204
Lancet, 106, 110, 261
Lask, Bryan, 234
Latvia, 254–7
Layard, Richard, 182, 183
learning difficulties (LD), 7–10, 91, 107, 109, 110, 129
left-wing politics, 241
Lehtinen, Laura, 91
LGBT Congressional Staff Association, 217
Libya, 252
Lloyd, Tony, 89
Lock, Margaret, 260
Lockheed Martin, 252
Long, Josie, 87
longitudinal studies, 120–21
looping effects, 74–5, 162–3, 232
Luckmann, Thomas, 242–3

Mad in America (Whitaker), 56
Madness and Civilization (Foucault), 292–3
major depressive disorder (MDD), 47–8, 50, 108–9, 150
Mandela, Nelson, 52
Manufacturing Consent (Chomsky and Herman), 243
marijuana, 42, 115

marketisation, 69–79, 81–3, 87–90, 129, 131–9, 158–70, 232–3, 245, 281
　ADHD, 72, 77, 87–90, 95–9, 163
　autism, 72, 77, 129, 131–9, 163
　compare and compete culture and, 245, 248–9
　'McDonaldisation', 158–62, 164, 187, 188, 281
　psychotherapy, 179–81, 187, 189–90
　relationships, 232–3, 244
Marx, Karl, 174, 242, 243
Marxism, 189
masking, 72, 134, 137, 148, 256, 259
Maté, Gabor, 69, 87
Maudsley Debate, 200
May Cause Side Effects (Siem), 273
'McDonaldisation', 158–62, 164, 187, 188, 281
McGuinness, Christine, 131
McPartlin, Ant, 87
Mead, George, 242–3
media, 36, 74, 136, 158–9, 251, 270, 279
　colonialism of, 236–6, 255, 262
　identity politics and, 218
　looping effects, 74–5, 162–3, 232
　neoliberalism and, 232, 243, 251
medical model, 28, 58
medication, 13–16, 55–63, 158–9, 177, 191–9, 273
　ADHD and, 13–16, 88, 94, 115–21
　chemical imbalance hypothesis, 16, 82, 88, 104, 111–12, 116–17, 191–9
　depression and, 23, 56, 59, 60–61, 158, 179, 184, 192–9, 273
　mortality gap and, 58–9
　numbing of feelings, 62*n*, 197
　trials, 51, 197–9, 202–3
meditation, 186–7
Mel B, 87
Mental Deficiency Act (1913), 83
Mental Health Act (1983), 157, 171

Mental Health First Aid (MHFA), 208
mental health Gap Action Programme
    (mhGAP), 257, 261
mental health industrial complex
    (MHIC), 54–5, 67, 99, 158, 184,
    190, 191–211, 292
  chemical imbalance hypotheses and,
    191–9
  data manipulation, 51, 202–3
  decline and, 249
  diagnosis and, 203–7
  emotional experiences and, 271–2,
    278
  gender dysphoria and, 228
  globalisation of, 193, 249, 253, 254–68
  identity politics and, 214, 228, 233
  looping effects and, 74
  'McDonaldisation', 158–62, 164, 187,
    188, 281
  organised crime, comparison with,
    50–51, 200–201
  propaganda, 207–11
  women and, 87
mental health models, 25–39
  awareness campaigns, 25, 59, 74, 88,
    129, 139, 159, 161, 162–5, 276
  concept creep, 75–7, 162
  diagnostic systems, 4, 20–21, 43–64
  economic deprivation and, 68, 71
  looping effects, 74–5, 162–3, 232
  marketisation of, 69–79, 81–3, 87, 129
  mental, definition of, 32–4
  physical illness, comparison with,
    27–32
  self, nature of, 32, 34–7
  subjectivity of, *see* subjectivity
meritocracy, 244, 246
meta-emotions, 269–72, 274, 278
methylphenidate, 13–16, 88, 94, 115–21,
    158
MeToo, 292

Mexico, 97
miasma, 48
Michaels, Walter Benn, 215
migraines, 30
militarism, 242
military industrial complex, 251–2
Miller, John, 61
Miller, Scott, 176
Milton, Damian, 212–13, 230
mindfulness, 136, 169, 186–7, 209
von Mises, Ludwig, 239
MMR vaccine, 129
Moncrieff, Joanna, 193–4
mood, 5, 26, 45–6, 72, 170, 259–60
  chemical imbalance hypothesis and,
    196
  medication and, 191–2, 194, 195
moral insanity, 83
More, Now, Again (Wurtzel), 115
mortality gap, 58–9
Mozart, Wolfgang Amadeus, 148
MTA study (1999), 12–16, 119
Murin, Marianna, 148
Musk, Elon, 251
Mussolini, Benito, 243
Myth of Normal, The (Maté), 69
Myth of the Chemical Cure, The
    (Moncrieff), 193–4

narrative therapy, 150
National Autistic Society, 133, 147
National Health Service (NHS), 7, 68,
    89, 182, 183, 192
  gender dysphoria and, 219–24, 226
National Institute of Clinical
    Excellence (NICE), 15, 119, 132
National Survey on Drug Use and
    Health, 68
natural kind, 28, 30
Nazi Germany (1933–45), 53–4, 125–8,
    165, 264, 267

NBC, 81
Neale, Miles, 187
neoliberalism, 207, 213, 215, 216, 228, 238–53
nervi, 254–6, 263
Netherlands, 98
neurasthenia, 260–61
neurodiversity, 97, 129–30, 136, 192, 210, 212–19
   'neuro' in, 212, 215, 230
   politics of, 212–19
neuroimaging, 57
   ADHD, 109–11
   autism, 152–4
neuroplasticity, 152–3
neurotransmitters, 111, 192–9
   dopamine, 82, 88, 111–12
   serotonin, 44, 192–9
New Zealand, 98, 285, 292
Newsnight, 219
Nigeria, 55
'noble savages', 264
normality, 52, 72, 165, 233, 242, 292
Northrop Grumman, 252
Norway, 110, 225, 288
Novartis Pharmaceuticals, 116
nuclear family, 35
nucleus accumbens (NA), 110
null hypothesis, 49–50, 104–12
   ADHD, 104–12
   autism, 151–4
numbing of feelings, 62n, 197, 276

obsessional personality disorder, 150
obsessive compulsive disorder (OCD), 150, 191
'On Being Sane in Insane Places' (Rosenhan), 204
one-way mirrors, 16
Open Dialogue, 285–6
Ophir, Yaakov, 98

organised crime, 50–51, 200–201
Orientalism (Said), 266
overdoses, 18
Ozsivadjian, Ann, 148

Pack, Joseph, 116
panic disorder, 87
paranoia, 66, 79
parenting
   belittlement, use of, 42, 63, 144
   corporal punishment, use of, 23–5, 42, 73
   marketisation and, 164, 165–8
   separation and, 42, 65, 66–7, 99, 171–2
Parkinson's disease, 121
Pasteur, Louis, 90
pathological demand avoidance, 146
pathology, 48
Paxil, 202
Pennant, Jermain, 87
Perkins, Sue, 87
personality disorders, 84
Peter Doshi, 198
Pfizer, 217
pharmaceutical industry, 50–51
pharmacotherapy, 158
philosophy, 179, 187–90
phrenology, 20
physical contact, schools and, 73
Pickett, Kate, 245–6
Pinochet, Augusto, 239
pollution, 246
polygenic risk score (PRS), 108–9
pornography, 228, 229, 232
Portugal, 98
post-natal depression, 259–60
post-traumatic stress disorder (PTSD), 43, 87
postmodernism, 189
poverty, *see* economic deprivation

Power Threat Meaning Framework, The,
    85, 286–7
Prozac, 158, 199, 202
psychiatric diagnosis, *see* diagnosis
Psychiatric Times, 61
psychiatry, 10*n*, 46, 56–7
    MHIC and, 202
    scientism and, 51
    social institution, 54
    women and, 83–7
Psychiatry UK, 89
Psychiatry Under the Influence (Cosgrove
    and Whitaker), 56, 201, 202
psychology, 10*n*, 35, 177–8
    philosophy, branch of, 179, 187–90
psychosis, 11, 18, 43
psychotherapeutic models, 21, 169,
    174–90
    brands, 179–81, 187, 189–90
    common factors paradigm, 175–6
    folk psychology, 174–5, 184–7, 188
    industrialisation of, 182–4
    narrative therapy, 150
puberty blockers, 221–4, 226, 229

race; racism, 12, 54, 97–8, 130–31, 193,
    215, 216–17, 219
    colonialism and, 263–8
Rain Man (1988 film), 129
Raytheon, 252
Reagan, Ronald, 135, 240
relationships, 232–3, 244, 276
religion, 32–3, 98, 136, 167, 259
replicability crisis, 49, 177–8
Republic of Korea, 98, 138
resilience, 38, 71, 160, 168, 269, 278
Restoring Invisible and Abandoned
    Trials (RIAT), 198–9
restricted imagination, 10
Rett's disorder, 146
Reynolds American, 217

Richard Fee Foundation, 273
Ritalin, 13–16, 88, 94, 115–21, 158
Road to Serfdom, The (Hayek), 239, 249
Robertson, Kyle, 88
Rosenhan, David, 204–5
Rousseau, Jean-Jacques, 264
Royal College of General
    Practitioners, 59
Royal College of Psychiatrists, 9, 12,
    59, 68, 87, 192, 267
Rüdin, Ernst, 53
Rush, John, 61
Russia, 252
Ruston, Phillipe, 265
Rutter, Michael, 128, 142

safeguarding, 23, 24–5
Said, Edward, 266
Saudi Arabia, 252
saviour fantasies, 176
schizoaffective disorder, 43
schizoid personality disorder, 150
schizophrenia, 43, 55–6, 59, 62,
    108, 285
    genetic research, 108
school systems, 12, 73, 92, 99, 159–62,
    168–70
    awareness campaigns and, 159, 161,
    162–5, 168–70, 276
scientism, 48–52, 245
Second World War (1939–45), 91, 165
Sedated (Davies), 208
selective serotonin reuptake inhibitors
    (SSRIs), 193, 195, 198, 209
self-esteem, 11, 35, 274
self-harm, 1, 5, 18, 22–5, 37–9, 87, 103,
    209, 276
separation anxiety, 177
serotonin, 44, 192–9
serotonin and norepinephrine
    reuptake inhibitors (SNRIs), 193

sexual harassment/violence, 86, 87, 219, 221
Sheffer, Edith, 126–7
Siem, Brooke, 273–4
Singer, Judy, 129
Skultans, Vieda, 254
slavery, 264
sleep, 19, 22, 41, 42, 46, 62, 75
   ADHD medication and, 115, 116, 118
   insomnia, 278–80
Smith, Matthew, 92
Smith, Shubulade, 268
SmithKline Beecham, 198
social class, see class
Social Construction of Reality, The (Berger and Luckmann), 242–3
social constructionism, 71–3, 189, 213, 230–32, 242–3
social looping, 74–5, 162–3, 232
social media, 36, 81–2, 86, 131, 135, 163, 164, 210
social phobia, 177
sociocultural dynamics, 52–5, 96–9, 137, 144, 177–9
   childhood and, 165–8
   eating disorders and, 236
   study population bias and, 177–8
sociopathic personality disorder, 149
Socrates, 212
Somalia, 252
Soteria, 288
soul, 32–3
South Africa, 138, 252
South Korea, 98, 138
Soviet Union, 92, 214, 249, 254–7
Spain, 98, 225
Spirit Level, The (Pickett and Wilkinson), 245–6
Spitzer, Robert, 205–6
Spivak, Gayatri, 266
Sputnik, 92

Sri Lanka, 262
St Mary Abbots Hospital, London, 83
standard mortality rates (SMRs), 58
Stanford University, 204
STAR*D study, 60–61, 170
Still, Frederick, 90–91
Strauss, Alfred, 91
stress, 26, 72, 136, 191
study population bias, 177–8
Su, Fen, 22–5, 37–9
subalterns, 266
subjectivity, 26–7, 31, 34, 43, 47, 50, 67, 69, 168, 178
   ADHD and, 81
   autism and, 133, 144
suicide, 18, 24, 56–7, 62, 64, 66, 67, 124, 225
   prevention programmes, 209
Suicide Prevention Australia (SPA), 209
Sunak, Rishi, 218
Sweden, 98, 121, 225, 226
Switzerland, 98
Sykes, Melanie, 131
symptoms, 4, 5, 26, 27–32, 113–14, 177, 205, 272–3, 287
Syria, 252
systemic philosophy, 189
Szasz, Thomas, 204

Taliban, 252
Talking Therapies Programme, 182
tautology, 45
Tavistock and Portman NHS Trust, 219–24
Terman, Lewis, 265
Thapar, Anita, 106
Thatcher, Margaret, 135, 240
therapeutic education, 168
Third Way, 70
TikTok, 80, 81–2, 163, 210
Time to Think (Barnes), 219

Tolstoy, Leo, 102
Tourette's, 163
trait versus state issue, 235
transgender people, 65–7, 77–9, 219–33
trauma, 25, 69–71, 72, 174, 287
   concept creep and, 76
Treatment of Adolescents with Depression Study (TADS), 198
treatment pathway model, 20, 176–7, 181
treatment resistance, 20, 173, 271
Trento, Italy, 283
Trieste, Italy, 284
Trump, Donald, 244, 253
Truss, Liz, 218
tsunami (2004), *see* Indian Ocean tsunami
twins, 104–6
type 2 diabetes, 29–30, 44
typology, 36

Ukraine, 253
United Arab Emirates, 252
United Kingdom, 68, 74–5
   ADHD in, 96, 98
   black population, 54
   decline in, 251, 253
   Defeat Depression campaign (1992–6), 59
   disability benefits in, 60, 196–7
   gender dysphoria in, 219–24, 226
   identity politics in, 218
   neoliberalism in, 135, 240
United Nations, 283
United States, 67–8, 75
   ADHD in, 96, 97, 98, 113
   civil rights movement (1954–68), 54
   Cold War (1947–91), 92, 252
   decline in, 249–53
   gender dysphoria in, 227
   identity politics in, 217–18, 267–8
   military industrial complex, 251–2
   neoliberalism in, 135, 240
   perception of world in, 178–9
   racism in, 264–5
   war on terror (2001–present), 242, 252
University of Bristol, 254
University of Exeter, 142, 212
Unstrange Minds (Grinker), 137–8
Users and Relatives as Experts (UFE), 283

Valencia, Spain, 225
Van Gogh, Vincent, 148
Vegas, Johnny, 87
voices, hearing of, 40–43, 62–4

Walmart, 217
war on terror (2001–present), 242, 252
Waste Management, 217
Watson, Tom, 87
Watters, Ethan, 236–7, 262
welfare, 57, 58, 60, 135, 196–7, 209, 241, 242
Western culture, 69, 85, 95, 113, 137, 138, 165, 174–5, 178–9
   body image, 222, 235, 236–7, 276
   colonialism of, 254–68
   compare and compete, 95, 135, 229, 237–8, 242–9
   individualism, 35, 37, 70, 77, 95, 134–5, 178
   study population bias and, 177–8
Whitaker, Robert, 55, 201, 202
'white man's burden', 263
Wilkinson, Richard, 245–6
Wing, Lorna, 128
women, 83–7, 133
   ADHD and, 82–3, 133
   autism and, 84, 133–4, 139, 144

sexual harassment/violence, 86, 87, 219
transgender politics and, 229, 231
workplace mental health, 207–9
World Bank, 240, 241, 268
World Health Organization (WHO), 26, 55, 138, 257–8, 283
World Trade Organization (WTO), 240
Wretched of the Earth, The (Fanon), 265

Wurtzel, Elizabeth, 115
Würzberg, Germany, 110

Yemen, 252
young-for-class children, 112–13, 247
Yugoslavia, 252

Zanzibar, 262
Zimbabwe, 262
Zoloft, 202

Sami Timimi is a consultant child-and-adolescent psychiatrist and psychotherapist in the NHS. He has written forty book chapters, mainly in academic books, on subjects related to critical psychiatry, childhood, psychotherapy, depression, behavioural problems and cross-cultural psychiatry. Timimi has authored six books, including *Naughty Boys: Anti-Social Behaviour*, and *ADHD and the Role of Culture*; co-edited four books, including, with Carl Cohen, *Liberatory Psychiatry: Philosophy, Politics and Mental Health*; and co-authored two others including, with Neil Gardiner and Brian McCabe, *The Myth of Autism: Medicalising Men's and Boys' Social and Emotional Competence*. His most recent book, published in 2021, is *Insane Medicine: How the Mental Health Industry Creates Damaging Treatment Traps and How You Can Escape Them*.